THE FORMATIVE PERIOD
OF THE
FEDERAL RESERVE SYSTEM

(During the World Crisis)

BY

W. P. G. HARDING
Former Governor of the Federal Reserve Board

AMS PRESS
NEW YORK

Reprinted from the edition of 1925, Boston
First AMS EDITION published 1970
Manufactured in the United States of America

International Standard Book Number: 0-404-03107-2

Library of Congress Card Catalog Number: 71-120221

AMS PRESS, INC.
NEW YORK, N.Y. 10003

PREFACE

In the personal narrative which follows there have been outlined the functions of the Federal Reserve Banks and the laws and principles under which they have been conducted. I have also touched upon some of the activities, policies, and experiences of the Federal Reserve Board during the eight years of my connection with it — the last six as its governor. Those years, which cover the entire period of the World War and four years of its aftermath, stand out as among the most eventful and critical in modern times. Every branch of the Government was constantly confronted with new and perplexing problems which affected all those engaged in banking and commerce, industry and agriculture. In dealing with many of the emergencies which arose in those abnormal times, it was difficult to reconcile the divergent interests of buyers and sellers, of employers and wage-earners, and of producers and consumers. Complaints and criticisms were inevitable, and during the period of world-wide reaction after the war, many were directed particularly against the Federal Reserve Board. It has been shown that in the main these were based on conditions not of the Board's making and entirely beyond its control.

This volume is submitted to the reader with the hope that its contents will aid in a correct appraisal of the part played by the Federal Reserve System during the world crisis, and of its value in the future.

W. P. G. HARDING

BOSTON, *June*, 1925

CONTENTS

CONTENTS

APPENDICES

ILLUSTRATIONS

THE FORMATIVE PERIOD

OF THE

FEDERAL RESERVE SYSTEM

• •

CHAPTER I

APPOINTMENT OF MEMBERS OF THE FEDERAL RESERVE BOARD — ORGANIZATION OF THE BOARD

ONE morning toward the end of March, 1914, before the Federal Reserve Bank Organization Committee had announced its decision as to the location of the Federal Reserve Banks, I received a telegram from Colonel E. M. House, whom I knew only by reputation, stating that he was leaving Houston for Washington, and requesting me to meet him the following day in New Orleans. I replied that I could not do so, and suggested that he stop over in Birmingham. He replied that he was taking another route, and asked me to meet him at his train, upon its arrival at Montgomery, at six o'clock the following Sunday morning. The train was scheduled for a stop of about two hours at Montgomery, and thus there would be ample time for a conference. Knowing something of his close relations with the President and the Secretary of the Treasury, I was anxious to meet him in order that I might have an opportunity of impressing upon him the claims of Birmingham for a Federal Reserve Bank. It happened, however, that his train was about two hours late, and made a stop only of about ten minutes at Montgomery. I therefore rode with him as far as Opelika, a junction point about sixty miles east, where I could take a train on another road back to Birmingham. Colonel House was not disposed to discuss the location of Federal Reserve Banks, but he asked a good many questions about business and banking conditions in the South, and he stated that he was particularly interested in the personnel of the Federal Reserve Board. He said that the President had many names under consideration, and he mentioned three, from which number one was likely to be chosen as the South's representative on the Board. He asked my opinion as to the qualifications of these gentlemen, but expressed no opinion as to which one was likely to be chosen. On the afternoon of the 4th of May, an evening paper was brought to my desk in the bank, and I saw on the front page that the President had announced his selections for the Federal Reserve Board. Greatly to my surprise, my name was on the list. At that time I had never seen President Wilson nor had I ever had any correspondence with him. My acquaintance with Secretary McAdoo was slight, and I had seen him only twice: once at the hearing before the Organization Committee in Atlanta, and first in the early summer of 1913, when I called at his office in order to ascertain his attitude toward national bank notes secured by two per cent consols, which were then selling on the market at a considerable discount.

I felt complimented upon my selection to be a member of the Federal Reserve Board, a body about which there had been so much talk for several months. I had no idea, however, at first of accepting the proffered appointment. I was a native of Alabama and had been for twenty-eight years a resident of Birmingham. I had seen the place grow from a town of ten thousand people to a city of more than one hundred and fifty thousand inhabitants, and had been promoted from a bookkeeper's desk to the presidency of the largest bank in the State. The Act provided that no member of the Federal Reserve Board should own any bank stock or be connected in any way with a bank, and, furthermore, that a member would be ineligible to hold any position or employment in a member bank for a period of two years after he had ceased to be a member of the Board. The salary attached to the position was not attractive, and altogether my acceptance of the post involved a very considerable sacrifice. I deemed it improper, however, to make any announcement of my intentions before receiving notice from the President of his intention to appoint me, and told representatives of the press that I should make no statement until after I had heard from the President. I found, however, that there was a general sentiment among my friends and business associates that the position was one of too much honor and importance to be declined, and that I ought to consider making the personal sacrifices necessary to enable me to accept the appointment. I was still undecided when I received a letter from the President, asking if I 'would not be willing to accept the eight-year appointment on the Board.' He said:

I feel that there is here a great opportunity to serve the country, and I hope sincerely that you will feel that you can make the sacrifices necessary to accept.

I must confess that the tone of this letter had a good deal to do with my final decision. The President's evident desire to have me become a member of the Board and his reference to the opportunity of rendering public service appealed to me, and after a few days I wrote the President of my willingness to accept.

The Honorable Richard Olney, of Boston, who was Secretary of State in the last Cleveland Administration, had been tendered appointment as a member and Governor of the Board, and Mr. Harry A. Wheeler, of Chicago, was offered a membership on the Board. Both of these gentlemen, however, declined to accept, and the President was therefore obliged to make new selections. Just at this time, the Secretary of the Treasury, Mr. McAdoo, married one of the daughters of the President and was away for about three weeks on a honeymoon trip. The newspapers stated that no selections would be made until his return to Washington. It was not, therefore, until the latter part of June that the President made formal nominations to the Senate of the following as members of the Federal Reserve Board: Charles S. Hamlin, of Boston, for a term of two years; Paul M. Warburg, of New York, for a term of four years; Thomas D. Jones, of Chicago, for a term of six years; W. P. G. Harding, of Birmingham, for a term of eight years; and Adolph C. Miller, of Berkeley, California, for a term of ten years.

Mr. Hamlin was a lawyer by profession, and had been Assistant Secretary of the Treasury during the second Cleveland Administration. He was occupying the same post at the time, of his nomination as a member of the Federal Reserve Board. Mr. Miller, who was at the time Assistant to the Secretary of the Interior, was an economist, and had been connected with the University of Chicago, and, later on, was Professor of Economics at the University of California. Mr. Warburg, who for many years had been deeply interested in the subject of banking reform and was a recognized authority on the subject, was a member of the New York banking firm of Kühn, Loeb and Company. Mr. Jones was a close personal friend of President Wilson and was a public-spirited business man. He was an officer of the New Jersey Zinc Company and had within a few years become a director of the International Harvester Company.

There was prevalent at the time, following the report of the committee to investigate the so-called 'money trust,' more than the usual amount of popular prejudice against 'big business,' and when the nominations came up for consideration in the Senate, opposition developed to Messrs. Jones and Warburg because of their banking and corporate connections. Action on their names was deferred, although the other three nominations were confirmed on July 6th. Later on, the President, at the request of Mr. Jones, withdrew his name, but he declined to act upon a similar request from Mr. Warburg, who had been invited to appear before a subcommittee to which his nomination had been referred. Mr. Warburg persistently declined to do so, and the Senate

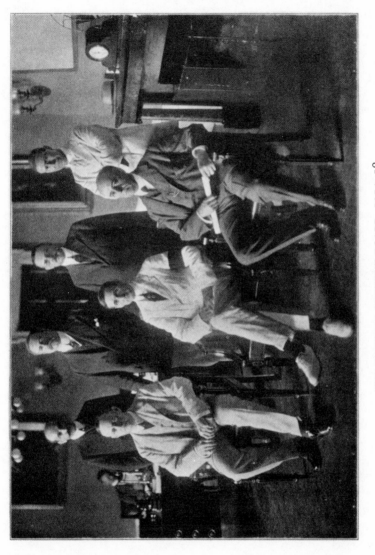

THE FEDERAL RESERVE BOARD, 1914–18

Left to right, seated: Charles S. Hamlin, William Gibbs McAdoo, Frederick A. Delano
Standing: Paul M. Warburg, John Skelton Williams, W. P. G. Harding, A. C. Miller

Committee refused to report his name unless and until he appeared before it. This deadlock continued for some weeks until just before the outbreak of the war in Europe. Mr. Warburg then agreed to appear before the committee and his confirmation by the Senate soon followed. Meanwhile, Mr. Frederick A. Delano, of Chicago, for many years a railroad executive, and who was then serving as a member of the Industrial Relations Commission, under appointments by Presidents Taft and Wilson, had been nominated and confirmed as a member of the Board.

The oath of office was administered to each member on the morning of August 10, 1914, at which time the organization of the Board was completed by the President's designation of Mr. Hamlin as Governor, and of Mr. Delano as Vice-Governor. Mr. M. C. Elliott, who had been Secretary of the Federal Reserve Bank Organization Committee, acted as Secretary of the Board for a short time. Upon the appointment of Dr. H. Parker Willis as Secretary, Mr. Elliott became Counsel, and served in that capacity until 1919, when he resigned in order to engage in private practice.

Up to this time no independent board or commission had been housed in the Treasury Building, but under authority given in the clause of Section 10 of the Federal Reserve Act 'The Secretary of the Treasury may assign offices in the Department of the Treasury for the use of the Federal Reserve Board,' the members of the Board were given offices on the second floor, on the west side of the Treasury Building; flanked on one side by the offices of the Secretary of the Treasury, and on the other by those of the Comptroller of the Currency.

It seems appropriate at this place to say something of my impressions, which I believe were shared by some other members of the Board, of the attitude of these two officials toward the Board. There had been a good deal of discussion, before the appointments were made, of the importance and dignity of the Board, and it was often alluded to as the Supreme

Court of Finance. This was obviously a misnomer, as the Board had no judicial powers. It was thought by some that the Board would rank in importance and dignity next to the Supreme Court and the Cabinet, especially as the Act fixed the salaries of the Board members on a parity with those of the Cabinet officers, which up to that time had not been the case with any other commission.

The office of the Comptroller of the Currency, ever since its creation in 1863, had been a bureau of the Treasury Department, and while the Federal Reserve Bank legislation was pending in Congress, there had been some discussion of the advisability of either abolishing the office and transferring its functions and duties to the Federal Reserve Board; or else to have the Comptroller placed under the jurisdiction of the Federal Reserve Board instead of the Treasury Department. All such suggestions, however, were disregarded, and under the Act as finally passed the Comptroller was made a member of the Reserve Bank Organization Committee, and a member *ex officio* of the Federal Reserve Board, with the further provision that, in addition to the salary paid him as Comptroller of the Currency, he should receive the sum of $7000 annually for his services as a member of the Board. This made the compensation of the Comptroller equal to that of other members of the Board.

There were, moreover, some provisions of the Act which were, from the time of the Board's organization, regarded as liable to create some misunderstanding and confusion.

Although the law requires any bank incorporated under State law desiring to become a member of the Federal Reserve System to make application to the Federal Reserve Board, no change was made in that section of the Revised Statutes of the United States which requires organizers of new national banks to make application to the Comptroller of the Currency, who can at his discretion grant or refuse a charter. Therefore, while the Federal Reserve Board has discretion in the admission of State banks as members, it has none in the matter of new national banks; nor does the Federal Reserve Act contain any clause which specifically requires the Comptroller of the Currency to furnish the Federal Reserve Board or a Federal Reserve Bank with a copy of the report of examination of a national bank made by a national bank examiner.

In view of the provisions of the Act, it was foreseen from the beginning that it might be difficult always to avoid differences between the Federal Reserve Board and the Comptroller of the Currency, for some of the duties of that officer related to matters which vitally concerned the operations of the Board, of which he was a member, although he was entirely independent of the Board in the exercise of the very important powers of his own office. During the eight years of my service on the Board, there were several instances where the Comptroller granted charters for new national banks against the recommendations of officials of Federal Reserve Banks, and where State banks which had been refused admission to membership by the Board were granted national bank charters by the Comptroller and thus became members without the consent of the Board. The Federal Reserve Board was authorized by law to have examinations made of all member banks, while the Comptroller was directed to have each national bank examined at least twice during each calendar year. The Board deemed it unnecessary, as a rule, to have examinations made of national banks, assuming that the Comptroller would furnish Federal Reserve Banks with copies of the examiners' reports of their national bank members. The Comptroller, as a matter of courtesy, furnished incomplete copies to the Reserve Banks, but for some time persisted in withholding from them certain information contained in reports made to him which Federal Reserve Bank officers regarded as essential.

The legislative history of the Act indicates that the Secretary of the Treasury was desirous that the Federal Reserve Board should be actually, if possible, but at any rate in

effect, a bureau of the Treasury, just as the Farm Loan
Board, which was created by the Act of July 17, 1916, was
made a Treasury bureau under the express terms of the Act
establishing it.

I do not believe, however, that Mr. McAdoo was at all
desirous of having the Federal Reserve Banks become political organizations, and, as a matter of fact, I recall several
statements of his which stressed the importance of keeping
them out of politics. The Federal Reserve Board has the
appointment of three ' Class C ' directors for each Federal
Reserve Bank, including the Federal Reserve Agent, a sal-
aried officer. Little, if any, attention was paid to the political
affiliations of these appointees, and it was afterwards ascertained, when the question had been raised, that the majority
of them were not of the then dominant political party. But
I do not think that Mr. McAdoo looked with favor upon the
establishment of independent boards and commissions, and
he always impressed me as sharing the views of those who
believed in having Cabinet supervision of all agencies of the
Federal Government. I do not recall any definite expressions of his to this effect, but my belief is that he would have
preferred that all boards and commissions be attached to
some executive department, and as many as possible to the
Treasury. At one time he advocated a change in the law
which authorized the Federal Reserve Board to levy an
assessment upon the Federal Reserve Banks for the payment
of its expenses, in order to make the Board dependent upon
a specific appropriation by Congress. The following is an
extract from Mr. McAdoo's memorandum to the Board on
this subject, written in February, 1916:

The Act should be so amended as to provide that the Federal
Reserve Board shall annually make an estimate to the Congress
of its requirements for the ensuing fiscal year, and secure an
appropriation therefor in like manner as the executive departments and other independent boards of the Government are required to do. If it should be desired to impose specifically upon

the Federal Reserve Banks the cost of maintaining the Federal Reserve Board, then the Treasurer of the United States should be required to levy an assessment annually upon the Federal Reserve Banks for the purpose of reimbursing the Treasury for the expenditures made by the Federal Reserve Board under authority of the Congress. The independence of the Federal Reserve Board as a Government body cannot be successfully maintained if it is made by law dependent upon the Federal Reserve Banks themselves for the means of support.

The views expressed in this memorandum were not in accord, however, with those of a majority of the members of the Board, and no further suggestion was ever made that the law be amended in the manner indicated.

The annual assessments levied by the Board under the provisions of the Act for the purpose of defraying the expenses of its organization, ranged during the years 1914 to 1922 inclusive, from .002 per cent to .005 per cent of the amounts of the average paid-in capital of the Federal Reserve Banks. The amounts of these assessments were, year by year, as follows:

1914	$191,897.30	1919	$594,668.63
1915	156,257.44	1920	700,766.52
1916	192,143.60	1921	741,436.29
1917	237,776.82	1922	722,544.61
1918	382,081.00		

After the year 1915 these assessments included also the cost of publication of the Federal Reserve Bulletin, and of the Board's proportion of the cost of operating the private wire system by means of which instantaneous transfers are made through the gold settlement fund. No department of the Government and no other independent board with comparable activities has been operated at so small a cost. Although the expenses of the Board were paid entirely out of assessments upon the Federal Reserve Banks, and not out of appropriations of public funds by Congress, the Attorney-General in the fall of 1914 ruled that the Board's accounts were subject to the Government audit, and the amounts received from the assessments were required to be covered into the Treasury to be paid out on warrants of a disbursing officer.

Mr. McAdoo also expressed himself at one time as favoring an amendment to the Federal Reserve Act under which the member banks would be permitted to elect only four of the nine directors, the other five to be appointed by the Board; but here again he failed to receive the support of a majority of the Board and his suggestion was never pressed.

It is of interest at this point to compare portions of the section which relate to the organization of the Board as embodied in the bill which passed the House on September 18, 1913, with the corresponding portions of the section in the bill which passed the Senate on December 19, and with section 10 of the bill as agreed upon in conference, which became law on December 23, 1913. Certain passages in the text below appear in italics in order better to attract attention.

BILL AS PASSED IN THE HOUSE

SECTION 11: That there shall be created a Federal Reserve Board, which shall consist of seven members, including the Secretary of the Treasury, the *Secretary of Agriculture, and the Comptroller of the Currency*, who shall be members ex officio, and four members appointed by the President of the United States, by and with the advice and consent of the Senate. Of the four members thus appointed by the President *not more than two shall be of the same political party*, and *at least one of whom shall be a person experienced in banking*. One shall be designated by the President to serve for two, one for four, one for six, and one for eight years, respectively, and thereafter each member so appointed shall serve for a term of eight years unless sooner removed for cause by the President. Of the four persons thus appointed, one shall be designated by the President as manager and one as vice-manager of the Federal Reserve Board. The manager of the Federal Reserve Board, *subject to the supervision of the Secretary of the Treasury* and Federal Reserve Board, shall be the active executive officer of the

Federal Reserve Board. . . . The Secretary of the Treasury shall be ex officio chairman of the Federal Reserve Board.

BILL AS PASSED IN THE SENATE

SECTION 10: A Federal Reserve Board is hereby created which shall consist of seven members, including the Secretary of the Treasury, who shall be a member ex officio, and six members appointed by the President of the United States, by and with the advice and consent of the Senate. *The members of said board, the Secretary of the Treasury, the Assistant Secretary of the Treasury, and the Comptroller of the Currency shall be ineligible during the time they are in office and for two years thereafter to hold any office, position, or employment conferred by any member bank.* Of the six persons thus appointed by the President *at least two shall be persons experienced in banking or finance.* One shall be designated by the President to serve for one, one for two, one for three, one for four, one for five, and one for six years, and thereafter each member so appointed shall serve for a term of six years unless sooner removed for cause by the President. Of the six persons thus appointed, one shall be designated by the President as governor and one as vice-governor of the Federal Reserve Board. *The governor of the Federal Reserve Board, subject to its supervision,* shall be the active executive officer. *The Secretary of the Treasury may assign offices in the Department of the Treasury for the use of the Federal Reserve Board.* Each member of the Federal Reserve Board shall within fifteen days after notice of appointment make and subscribe to the oath of office. . . . The Secretary of the Treasury shall be ex officio chairman of the Federal Reserve Board.

FEDERAL RESERVE ACT AS AGREED UPON
AT CONFERENCE AND PASSED

SECTION 10: A Federal Reserve Board is hereby created which shall consist of seven members, including the Secretary of the Treasury and the Comptroller of the Currency, who shall be members ex officio, and five members appointed by the President of the United States, by and with the advice and consent of the Senate.

The members of said board, the Secretary of the Treasury, the Assistant Secretaries of the Treasury, and the Comptroller of the Currency shall be ineligible during the time they are in office and for two years thereafter to hold any office, position, or employment in any member bank. Of the five members thus appointed by the President, at least two shall be persons experienced in banking or finance. One shall be designated by the President to serve for two, one for four, one for six, one for eight, and one for ten years, and thereafter each member so appointed shall serve for a term of ten years unless sooner removed for cause by the President. Of the five persons thus appointed, one shall be designated by the President as governor and one as vice-governor of the Federal Reserve Board. The governor of the Federal Reserve Board, *subject to its supervision, shall be the active executive officer.* The Secretary of the Treasury may assign offices in the Department of the Treasury for the use of the Federal Reserve Board.

The House bill went much further than did the Senate bill toward making the Federal Reserve Board subordinate to executive departments. It not only made the Secretary of the Treasury chairman of the Board, but included as *ex officio* members also the Secretary of Agriculture and the Comptroller of the Currency, with only four appointed members; and the active executive officer of the Board was to be designated by the President as manager, and was made subject to the supervision of the Secretary of the Treasury and the Federal Reserve Board. The Senate bill provided for six appointed members and made the Secretary of the Treasury the only *ex officio* member. Had the House bill become law, all that could have prevented the Federal Reserve Board from becoming a mere instrumentality of the Treasury would have been possible differences between the Secretary of the Treasury and the Secretary of Agriculture. There would have been three *ex officio* members, all having exacting duties of their own, on a Board with four appointed members required to devote their entire time to the business of the Board. It would have been necessary to consult the convenience of the three *ex officio* members in arranging for meetings, and as an additional complication, the active executive officer of the Board would have been subject to the supervision of the Secretary of the Treasury, as well as of the Board as a body. It will be observed that the Conference Committee in reporting section 10 of the bill as finally passed, adopted in the main the language of section 10 of the Senate bill, including the following clause, which has been commented upon unfavorably by each of the three Secretaries of the Treasury who have served since 1918:

The members of said Board, the Secretary of the Treasury, the Assistant Secretaries of the Treasury, and the Comptroller of the Currency shall be ineligible during the time they are in office and for two years thereafter to hold any office, position, or employment in any member bank.

This was amended by the Act of March 3, 1919, to read:

The Secretary of the Treasury and the Comptroller of the Currency shall be ineligible during the time they are in office and for two years thereafter to hold any office, position, or employment in any member bank. The appointive members of the Federal Reserve Board shall be ineligible during the time they are in office and for two years thereafter to hold any office, position, or employment in any member bank except that this restriction shall not apply to a member who has served the full term for which he was appointed.

The Organization Committee had framed a set of by-laws to govern the operations of the Federal Reserve Board, and at one of the early meetings these were presented to the Board for adoption. One clause of the proposed by-laws provided that whenever the Secretary of the Treasury was absent from a meeting, the Comptroller of the Currency should preside. This was not agreed to by the Board, however, and the by-laws as adopted provided that, in the absence of the statutory chairman, the Secretary of the Treasury, the Governor of the Board should preside; and in the absence of both the Chairman and the Governor, the Vice-Governor should preside.

CHAPTER II

Economic Disturbances Occasioned by the World War— Gold Exchange Fund — Cotton Loan Fund

No governmental board was ever confronted with a more difficult task than that which faced the Federal Reserve Board at the time of its organization. The passage of the Federal Reserve Act was a great achievement, for which all of those who had a part in placing the law upon the statute books are entitled to much credit. The consensus of banking opinion, when the Board took office, was that the Act was about eighty-five to ninety per cent good, but there was a diversity of opinion as to just what provisions comprised the defective ten to fifteen per cent. The public mind, furthermore, was led to expect too much of the new law. Its object was well described in the caption, or short title of the Act, which reads as follows:

An Act to provide for the establishment of Federal Reserve banks, to furnish an elastic currency, to afford means of rediscounting commercial paper, to establish a more effective supervision of banking in the United States, and for other purposes.

But no constructive law of this kind can possibly be self-executing, and a great deal must depend upon the manner in which it is administered. The Act was a result of many compromises, and the meaning of some clauses was somewhat obscure and ultimately called for judicial interpretation. Moreover, no matter how wisely the law might be administered, it was folly for any one to assume that its operation would usher in a financial and economic millennium, or that the farmer, the manufacturer, the business man, or the banker could disregard in future the dictates of common-sense and business prudence, and rely upon the Federal Reserve Board to do his thinking for him or to pilot him safely through stormy seas, without reasonable coöperation on his own part. Under the most favorable circumstances the task of the Board would have been difficult, for it had to organize a system of banking entirely new in this country; it had no well-established precedents to guide it, and it had many deeply rooted prejudices to overcome.

The members of the Board had been appointed from different sections of the country and some of the members had never seen each other until they met in Washington. World conditions were such when the members of the Board took office as to make their problems even more difficult than had been anticipated. During the preceding week, the war in Europe had broken out, and when the members of the Board assembled for their first meeting, the German artillery was shelling the defenses of Liège. Ocean transportation was paralyzed, for at that time most of the shipping was under the flags of the various belligerent nations, and merchant ships were seeking safety in neutral ports. For a week or ten days before the declaration of war, American securities held abroad had been rushed in great volume to American markets for sale. There was also a great disturbance in the commodity markets, and in order to avert disaster, some of the leading exchanges, such as the New York Stock Exchange, and the New York and New Orleans Cotton Exchanges, had suspended operations entirely and remained closed for several months.

A currency panic would have been inevitable but for the operation of the emergency law of 1908, known as the Aldrich-Vreeland Act, which as originally enacted was to expire by limitation on June 30, 1914. The framers of the Federal Reserve Act had, however, with wise foresight inserted a section in the new law which continued the Aldrich–Vreeland Law in effect for a period of one additional year, or until June 30, 1915. Under this law, national banks were permitted, through national currency associations, to receive additional circulating notes upon the security of good assets (other than

Government bonds) specifically pledged. This additional circulation was subject to a special tax, beginning at three per cent and increasing at the rate of one half of one per cent a month until the tax reached six per cent per annum.

It had not been anticipated, however, that so great an emergency would arise, and it was evident that the terms of the law were not sufficiently liberal to enable the national banks of the country to meet the demand for additional currency. The Secretary of the Treasury, Mr. McAdoo, urged Congress to amend this section immediately in order that an adequate volume of additional national bank notes might be issued through the national currency associations, which were authorized under the Act of May 30, 1908. A bill was quickly passed (August 4th) which amended some of the provisions of the Aldrich–Vreeland Act, so as to give the Secretary of the Treasury more latitude in permitting increases in the circulation of national bank notes. This legislation enabled the national banks to meet the unusual demands for currency without resorting to clearing-house certificates or other expedients which had been employed in acute financial crises and panics in the past. The maximum amount outstanding of this additional national bank note circulation, secured by collateral other than Government bonds, was about $386,000,000, all of which was retired before the expiration by limitation of the law which authorized it.

There were numerous conferences held at the Treasury during the summer of 1914. The war had broken out at a time when the major crops of the country were beginning to move, and there was a heavy export demand for wheat and other food products. Because of the demoralization of ocean transportation, these commodities had accumulated at the ports, resulting in embarrassing congestion of railroad and warehouse facilities, as well as of bank credits. One of the first effects, however, of a great war is to stimulate demand for grain and foodstuffs, and after a few weeks this demand was strong enough to cause a movement of these products abroad, notwithstanding higher freights and increased insurance rates. As the German cruisers were driven from the seas, this movement was accelerated.

The most serious embarrassment caused by the unexpected outbreak of the war was felt by the producers of cotton and by business interests located in, or which dealt with, the cotton-growing sections.

Those who had large payments to make abroad were also much embarrassed because of the high rates of exchange on London and other European money centers. The United States was at the time a debtor nation. For some years the apparent balance of trade — that is, the difference between exports and imports — usually had been in our favor to a moderate extent, but the favorable balance was created by exports of cotton and grain. Payments of interest and dividends on securities owned abroad, interest on borrowed money, expenditures of tourists, ocean freights and insurance premiums paid to foreign companies, often more than offset our favorable trade balance; and up to the middle of the year 1914, it had always been the custom of American banks, early in the year, to draw finance bills against credits arranged with foreign banks. These bills would be liquidated in the autumn by the sale of bills of exchange drawn against shipments of grain and cotton.

The shortage of ocean transportation caused by the war made it impossible for a while to export commodities in anything like the usual volume. It was found in most cases impracticable to secure an extension of maturing obligations abroad. For some weeks the Bank of England rate was ten per cent and sterling sold above seven dollars. At the same time, the largest crop of American cotton ever produced was coming upon the market. The export demand was greatly curtailed, and, besides, it was practically impossible to secure space for cotton in foreign bottoms, the preference being given to grain.

The Federal Reserve Banks were not open for business

until November 16th, and the Federal Reserve Board had, therefore, no financial machinery available for extending relief. The Secretary of the Treasury, however, at a meeting with New York bankers on the evening of August 2, 1914, had informed the bankers present — and his message was carried to the country by the press — that, through the issue of emergency currency, already described, the banks would be expected to maintain themselves on a cash basis, and that ample currency was ready for immediate delivery.

After the members of the Board had taken the oath of office, they were requested by Secretary McAdoo to coöperate with him in various matters which concerned the Treasury directly, but in which the Federal Reserve Banks when ready for business would be concerned. Obligations aggregating a large amount and payable in sterling were approaching maturity, and the British Government sent Sir George Paish and Sir Basil P. Blackett to Washington to discuss the exchange situation. These gentlemen remained in Washington for some weeks and were in frequent conference with Secretary McAdoo and members of the Board.

I believe that it was Mr. Warburg who made the suggestion, which was adopted, that an exchange pool of $100,000,000 be formed by some of the larger banks throughout the country, outside of the cotton belt, which at that time was in dire distress. The members of this pool obligated themselves to make payments in gold as called for by the Managing Committee for the purpose of forcing the rate for sterling down to a figure approximating the cost of shipping gold.

In the annual report of the Federal Reserve Board for the year 1914, the following reference is made to the gold exchange fund:

In order to cope with this extraordinary situation, it was felt that joint action on a comprehensive plan would become necessary. The Federal Reserve Board, in conjunction with the Secretary of the Treasury, therefore, took the initiative in calling, September 4, a conference of representatives of the clearing-houses of all the Reserve cities. The conference had a twofold purpose. On the one hand, it sought to establish, so far as that could be done, the aggregate amount of the actual current indebtedness of the United States to Europe, and, on the other hand, to devise a means of coöperation in dealing with the situation.

The investigation undertaken by the Federal Reserve Board and the conference above mentioned disclosed the opinion that the current indebtedness of the United States to foreign countries was to be stated at approximately $500,000,000, a sum the maturity of which was spread over a period of months. The conference also resulted in the formulation of a plan of relief. A committee of bankers appointed at this conference subsequently recommended a plan for the formation of a gold fund of $100,000,000, which was approved by the Board on September 19, and a letter was sent to the presidents of the clearing-house associations throughout the country under date of September 21, 1914, in which subscriptions aggregating this sum were asked. The Federal Reserve Board had been requested to allot the *pro rata* of the contributions to be made to each clearing-house district, and such allotment was made. Action upon these allotments was prompt and effective, and a total of over $108,000,000 was subscribed.

As had been expected, the beneficial effect of the establishment of this fund became evident almost immediately, notwithstanding that only a comparatively small percentage of the amount subscribed was actually called for, and not more than $10,000,000 was actually exported to furnish a basis for selling foreign exchange. By the time of the opening of the Federal Reserve Banks, the premium had disappeared and the danger of immediate gold exports had been removed.

The freer movement of grain and foodstuffs to Europe aided also in reducing the sterling rate, and by the time Sir George Paish and his associate returned to London, the excessive premium had disappeared. Later on, sterling went to a discount and did not regain its normal parity until May, 1925.

Meanwhile the cotton situation was a subject of grave concern. Congress was in session and many plans for relief were suggested. One does not have to be long in official life in Washington to learn that while public officials are anxious to serve, and as a rule are extremely desirous of getting full credit and publicity for good things accomplished, there are some who are not looking for difficult problems which admit of no immediate spectacular solution. There are always many in Washington who are adepts in the gentle art of 'passing the buck.' There was, indeed, some talk in Congress of legislation which could not possibly be obtained, and which would have been ineffective and vicious, but there was general acquiescence in the idea that the problem was one which should be worked out by the Treasury Department and the Federal Reserve Board. The situation was distressing and unique, and, while it resembled in some respects the situation which afterward developed in the fall of 1920, it was strikingly different in others. The cotton crops of 1912 and 1913 had been sold at from twelve to fourteen cents a pound, which in those days was regarded as a satisfactory price. A large acreage had been planted in the spring of 1914, and the season having been favorable, the result was the largest production of cotton ever known before or since — nearly seventeen million bales. The actual growth, no doubt, was even greater, but owing to the depression much cotton was left in the field unpicked. The war had destroyed for the moment the export demand for cotton, and, as the New York and New Orleans Cotton Exchanges were closed, there was no means of obtaining official quotations. Domestic mills bought from hand to mouth at varying prices depending upon the immediate requirements of the mills and the necessities of the producers. It was recognized that the prices, indefinite as they were, were absurdly low as compared with the standards of preceding years and with the actual costs of production. Few mills, however, were disposed to stock up in the absence of an organized market, and altogether the situation was chaotic. Some well-disposed persons started what is known as the 'buy-a-bale' movement, hoping in this way to create an artificial demand of sufficient breadth to relieve in some degree the distress of the producers. Several hundred individuals coöperated by buying a bale at ten cents a pound, but the futility of this movement soon became evident. The idea of being looked upon as objects of charity was revolting to producers, and even if it had been possible to induce five hundred thousand individuals to buy a bale in this way, the relief afforded would have been negligible. The cotton situation in 1914 is comparable with the wheat situation in 1923 rather than with the cotton marketing problems of 1920. In the latter year there was an insistent demand for credit to enable producers to hold their cotton. The feeling then was strong that, despite the large stocks carried over from previous years, and although the current crop was the second largest in the history of the country — 13,400,000 bales, being next in size to that of 1914 — the cost of production, estimated to be around thirty cents a pound, could be realized presently if credits could be arranged sufficiently liberal in volume and terms to enable the producers to keep their cotton off the market.

In the fall of 1923 the producers of wheat were not asking for ordinary credits, but they were clamoring for a market just as the cotton producers in 1914 were practically unanimous in demanding a market rather than credit. In September and October, 1923, there were many in the Northwest who urged that the Government through some instrumentality should purchase wheat at $1.50 a bushel, and in 1914 there were many in the South who demanded that the Government should purchase cotton at ten cents a pound. There were others, however, including some leaders in Congress, who thought that the situation could and should be relieved by the deposit of a large volume of Government funds in Southern banks (to be raised by an issue of 'greenbacks' and by the sale of Government bonds), to be loaned on cotton exclusively. Secretary McAdoo replied, on October 9th, to a suggestion of this kind made by Honorable Robert L. Henry, of Texas, Chairman of the House Committee on Rules, in a letter from which these excerpts are taken. Much of the Secretary's letter would have been apropos in later years.

Your proposition is, in essence, to issue $400,000,000 of Government bonds, $200,000,000 of which are to be deferred obligations bearing 3 per cent interest, and $200,000,000 are to be demand obligations, or greenbacks, and to deposit the proceeds in the cotton States exclusively, to be loaned on cotton exclusively, through some method too vaguely outlined in your letter to admit of judgment.

It is extremely doubtful if so large amount of 3 per cent Government bonds could be sold at par in the present condition of the money market. The rate of interest would in all probability have to be increased. Moreover, the Secretary of the Treasury has no power, under existing law, to do this. You admit his want of power because you suggest that if he needs 'a little more legal authority' he can get it from Congress.

I cannot believe that this is true. You have been a member of Congress for seventeen years; you are the head of its powerful Committee on Rules, which determines what legislation may be specially considered and advanced by the House of Representatives. If you think the necessary 'legal authority' can be had, why do you not prevail upon Congress to give it?

Is it not because the Congress itself thinks the constitutionality of such legislation is open to the gravest doubt, and the policy of it even more questionable? Is it wise to issue $400,000,000 of Government bonds and greenbacks, merely to lend on cotton? Tobacco, naval stores, copper, silver, lumber, and other things have been hurt by the European War. All have applied to the Treasury for relief. If we disregard every suffering interest except cotton and make it the sole beneficiary of governmental favor, what becomes of the Democratic principle 'equal rights for all, special privileges to none'? If we enter upon the course you suggest, we must help every distressed industry impartially. To do that would necessitate the issue of many more than $400,000,000 in bonds and greenbacks and dangerously involve the credit of the Government. It would be a hopeless undertaking, in defiance of every sound principle of finance and economics, with certain disaster at the end. . . .

On the 24th of August a special conference of representative men in the different sections of the country interested in the production, manufacturing, and financing of cotton assembled in Washington upon invitation of the Secretary of the Treasury. At the conclusion of that conference the Secretary of the Treasury announced that he would accept, from national banks, through currency associations, notes secured by warehouse receipts for cotton, tobacco, and naval stores at 75 per cent of their face value. This left the bankers free to lend such amount as they thought safe upon the security of cotton, and made it possible for them to convert 75 per cent of the notes so received into national bank currency. Since the 1st of August there has been issued to national banks in the Southern States, including Missouri and Maryland, $68,000,000 of additional national bank currency. The national banks in these same States may, by complying with the law, receive $151,443,000 of additional national bank currency. . . .

After pointing out that there was already available, to the national banks in the Southern States, Government deposits and additional national bank currency amounting in the aggregate to $246,845,000, the Secretary continued:

Aside from the foregoing, I may say that the Secretary of the Treasury has authorized the issuance, since the outbreak of the European War, to national banks throughout the country, of additional national bank circulation aggregating $348,795,210. A large part of this currency has found its way to the South. Recently the Comptroller of the Currency, at my request, called on the national banks of New York City for a statement of the amount of loans which they had made to banks in the Southern States from August 1, 1914, to date. These reports show that the New York City national banks are lending to Southern banks more than $40,000,000.

Moreover, existing law authorizes the Secretary of the Treasury, in his discretion, to issue more than $1,000,000,000 of additional currency to national banks throughout the country.

The banks, therefore, have ample opportunity to get more than enough currency to meet every conceivable demand, if more currency is, as many seem to think, the remedy for the cotton situation. I do not believe it is. *I am firmly convinced that neither additional nor unlimited issues of paper money will help the cotton planter. I am equally convinced that the inevitable inflation which such issues would cause would hurt him and hurt the country. What is really wanted is a restored market for cotton at a profitable price. This is the real fact, the real truth in the situation. It is impossible by legislation to create a market for cotton or to establish a price for it. The value of cotton has been injured this year by the European War. This injury cannot be retrieved nor the market restored by legislation any more than the injury to corn which was caused by the drought last year in the great corn States of the West could have been repaired by legislation.*

Up to the present time there has been a disposition everywhere to look exclusively to and rely wholly upon the National Government for assistance. There are many things which the Cotton States and the people of the South can do for themselves which the National Government cannot do for them. The powers and resources of the Southern States should be employed for the benefit of their people and the National Government should not be expected to do things which are beyond its power.

The Secretary of the Treasury has exercised, and will continue to exercise, all the lawful powers he possesses, consistent with sound economics and safe financing, for the assistance of the cotton producers of the South and all other industries which have been injured by the European War or which are entitled to assistance for any cause. . . .

Reference has already been made to the effect of the closing of the cotton exchanges in Liverpool, New York, and New Orleans upon the cotton market. There was no way for the mills to contract for their future requirements or to 'hedge' against their spot purchases, nor was there any established or authentic price for cotton. In these circumstances, bank loans on cotton as security were made sparingly, with reluctance, and always on a very low valuation.

Mr. Festus J. Wade, of St. Louis, at a conference held in Washington during the latter part of August had suggested that a fund of $100,000,000 be subscribed by banks out of which loans on cotton should be made on a reasonable basis, an arbitrary valuation to be fixed high enough to afford some measure of relief and low enough to ensure the safety of the fund. Many banks indicated their willingness to subscribe to this fund provided that the members of the Federal Reserve Board, even though not acting in their official capacity, should give their support and sanction to the undertaking. The Attorney-General having given an opinion that the operation of such a fund would not be in conflict with anti-trust laws, the members of the Board, while reluctant to assume any additional responsibilities, felt impelled by

the same sense of public duty which had actuated them in the case of the gold fund to respond to the call and to act as a central committee of the cotton loan fund. After the members of the Board had consented to act in this capacity, many conferences were held, with the ultimate result that banks in New York City agreed to pledge a subscription of $50,000,000 to the fund upon the condition that an equal amount be raised by banks in other than cotton-producing States. The plan provided that to the $100,000,000 to be raised in this manner there should be added a further sum of $35,000,000 to be contributed by banks in the cotton-producing States, and that the $100,000,000 should be called for in proportion as the $35,000,000 fund should be subscribed and paid in. Under this plan, if borrowers should absorb the entire amount of $135,000,000, $100,000,000, or practically two thirds, would be furnished by banks located outside of the cotton-producing States, while only $35,000,000 would be supplied by Southern banks. In this way material relief would be afforded, while the banks not located in cotton sections which furnished $100,000,000 would have additional protection in that they would have preference as the loans were paid; Southern banks thus having in effect a second lien. The loan value was fixed by the committee at approximately six cents per pound.

It was impossible, however, to put the plan into operation until November 30, 1914, by which time the Federal Reserve Banks had been opened for business, thereby releasing a large amount of reserve funds which enabled member banks to make new loans and grant extensions which otherwise would have been impossible. At the same time there had been some improvement in shipping conditions, and less than $30,000 of the fund was ever applied for and only about $20,000 actually loaned. As the cotton exchanges were not reopened until after January 1, 1915, the loan value of six cents per pound fixed by the committee was generally accepted as a bedrock valuation of cotton, basis middling, and cotton sold in December, 1914, brought about that figure.

CHAPTER III

THE FEDERAL RESERVE BANKS BEGIN BUSINESS — THEIR POLICY OUTLINED

WHILE the cotton situation was engrossing public and official attention, the Board was confronted with the problems of organization, for upon it fell the duty of completing the directorships of the Federal Reserve Banks by appointing the three 'Class C' directors for each and of speeding up the preparations for opening the banks. In view of conditions prevailing at the time the Board took office, there were frequent expressions of the belief that the opening of the Federal Reserve Banks should be deferred until the return of more normal conditions. These expressions of opinion led to many conferences and to many discussions at Board meetings. During the unusually hot summer of 1914, the Board frequently remained in session five or six hours a day, and the discussions impressed me as being generally interesting, sometimes amusing, and occasionally tiresome. As a result of many conferences and of long discussions and of the insistence of Secretary McAdoo, the Board concluded in October to proceed forthwith with the organization of the Reserve Banks with the view of having them begin business as soon as suitable quarters could be secured, and competent operating staffs selected. The following extract from the Board's annual report, which was signed by all the members of the Board after prolonged consideration of the draft first submitted, throws a better light upon some of the primary problems of the Board than would anything written by an individual after this lapse of time, and I have therefore incorporated it below:

The Board was also, however, firmly of the opinion that in undertaking thus early to establish the Federal Reserve Banks it would be necessary to enlist the hearty coöperation of all the member banks in two matters which were deemed of fundamental importance: (1) payment by the member banks in gold out of their own vaults of the reserves they were required to contribute to the new banks, thus diffusing the burden of providing the cash resources of the Federal Reserve Banks; (2) the adoption of a discount policy which would prevent the accumulated strength of the banks from being dissipated and protect their resources from being used to finance operations not calculated to add to the strength or solidity of general banking conditions.

Before the banks could be set in actual operation, however, it was necessary for the Board to complete the organization prescribed in the Federal Reserve Act by the appointment of three Government directors in each of the several institutions. Pursuant to the requirements of law, the Reserve Bank Organization Committee, consisting of the Secretary of the Treasury, the Secretary of Agriculture, and the Comptroller of the Currency, had already taken preliminary steps, resulting in the election by the banks of six directors in each Federal Reserve District, and the results of these elections were reported to the Federal Reserve Board upon its organization.

There remained to be appointed by the Board three Government directors for each district, the first of whom was to be designated Federal Reserve Agent and Chairman of the board of directors, the second as Deputy Reserve Agent and Vice-Chairman. Particular importance was felt to attach to the choice of all the Government directors, and especially of the Federal Reserve Agents. The Federal Reserve Act specifically designates the Federal Reserve Agent as the representative of the Federal Reserve Board at the bank to which he is accredited, and invests him with very large responsibilities. It was not, in the opinion of the Board, the intent of the Act to constitute the Federal Reserve Agent the operating head of the bank, but, rather, that he should be vested with the function of promoting the general interests and purposes of the system, assuring himself and this Board of the sound and impartial administration and efficient operation of the bank to which he was accredited, and giving both to the Federal Reserve Board and to the executive officers and his fellow directors of the bank, over whom he had been appointed Chairman, the benefit of his advice and knowledge. The office is undoubtedly one which calls for exceptional qualifications, and is, therefore, difficult to fill, since by the very terms of the Act, 'tested banking experience' is made a prerequisite, while consideration for the general welfare of the bank's administration requires that the incumbent be a man of solidity, independence, and tried character.

Believing that the choice of the Government directors was a matter of fundamental importance and that errors made in their selection would produce serious consequences in the later working of the banks, the Board deemed it essential to scrutinize every name submitted for appointment, or suggested from any source, with the utmost care. The process was one which required time, and necessitated visits by members of the Board to various and distant parts of the country, as well as the invitation of competent advisors to Washington for consultation. As the outcome of these investigations and deliberations, the Board announced to the public at different dates early in October the three selections made for Government directors for each of the Reserve Banks, or 36 in all. . . .

In order to obtain persons of satisfactory banking experience, as required by law, it was found necessary to give to Federal Reserve Agents salaries commensurate with, or approximating, those prevailing in the banking community in each district for men of similar attainments, abilities, and experience. In a number of cases it was found possible to attract to the service of the Reserve Banks men of high qualifications at a rate of compensation substantially lower than they had been receiving or were in a position to obtain. The action of the appointees in accepting office on short notice and at the compensation established was the more to their credit in that in not a few cases it was necessary for them to incur substantial financial sacrifice because of the unfavorable conditions under which they were obliged to dispose of their holdings of bank stock, the Federal Reserve Act making it mandatory that each Federal Reserve Agent and each director of Class C should divest himself of ownership of this class of securities. . . .

As soon as the directors of the several banks had been chosen, they proceeded to select the nucleus of a suitable staff, in order that the banks might be ready to begin active operations when qualified to do so. The Board particularly enjoined upon them the choice of a suitable chief executive officer in each institution, with the suggestion that this officer be given the title of governor in order to differentiate his functions from those of the president of a member bank.

While some members of the Board may have preferred that the Board's own appointees and representatives, the Federal

Reserve Agents, be made the operating heads of their respective banks in order to strengthen the Board's control over the banks, the conclusion was finally reached, and, if I remember correctly, unanimously, that under the terms of section 4 of the Federal Reserve Act this was impossible.

The plain intent of the law was to establish a regional as opposed to a central banking system. Provision was made that six of the nine directors of each Federal Reserve Bank should be chosen by its stockholding banks. Each Federal Reserve Bank was made a body corporate, to have succession for a period of twenty years, and was empowered

to make contracts . . . to appoint by its board of directors such officers and employees as are not otherwise provided for in this Act, to define their duties, require bonds of them and fix the penalty thereof, and to dismiss at pleasure such officers or employees . . . to prescribe by its board of directors, by-laws not inconsistent with law, regulating the manner in which its general business may be conducted, and the privileges granted to it by law may be exercised and enjoyed . . . to exercise by its board of directors, or duly authorized officers or agents, all powers specifically granted by the provisions of this Act, and such incidental powers as shall be necessary to carry on the business of banking within the limitations prescribed by this Act.

And again it is expressly prescribed in section 4 that

Every Federal Reserve Bank shall be conducted under the supervision and control of a board of directors. The board of directors shall perform the duties usually appertaining to the office of directors of banking associations and all such duties as are prescribed by law.

The law requires the Federal Reserve Board to designate one of the three directors appointed by it as Chairman of the board of directors of the Federal Reserve Bank and as Federal Reserve Agent. His compensation is fixed, not by the directors of the bank, but by the Federal Reserve Board, and his duties in each of his dual capacities are clearly and specifically defined in the Act. As Federal Reserve Agent he is the direct representative of the Federal Reserve Board to which body he is required to make regular reports. His duties, as defined in the Act, relate chiefly to the custody, issue, and redemption of Federal Reserve notes; to the custody of gold and other collateral held to secure Federal Reserve notes; and to examinations of member banks, and of banks applying for membership. By direction of the Federal Reserve Board he is required to keep it informed of the personnel of the directorates of large member banks in his district, and to forward with his recommendation applications from any individuals who wish to serve at the same time as directors of two or more banks, one of which comes within the purview of the so-called Clayton Act, which regulates interlocking directorships.

He is charged also by the Board with the duty of assembling statistical matter and of making reports on financial and economic conditions in his district.

As Chairman of the board of directors of the Federal Reserve Bank to which he is accredited, he presides at meetings of the directors and shares with the other directors in their duties and responsibilities as such.

He is required by law to supervise the election of directors of Classes A and B, and to announce the result; and 'under regulations to be established by the Federal Reserve Board' to maintain a local office of said Board on the premises of the Federal Reserve Bank.

Nowhere in the law is there any provision requiring or permitting him to act as the chief executive officer, and the Board felt that it could not vest him with such power without infringing upon the rights of the directors as defined in section 4 of the Act. The law imposes upon the board of directors of a Federal Reserve Bank serious duties and responsibilities, in the discharge of which the directors are clearly entitled to choose their own officers and agents.

As a rule there has been no friction between the Chairman and Federal Reserve Agent and the Governor of a Federal

Reserve Bank, and in those cases where friction has occurred, it has been found to have been due either to personal considerations of a trivial character, or to a disregard or misconception of their respective duties as defined by law or as delegated under the by-laws of the bank.

A few years after the organization of the System, the directors of one of the Federal Reserve Banks sought by resolution to make the Chairman of the board of directors the operating head of their bank, but the Federal Reserve Board was not willing to assume responsibility for the routine management of the Federal Reserve Banks which it would have incurred had it permitted its own appointee and agent to assume executive duties, and therefore declined to approve the change proposed.

Notwithstanding the unusually difficult conditions which confronted the Board upon its organization, which led many to express the opinion that the Federal Reserve Banks could not be opened before the first of January, 1915, conditions had improved sufficiently to warrant an earlier date for the opening, and the work of organization being well advanced, the Board on October 26th notified all member banks to pay in their first installment of capital stock on November 2d. At about the same time the Secretary of the Treasury, acting under the authority conferred upon him by section 19 of the Federal Reserve Act, fixed November 16th as the date for opening the Federal Reserve Banks, at which time the reserves of the member banks were to be readjusted in accordance with the requirements of section 19 of the Act.

Many sections of the Federal Reserve Act require that the functions described therein shall be exercised under regulations to be prescribed by the Federal Reserve Board. In formulating regulations it was necessary for the Board to agree upon the general principles or policies which should govern the operation of the banks. While it was clear that the Federal Reserve Banks are not authorized by law to make loans direct to individuals, but can only rediscount paper for eligible banks upon their endorsements, the open-market powers, in which the Federal Reserve Banks might legally engage under regulations to be prescribed by the Federal Reserve Board, opened to them an independent avenue for the employment of their funds and a means of exerting a direct influence in the money market. There were some who sought to convince the Board that the Federal Reserve Banks should be emergency institutions, and that ordinarily they should not be allowed to engage regularly in many transactions permissible under the terms of the Act; others took the position that the banks should, on the contrary, actively and continuously exercise all their functions at least to a moderate extent. The Board after much deliberation and discussion agreed that the banks should not be operated only as emergency institutions, and while merely for the sake of profit they should not undertake to engage in business to the full extent of their legal power, they should nevertheless be organized in such a manner as to admit of the fullest exercise of all their activities when occasion demanded, and that as a matter of policy they should regularly and constantly employ a part of their resources in the exercise of their proper functions without exceeding the bounds of prudence and moderation.

Under the caption 'Place of Reserve Banks,' in its first annual report to Congress the Board said:

It should not, however, be assumed that because a bank is a Reserve Bank its resources should be kept idle for use only in times of difficulty, or, if used at all in ordinary times, used reluctantly and sparingly. Neither should it be assumed that because a Reserve Bank is a large and powerful bank, all its resources should be in use all the time or that it should enter into keen competition with member banks, distributing accommodations with a free and lavish hand in undertaking to quicken unwisely the pace of industry. Such a policy would be sure, sooner or later, to invite disaster. Time and experience will show what the seasonal variations in the credit demands and facilities in each of the Reserve Banks of the several districts will be and when and to what extent a Reserve Bank may, without violating its special function as a guardian of banking reserves, engage in banking and credit operations. The Reserve Banks have expenses to meet, and while it would be a mistake to regard them merely as profit-making concerns and to apply to them the ordinary test of business success, there is no reason why they should not earn their expenses, and a fair profit besides, without failing to exercise their proper functions and exceeding the bounds of prudence in their management. Moreover, the Reserve Banks can never become the leading and important factor in the money market which they were designed to be unless a considerable portion of their resources is regularly and constantly employed.

There will be times when the great weight of their influence and resources should be exerted to secure a freer extension of credit and an easing of rates in order that the borrowing community shall be able to obtain accommodations at the lowest rates warranted by existing conditions and be adequately protected against exorbitant rates of interest. There will just as certainly, however, be other times when prudence and a proper regard for the common good will require that an opposite course should be pursued and accommodations curtailed. Normally, therefore, a considerable proportion of its resources should always be kept invested by a Reserve Bank in order that the release or withdrawal from active employment of its banking funds may always exercise a beneficial influence. This is merely saying that to influence the market a Reserve Bank must always be in the market, and in this sense Reserve Banks will be active banking concerns when once they have found their true position under the new banking conditions.

It would be a mistake, therefore, and a serious limitation of their usefulness to regard the Reserve Banks simply as emergency banks. Regulation in ordinary times, as well as protection in extraordinary times, may be expected to become the chief service which these institutions will perform.

It is evident, therefore, that the open-market operations, in which, in recent years, the Federal Reserve Banks have engaged, are entirely consistent with the policy announced by the Board immediately after the Reserve Banks began business.

CHAPTER IV

PRIOR to the appointment of the Board members the twelve
Federal Reserve districts and the Federal Reserve Bank cities
had been designated by the Organization Committee. Bankers in certain cities, and in the territory adjacent thereto,
were not satisfied with the decision of the Organization Committee, which the law prescribed in section 2 of the Act
should 'not be subject to review except by the Federal Reserve Board when organized.' Soon after the Board took
office, it was requested in certain instances to review the
decision of the Organization Committee, but no immediate
action was taken because of the urgent duties imposed upon
the Board in the organization of the banks. That work having been completed, the Board announced that it would
proceed with the hearing of these appeals shortly after the
first of January, 1915. The applications generally were for
the transfer of certain territory from one district to another,
but there were two cases in which it was sought to change the
location of the Federal Reserve Bank of the district. One of
these was a petition from Pittsburgh member banks requesting that Pittsburgh be designated as the seat of the Federal
Reserve Bank instead of Cleveland in District No. 4, and
the other was a petition from Baltimore member banks requesting that Baltimore instead of Richmond be designated
as the seat of the Federal Reserve Bank in District No. 5.
Much of the Board's time during the whole year of 1915 was
taken up with the consideration of these cases, as well as with
the discussion of a proposition to reduce the number of Federal Reserve districts from twelve to eight or nine. There
was during that year an abnormally easy money market due

to the rapid growth of bank deposits throughout the country, and to the large importations of gold for foreign account. Some of the Federal Reserve Banks were not earning their operating expenses, while only one of them, the Federal Reserve Bank of Richmond, had been able on the 30th of June to pay its semiannual dividend.

Section 2 of the Federal Reserve Act provided that the Organization Committee 'shall designate not less than eight or more than twelve cities to be known as Federal Reserve cities,' and to divide the United States into districts corresponding to the number of Federal Reserve Banks determined upon. The law also prescribed that

The determination of said Organization Committee shall not be subject to review except by the Federal Reserve Board when organized: *Provided*, That the districts shall be apportioned with due regard to the convenience and customary course of business and shall not necessarily be coterminous with any State or States. The districts thus created may be readjusted and new districts may from time to time be created by the Federal Reserve Board, not to exceed twelve in all.

Provision was also made in the Act, section 3, for the establishment of branches of Federal Reserve Banks.

Messrs. Warburg and Delano took the view that before changing district lines the Board should consider the propriety of making some reduction in the number of districts, and that in any case where a Federal Reserve Bank was abolished, a branch should be substituted in its place in order not to disturb the customary course of business. At that time I shared with them the opinion that the System could be more efficiently and economically operated with a smaller number of banks, and I believe that Mr. Miller held the same view. There was a question, however, as to the extent of the Board's powers, and the opinions rendered by the Board's counsel were somewhat vague, although the consulting counsel, Joseph P. Cotton, formally rendered an unqualified opinion that the Federal Reserve Board was fully authorized by the Act to reduce the number of districts. Although I was at the time in favor of reducing the number of districts to ten, I did not overlook the difficulties in the way of effecting such a reduction, nor did I ever believe that the reduction would be made. It would have been necessary to have an agreement as to which of the banks should be eliminated, and, as three members of the Board were strongly opposed to any reduction, it seemed to me probable that there might be a disagreement among the four members who favored a reduction in principle as to how the districts should be readjusted.

While all these matters were under discussion, the Attorney-General on November 22, 1915, addressed a letter to the President which was transmitted by him to the Board. In this letter the Attorney-General expressed the opinion that the Federal Reserve Board had no power to abolish any one or more of the Federal Reserve districts, nor any one or more of the Federal Reserve Banks located in the cities designated by the Reserve Bank Organization Committee.

Earlier in the year Governor Hamlin had appointed a committee on redistricting composed of Messrs. Delano, Warburg, and myself. Upon receipt of the Attorney-General's opinion, this committee made a report to the Board reviewing the whole subject. In this report the committee reiterated the opinion which had often been expressed that the number of the banks and districts was larger than was conducive to the most efficient operation of the System. This the committee reported was not the fault of the Act, but was due to the circumstance that the Organization Committee, although acting in the best of faith, could not, in the short time allotted to it, acquire such knowledge and experience as was absolutely necessary for a final determination of such an important question.

The committee, however, recognizing the authority of the Attorney-General's opinion, and submitting to the conclusion reached therein, recommended that the Board abandon any plan of redistricting which involved the consolidation of any districts, and address itself to the specific appeals pending and to such readjustments as might be permissible and practicable under the Attorney-General's opinion.

In view of the applications from Pittsburgh and Baltimore to be designated as Federal Reserve cities in place of Cleveland and Richmond respectively, and of other applications for the transfer of territory from one bank to another, which transfers would reduce the capital of a Reserve Bank below the statutory limit of $4,000,000, the committee recommended that the Board instruct the Governor to address a letter to the President requesting him to obtain the opinion of the Attorney-General on the following questions:

(1) Can the Federal Reserve Board legally change the present location of any Federal Reserve Bank?
   (a) In the case where there has been no alteration in the district lines? and
   (b) In the case where there has been such a readjustment of district lines as in the opinion of the Board necessitates the designation of a new Federal Reserve city in order that the convenience and customary course of business may be accommodated as required by law?
(2) Must the Board, in exercising its admitted power to readjust, preserve the $4,000,000 minimum capitalization of each and every Federal Reserve Bank?

On the 14th of April, 1916, the Attorney-General addressed a letter to the President in which he expressed the opinion that the Federal Reserve Board had no power to change the location of any Federal Reserve Bank, and reiterated his previous opinion that the Board could not reduce the number of Federal Reserve districts or abolish a Federal Reserve Bank. He did, however, express the opinion that the Board had power to make reasonable readjustments of Federal Reserve districts by changing their boundary lines. This opinion made it unnecessary for the Board to give further consideration to the petitions of Pittsburgh and Baltimore. It was clear and explicit, and effectively disposed of a question which bid fair to be highly controversial.

Meanwhile the Board had made some readjustments of district lines, some of the most important of which were as follows: The transfer of Fairfield County, Connecticut, and several counties in northern New Jersey to the New York District. Originally, Jersey City and Newark had been placed in the Philadelphia District. Mr. McAdoo was reminded that, while as builder of the Hudson tunnels he had put these cities within ten minutes' touch of the financial district of New York City, he had as chairman of the Federal Reserve Organization Committee attempted to make them tributary to Philadelphia, thus giving their banking business a back haul, which would involve two days in getting into New York.

Other changes in district lines made at this time involved the transfer of two counties in the panhandle region of West Virginia from the Richmond to the Cleveland District, and of all but seven counties in southern Oklahoma (south of the Arkansas River) from the Dallas to the Kansas City District. The application of bankers in Nebraska and Wyoming to have those States transferred from the Kansas City to the Chicago District was denied, but later on their wishes were complied with substantially by the establishment of a branch of the Federal Reserve Bank of Kansas City at Omaha. A year or two later other slight adjustments in district lines were made involving the transfer of two additional counties in West Virginia to the Cleveland District, and a few counties in Wisconsin from the Minneapolis to the Chicago District, and of several parishes in southern Louisiana from the Dallas to the Atlanta District.

Another problem to which the Board as well as the officers of the Federal Reserve Banks devoted much attention during the year 1915 related to the establishment of a check clearing and collection system. This problem was to be one of the most difficult which was ever presented to the Board, and events have proved that it could not be easily or speedily solved. Even before the passage of the Federal Reserve Act, a large number of banks, those located in small towns especially, were outspoken in their opposition to any steps which would tend to the abolition of what they called their 'exchange charges'; that is, a charge that they had been accustomed to make in remitting their own checks drawn on correspondent banks in larger cities in payment of checks on themselves which had been forwarded by holders residing elsewhere. In every step taken by the Board and the Federal Reserve Banks to establish a universal par clearance system, they were confronted with persistent opposition which finally culminated in long-drawn-out litigation. In a subsequent chapter will be found a review of the successive steps which were taken to establish an efficient system for par clearance of checks by Federal Reserve Banks, as well as of the litigation which followed.

During the year 1915 some of the collateral effects of the war in Europe became increasingly noticeable in Washington. At the time of the outbreak of the war, the President issued a proclamation enjoining strict neutrality, but it was impossible to smother human preferences and prejudices. Social amenities in Washington cut more of a figure in current affairs than they do elsewhere. It is not unusual for matters of national, and even international, importance to be discussed over coffee-cups and cigars after dinner at the home of some official or unofficial hostess in Washington. Great care was exercised by those giving receptions or dinners not to invite at the same time those whose sympathies were with the Allies and those who were pro-German in their feelings. The diplomatic corps was divided into two distinct parts, and, instead of there being the usual diplomatic dinner at the White House in the winter of 1915–16, there were two such dinners; one each to the envoys of the belligerent groups, with the neutral ambassadors and ministers distributed between the two. Official circles were supposed to be neutral, and while the preponderance of sentiment in Congressional and social circles was pro-Ally, there were prior to the sinking of the Lusitania not a few partisans of the German cause. While that event changed the feelings of many, there were nevertheless some prominent German sympathizers up to the time of our own entry into the war in 1917.

There were many evidences of propaganda work in behalf of the German as well as of the Allied cause, but it seemed to me that the German propaganda was far more insidious and persistent.

The Allies had maintained an effective blockade of the German ports ever since the beginning of the war, while the German counter-offensive — the submarine terror — was not nearly so effective in 1915 as it afterward became. England and France particularly were importing from this country large quantities, not only of foodstuffs, but of metals and munitions of war. Cotton began to be used in appreciable quantities in the manufacture of explosives such as guncotton, and it appeared that large quantities were getting into Germany through the port of Gothenburg, Sweden.

There appeared before the Federal Reserve Board on several occasions during the year a delegation of about a half-dozen men who called themselves Labor's National Peace Council. These people endeavored to convince the Board that it was its duty to declare as ineligible for rediscount or purchase by Federal Reserve Banks all paper growing out of the exportation of war material or munitions. There were at the same time rumors that the British Government proposed to issue an order making cotton an absolute contraband of war, and claiming the right of search and seizure, in order to prevent that commodity from being taken into those neutral ports from which it might enter the German lines. The cotton market had recovered to some extent from its extreme depression of the previous autumn, and the better grades were selling at from eight to nine cents a pound. Southern producers felt that the effect of any further restrictions upon the export of cotton would be unfavorable to them, and some of the Southern Senators and Representatives were insisting that if cotton was placed on the contraband list by Great Britain, the United States Government should retaliate by putting an embargo upon shipments of war material and munitions.

Meanwhile, bankers' syndicates were arranging for the flotation of both long- and short-term loans in the United States for the benefit of belligerent powers, but mainly for British and French account. The Board was not concerned directly with long-term obligations, for the Federal Reserve Act expressly prohibits Federal Reserve Banks from financing purchases of any bonds except those of the United States.

There were, however, some short-time credits of the type technically known as 'revolving credits,' the eligibility of which the Board was asked to consider. It was proposed that drafts be drawn against shipments of goods abroad, having a maturity of three months, as provided by the statute, with the understanding that there might be three successive renewals. The question submitted to the Board was whether renewal agreements, if the Federal Reserve Banks were not a party to them, affected the eligibility of the paper. There was also a question whether these drafts were drawn to finance exportations of munitions, and whether, in such event, the Board should declare them ineligible. The Board decided that munitions and war material were 'goods, wares, or merchandise' within the meaning of the Act, and that drafts drawn against such shipments, if otherwise eligible under the terms of the Act, were not rendered ineligible by reason of the fact that the 'goods, wares, or merchandise' happened to be war munitions. This was based upon the conclusion that it was the province of the President and the Department of State, and not of the Board, to determine whether shipments of munitions should be made from this country to nationals of belligerent powers.

The price of cotton, which had advanced from six cents a pound in December, 1914, to about nine cents early in June, 1915, declined during the months of June and July, and when it had reacted to eight cents, much alarm was felt in the cotton-producing sections. Heavy losses had been incurred by cotton producers because of the drastic decline in 1914, and it was felt that, unless the new crop could be sold on a basis of at least ten cents a pound, financial distress throughout the South would be aggravated. German propagandists, no doubt, made the most of this situation, for the decline in cotton was associated in the public mind with the report that the British Government intended to put cotton on the contraband list. As has already been stated, some of the Southern Senators and Representatives were insisting that, if this were done, our Government should put an embargo on the shipment abroad of munitions.

Sir Richard Crawford, who was the commercial advisor of the British Embassy, used to call at my office quite frequently, and he seemed to be especially interested in the cotton situation. One morning late in July he came to see me and said that the British Ambassador, Sir Cecil Spring-Rice, would like to have me take tea with him at the Embassy that afternoon. I called there at five o'clock, and, after insisting that I follow his example and doff my coat, the Ambassador came immediately to the point. He stated that the British Government had no desire whatever to injure the South, but, as Germany was getting so much cotton through neutral ports, it had become absolutely necessary to declare it a contraband. It would be very embarrassing, he said, to have an embargo placed upon the shipment of munitions, but that, come what may, his Government would be compelled to put cotton on the contraband list. He had asked me to come to see him as an individual and as a Southern man, he said, and he wished particularly to know whether the South would be benefited by a delay of sixty days of the proposed order in council, which was even then ready to be signed.

I replied that I was of the opinion that there would be no advantage to the South in delaying for sixty days the order making cotton contraband, for by that time the new crop would be coming in rapidly, and the market would have to sustain not only the shock occasioned by the order, but also the weight of largely increased offerings of cotton. I suggested that the order be signed promptly and that it be made public the following Saturday afternoon after the close of the market, and that the British Government take steps to give strong support to contracts for fall deliveries the following Monday morning on the Liverpool, New York, and New Orleans Cotton Exchanges. I suggested that this support be continued steadily for some time with the view of forcing prices beyond the ten-cent level. If this could be done, I felt sure that there would be no agitation in the South in favor of an embargo on exports of munitions.

The order in council was signed the next Saturday afternoon. The markets in Liverpool, New York, and New Orleans were strong the following Monday, and in all of them cotton advanced steadily day by day almost without reaction, until, in November, the quotations were above twelve cents a pound. As I had predicted, Southern agitation for an embargo on shipments of munitions ceased.

The acquaintance which I formed at this time with Sir Cecil Spring-Rice ripened into a personal friendship, the memories of which are most pleasant. The Ambassador was entirely lacking in the aggressiveness and effrontery which characterized some of the envoys at that time. He was modest and unassuming in his demeanor, and it was sometimes said that his diplomacy was of the negative type. However this may be, he was an able representative of his Government, and a most attractive personality. He was a good raconteur and his stories of some of his diplomatic experiences were most interesting. He told me on one occasion that his first assignment as ambassador was to the Court of Czar Nicholas at St. Petersburg. This was in 1906 when Mr. Asquith was the British Prime Minister. The Ambassador said that, in accordance with custom, before leaving for his post he called on King Edward VII, in order to receive any personal messages which the King might wish to have delivered to the Czar. The conversation turned to the autocratic powers of the Emperor of Russia as contrasted with the limited actual authority of a constitutional king, and in parting King Edward said, 'You tell Nicholas that after all I am better off than he is; for if it rains in Siberia it is his fault, while if it rains in Scotland it is Asquith's fault.' Subsequent events certainly proved the soundness of King Edward's philosophy.

The Federal Reserve Board in its annual report for 1915 gives the following account of the steps it took during the summer to assist the orderly marketing of cotton and other staple crops:

Because of the difficult international conditions, the Federal Reserve Board early in the summer felt that it would be advisable to be prepared for any contingency that might arise in connection with the marketing of the cotton crop. Fears for the situation were widespread in the South, some pessimistic observers predicting a repetition of the disastrous experiences of 1914. The Board, therefore, in June, 1915, appointed a special committee to study the condition and needs of the cotton-growing districts. The committee, realizing the importance of fostering a financial condition in which producers would not be obliged to sacrifice their cotton, but would be assisted in the gradual and orderly marketing of the crop, began its work by investigating warehouse facilities in the cotton belt and by making a careful study of the laws governing warehousing in the Southern States. It also informed itself regarding the extent of crop diversification, which early in the year had been strongly urged by the Department of Agriculture and by bankers' associations in the South. It ascertained that the cotton acreage had been greatly reduced and that food crops had been planted to a greater extent than in previous years, and it was not long in reaching the conclusion that the yield of cotton would be much less than was the case in 1914. Finding the storage facilities for such portion of the crop as might have to be carried over generally adequate, it recommended the creation of a special kind of accommodation to assist those producers who, having made their crop, might desire temporarily to withhold a portion of it from the market. The committee entertained the view that warehouse receipts for cotton, grain, and other staple, non-perishable agricultural products of a readily marketable character, form an excellent basis for bank loans, particularly as under the terms of the Federal Reserve Act and the regulations of the Board, notes thus secured are eligible for rediscount by Federal Reserve Banks.

During the summer, the committee developed a method by which producers could secure low rates upon loans secured in this manner, and in order to encourage coöperation between member banks and producers, the Board issued on September 3, 1915, its commodity paper regulation which provided that notes secured by non-perishable staple commodities, having a specified date of maturity, and upon which member banks had not charged a rate of interest or discount, including all commissions, of more than six per cent per annum, should be eligible for rediscount in Federal Reserve Banks at a preferential rate. It should be especially noted that this commodity rate, so called, was not confined to any section of the country or to loans secured by any one commodity, but was general in its nature. It applied not to cotton alone, but to other staple products, such as grain, sugar, and wool. It was, in fact, adopted by several of the reserve banks, some of them, however, receiving but little business under it owing to the abundance of funds in member banks.

The Board, moreover, in the exercise of the powers conferred upon it by the Federal Reserve Act, was fully prepared to set in operation, if it should become necessary, at rates to be fixed by it, the machinery of interbank rediscounting, in order to make available for Federal Reserve Banks requiring larger resources the available funds of other reserve banks, the collective strength of the reserve system as a whole being far in excess of any demands that might reasonably be expected to be brought to bear upon it at that time.

The Board's commodity paper regulation was issued September 3, 1915, well before the time when the movement of the cotton crop could be expected to give rise to drafts upon the southern banks, and it was some time, therefore, before any considerable number of applications for loans at the commodity rate was made. During the month of November the southern reserve banks converted many of their loans into the commodity form. Such loans aggregated $10,300,000 to the end of the year, $7,500,000 being the volume outstanding on December 30, 1915.

The effect of the commodity paper regulation was mainly anticipatory and protective. The certain assurance that whatever funds might be necessary for the gradual and orderly marketing of the cotton crop would be available at moderate rates had an immediate and stimulating effect on sentiment. Other factors which contributed to the same result were the evidences of an early and active buying movement and the realization that the cotton yield would be much less than that of 1914. Within sixty days, prices advanced from eight cents to twelve cents per pound. There was a steady movement of the staple to primary markets, the price of cotton seed advanced to a figure that added from $20 to $25 a bale to the farmer's income, and comparatively little cotton had to be carried by banks for producers.

It is difficult, however, to find any real justification for preferential rates on commodity paper. They were in force at three or four of the banks for two years, but were finally suspended in December, 1917. A majority of the Board then regarded them as unsound in principle, and they were found to be of practically no benefit to producers, having been availed of very little. In most of the agricultural States banks may legally charge more than six per cent interest, and outside of the larger centers in those States banks generally were unwilling to make loans at a six per cent rate, particularly where they received no compensating deposits. It was also feared in 1917 that the special commodity rate might have a tendency in some places to promote speculative holdings of commodities which were needed in the conduct of the war. There was never, however, any difference of opinion among members of the Board as to the propriety of encouraging gradual and orderly marketing of staple crops.

One of the important developments of the year 1915 was the establishment by the Federal Reserve Board of

a gold fund for the immediate settlement of balances arising out of transactions among the twelve Federal Reserve
Banks.

Section 16 of the Federal Reserve Act authorizes the Federal Reserve Board, at its discretion, to exercise the functions of a clearing-house for the Federal Reserve Banks.
Pursuant to this authority, the Board on May 8, 1915, issued
a regulation covering the establishment and operation of a
gold fund. Each Federal Reserve Bank was required to deposit with the Treasurer of the United States at Washington,
or at any Sub-Treasury, the sum of $1,000,000 plus the net
amount of its indebtedness to other Federal Reserve Banks.
The Treasury Department coöperated with the Board in operating this fund, and the several assistant treasurers were
instructed to forward telegraphic advice of deposits received
to the Treasurer of the United States at Washington, who in
turn would issue gold order certificates in the denomination
of $10,000, payable to the Federal Reserve Board.

In the beginning, settlements were made on Thursday of
each week. On Wednesday evening each Federal Reserve
Bank transmitted to the Board advice of the amount due to
it by, or by it to, every other Federal Reserve Bank. After
completion of the settlement, a telegram would be sent to
each bank giving the amounts which other Federal Reserve
Banks had reported as due, together with the net amount by
which it was debtor or creditor at the clearing. Upon receipt of this telegram each bank charged the accounts of
other Federal Reserve Banks with the amounts reported due
by them, and credited their accounts with the amounts which
were due to them, the debits in each case having been ex-
tinguished by the operation of settling and the transfer of
title to gold held in the gold settlement fund. The principal
object of the fund was to make unnecessary the shipment of
funds by one Federal Reserve Bank to another.

Subsequently the Federal Reserve Agents' fund was established, this fund consisting of gold held by Federal Reserve

Agents to reduce the liability of Federal Reserve Banks against Federal Reserve notes outstanding.

In 1916 the Act was amended to permit the Treasurer of the United States to carry a special account on his books to the credit of the Federal Reserve Board, as agent for the respective Federal Reserve Banks, payments being made by checks signed by officials of the Board.

Upon the leasing of a system of private wires between all Federal Reserve Banks and branches and the Federal Reserve Board, the operation of the fund was greatly simplified, and settlements were made daily instead of weekly. Arrangements were made also with the Treasury to assume direct custody of the fund as a special gold account, and, while the fund was intended originally as a means of making immediate settlements of balances between Federal Reserve Banks, its scope was afterward extended, and provision was made in 1921 for a daily settlement between Federal Reserve Banks for Federal Reserve notes, whether fit for use and returned to the bank of issue, or unfit for use and returned to the Treasury for redemption. Transfers were also arranged for national banks to their five per cent redemption fund against shipments of national bank notes.

The combined clearings and transfers through the gold settlement fund from 1915 to 1922 were as follows:

1915	$1,052,649,000	1919	$73,984,252,000
1916	5,533,966,000	1920	92,625,805,000
1917	27,154,704,000	1921	68,223,882,000
1918	50,251,592,000	1922	76,489,962,000

making a grand total of $395,316,812,000. The average cost of making these transfers, including rental of leased telegraphic wires and clerical services, was less than one half of a cent per thousand dollars.

CHAPTER V

PAR CLEARANCE OF CHECKS

REFERENCE has already been made to the problems incident to the establishment of a check clearing and collection system. The framers of the Federal Reserve Act foresaw that if Federal Reserve Banks were to act as reserve depositories for all member banks, it would be necessary for the Reserve Banks to receive, as deposits from member banks, checks as well as gold and currency. The establishment of a clearing system, however, proved to be no simple task, and before outlining the steps which were taken, and the problems which were encountered in this connection, it would be well to review the methods employed in making domestic exchanges before the Federal Reserve Banks were established and the changes which became inevitable after the passage of the Federal Reserve Act.

Prior to December 23, 1913, the only laws of national application which were designed to regulate the operations of banks were those sections of the Revised Statutes which are commonly called the National Bank Act. While these were applicable to national banks only, the State banks and trust companies, in collecting checks deposited with them which were drawn on banks in other places, adopted practically the same system which was employed by the national banks.

The National Bank Law provided for central reserve cities and for reserve cities, and banks in other towns or cities were permitted to count, as a part of their required reserves, balances which they carried with correspondent banks in the reserve and central reserve cities. Some of the larger State banks and trust companies also received deposits from country banks, and all country banks carried balances with one or more banks in the larger cities. While many of the so-called country banks maintained reciprocal accounts with banks in their immediate vicinity for mutual convenience in making collection of checks, it was the general practice of all country banks to send checks drawn on banks in more distant places to their city correspondents. City banks as a rule adopted the practice of sending checks for direct collection only to banks which maintained accounts with them, and would in addition send to such banks checks drawn upon other banks in their State or in their immediate vicinity. As a rule the checks sent in this way for collection were not charged by the city banks against the regular accounts of their country bank correspondents, but were entered in a separate account called the 'collection account.' It was the usual practice of the country banks, in remitting or giving credit for items received from city bank correspondents, to make a so-called exchange charge of one tenth to one quarter of one per cent. Out of these charges the country banks in the course of a year would make substantial apparent profits, but these profits were more apparent than real, when it is considered that in order to get this business the country banks were obliged to maintain balances with the city banks on which they received interest usually at a rate of two per cent per annum, which otherwise could be loaned to customers at six per cent or more; and that, in order to maintain these balances with the city bank correspondents, country banks were often obliged to buy exchange at a premium or else bear the expense of shipping currency. This routine resulted in circuitous methods of collection, so that frequently checks in process of collection were outstanding three or four times as long as would have been the case if they had been sent direct. In the course of an investigation made by the Federal Reserve Board, it was brought out that there were frequent cases where a check originating at a city bank would in process of collection come back to another bank in the same city, or to a bank in a near-by city, before it was finally forwarded for presentation to the bank on which it was drawn.

I recall an instance where a national bank in Rochester, New York, sent a check drawn on a bank in North Birmingham, Alabama, to a correspondent bank in New York City, by which it was sent to a bank in Jacksonville, Florida, which sent it for collection to a bank in Philadelphia, which in turn sent it to a bank in Baltimore, which forwarded it to a bank in Cincinnati, which bank sent it to a bank in Birmingham, by which bank final collection was made. Not only were the methods of collection circuitous, but the routine resulted in the creation of fictitious reserve balances. In the case above cited, had the national bank in Rochester, New York, sent the check direct to the North Birmingham bank for collection, or had it sent it to a bank not an approved reserve agent, the amount of the check would not have been included in the Rochester bank's lawful reserve; but as it was sent to its correspondent bank in New York City, its approved reserve agent, and was charged to the account of the New York bank at the time it had left Rochester, it counted from that moment as a part of the Rochester bank's legal reserve, although more than two weeks elapsed before it was finally collected.

The Federal Reserve Act as amended has made substantial reductions in bank reserves, but permits member banks to count as lawful reserve only collected balances in their respective Federal Reserve Banks. Consequently, checks in transit, or 'float,' to use a technical term, no longer count as reserve, and this element of inflation has been eliminated. The Federal Reserve Board conceived it to be its duty under the terms of the Act to establish a par clearance system for making domestic exchanges throughout the country, and, in carrying this plan into effect, met with determined opposition from many of the smaller banks which were reluctant to give up their profits, real or imaginary, which they had derived under the old system. Some of the city banks also looked upon the plan as an encroachment upon their functions and as a menace to their relations with country bank correspondents. At the outset the Board was hampered by lack of facilities, which were afterward provided, such as the leased wire system and the daily clearing through the gold settlement fund, and no attempt was made to establish a comprehensive par clearance system, but instead the plan was to establish a voluntary system, necessarily of limited scope and efficiency. One of the first suggestions made was that Federal Reserve Banks should give immediate credit at par for all checks deposited with them, and the checks on member banks should be charged as received against their reserve accounts. It was soon realized, however, that this procedure would not be equitable, as it would be tantamount to forcing a bank to pay a check in advance of actual presentation. It was finally decided to give deferred credit, based upon the time in transit from the Reserve Bank to the banks upon which the checks were drawn. At first the actual initiative for the inauguration of a check collection system was left to the respective Federal Reserve Banks, which established a voluntary system of clearance and collection in which member banks might or might not participate as they chose. Experience, however, soon demonstrated that this plan was not sufficiently comprehensive and that there were many factors militating against its success. The number of member banks assenting to the plan did not increase materially and some districts declined. The plan adopted proved to be a hardship to some banks, while it did not attempt and seemed unlikely ever to reach such a plane of efficiency as to make it a substantial factor in making domestic exchanges. For these reasons the Board decided in April, 1916, to establish a more uniform and more comprehensive system, and it formulated a new plan which was put into effect by the Federal Reserve Banks on July 15th. Under the revised plan, member banks were left free to carry accounts for collection purposes with other banks, but were required to pay, without deduction, checks drawn upon themselves upon presentation at their own counters. Remittances of such checks through the mail to a member bank by the Federal Reserve Bank was construed as presentation at the member bank's counter, and the member bank was requested to settle with the Federal Reserve Bank for these checks by permitting a charge against its reserve account, or by sending a check on some other bank acceptable to the Federal Reserve Bank. The member banks were also allowed to make remittances of currency to the Federal Reserve Banks with the understanding that the expense of transportation would be borne by the Reserve Bank. This plan provided also that a small service charge, not to exceed two cents per item, be made at stated intervals against those banks which sent to the Federal Reserve Banks checks on other banks for collection and credit. Member banks were not deprived of any income which they were accustomed to receive from the collection of drafts (other than bank checks) or from the purchase or discount of commercial bills of exchange.

It was estimated by the Board that, as soon as a new clearing system could be put into operation, checks drawn upon about fifteen thousand national banks, State banks, and trust companies throughout the United States would be collected by the Federal Reserve Banks at par, subject to the small service charge to which reference has been made. Some members of the Board were optimistic enough to believe that in a short time checks drawn upon practically all banks in the United States could be collected at par by the Federal Reserve Banks, upon the theory that a bank would be likely to lose desirable business when checks drawn upon it would be at a discount outside of its own neighborhood, while checks drawn on a near-by competitor would be taken at par. If the merchants and manufacturers of the country and other recipients of checks had insisted that checks sent them in payment of bills be free of exchange, perhaps this roseate anticipation would have been realized; but in many cases large dealers were able to induce banks with which they deposited to absorb collection charges, and in other cases they were not willing to return a check, say for a hundred dollars, sent in payment of an account, merely because its collection would involve a charge of from ten to twenty-five cents, nor did they care to risk losing the good-will of a customer in a controversy over an exchange charge.

In June, 1917, the Federal Reserve Act was amended so as to allow Federal Reserve Banks to receive accounts for collection and exchange purposes from any non-member banks and trust companies which might agree to remit to Federal Reserve Banks at par for checks drawn upon themselves, and which were willing in addition to maintain balances with the Federal Reserve Banks sufficient to offset the items in transit held for their account by the Federal Reserve Banks. Very few non-member banks availed themselves of this privilege, however, and the Federal Reserve Banks were still unable to collect checks drawn on many non-member banks except at a heavy expense. Determined effort was made in the interest of non-member banks and some member banks to amend the Federal Reserve Act by providing for a standardized exchange charge not to exceed one tenth of one per cent, to be made by any bank so desiring against Federal Reserve Banks for checks sent for collection. This effort, however, was not successful, and the Act as finally amended provided that a member or non-member bank may make

reasonable charges, to be determined and regulated by the Federal Reserve Board, but in no case to exceed ten cents per hundred dollars or fraction thereof, based on the total of checks and drafts presented at any one time, for collection or payment of checks and drafts and remission therefor by exchange or otherwise; but no such charges shall be made against the Federal Reserve Banks.

In the opinion of the Attorney-General of the United States, this required member banks to make remittances without deduction for checks sent them by Federal Reserve Banks, but this requirement did not apply to non-member banks. The Attorney-General held also that Federal Reserve Banks were not permitted to pay exchange charges to banks, although they might decline to receive checks which they could collect only by sending to banks which would impose a charge. Consequently, the difficulties in the way of the establishment of a comprehensive par clearance system, applicable to member and non-member banks alike, were not resolved by this legislation. With the view of making the clearance system more attractive, there was put into operation by all Federal Reserve Banks a system of transfer drafts by which any member bank might have its check drawn upon the Federal Reserve Bank of its district, paid immediately without time allowance or deduction at any other Federal Reserve Bank. In this way every member bank was given the same exchange facilities it would have had if it carried accounts in each of the twelve Federal Reserve cities; but little use, however, was ever made of these facilities.

During the year 1918 the conclusion was reached that every effort should be made to increase the number of banks on the par list. It was felt that the public and the banks themselves needed a system which should be able to collect all items. At the beginning of the year 1919 checks on two thirds of all banks in the country could be collected at par through the Federal Reserve Banks, and the banks which had agreed to remit in this way represented about ninety per cent of the banking resources of the country. Yet the number of banks which would not agree to remit at par, including some of substantial size and located in important cities, was sufficiently large to make many banks hesitate to use the Federal Reserve collection system because of the number of items which could not be collected by the Federal Reserve Banks.

The service charge which was àt first made by Federal Reserve Banks for collecting checks was soon modified and later on was entirely abrogated. Additional facilities were given member banks and their customers through the absorption by the Federal Reserve Banks of all costs of postage, insurance, and express charges incident to the shipments of currency to and from member banks; and the same facilities were extended to those non-member banks which maintained clearing accounts. Other non-member banks were provided with stamped envelopes for use in returning remittances for checks sent them, and all their expenses incident to shipments of currency made in payment of items sent for collection were borne by the Federal Reserve Banks. Many non-member banks, however, still persisted in opposition to the par clearance system despite repeated efforts to induce them to make remittances without charge for checks sent them by Federal Reserve Banks. These non-member banks, however, were able to avail themselves of the facilities of the par clearance system, and, while they were able to collect their own items without apparent expense through some correspondent bank, they were in many cases disinclined to reciprocate and refused to give up their profits from so-called exchange charges, which profits, as has already been explained, were much overestimated. It was therefore decided that the Federal Reserve Banks should undertake to collect all checks received from member banks, and that, in cases where the drawee banks declined to remit at par, checks should be collected through an intermediate bank, through an express company, or by means of personal presentation. It was, of course, anticipated that any method of collection except through a bank would necessarily be expensive, but in view of the demonstrated value of the par clearance system and of the large number of banks which had assented to it, it was hoped that the opposition of the non-assenting banks would gradually disappear. This hope, however, proved to be illusive, and the opposition became more aggressive and more thoroughly organized. Although the administrative officers of the American Bankers' Association have always assumed a friendly attitude toward the Federal Reserve System, so large a portion of the membership of that Association is composed of banks which prefer the old method of collection that the Association has been put in the position, on the one hand, of according cordial support to the Federal Reserve System, and on the other of fostering opposition to one of its important functions. At an annual meeting of the Association a committee of twenty-five was formed, which was afterwards reduced to five, and this committee has been active in throwing every possible obstacle in the way of the establishment of a comprehensive par clearance system by the Federal Reserve Banks. Due partly to efforts of this committee, legislation was obtained in a number of States, mainly in the South, requiring or permitting State banks to impose a collection charge, and numerous proceedings have been instituted in the courts. In most of the legislation to which reference has been made, it was provided that there shall be no right of action, either at law or in equity, against any bank for refusal to pay a check when such refusal is based alone on non-payment of exchange.

Meanwhile, in several of the districts, the Federal Reserve Banks had appointed agents at various points to whom they would send checks for presentation to drawee banks which refused to remit at par.

The lower courts generally decided all questions raised in the litigation in favor of the Federal Reserve Banks, and, despite adverse legislation, the Federal Reserve Banks on January 1, 1921, had on their par lists all but 1755 of the 30,523 banks at that time existing in the United States. All these banks were located in seven States in the Southeast: Tennessee, South Carolina, Louisiana, Mississippi, Alabama, Georgia, and Florida. During the year 1921 the legislatures of North Carolina, Tennessee, and Florida, in addition to the five States which had already enacted similar laws, put upon the statute books of their respective States laws designed to require or permit banks to make charges for collecting and remitting checks which are presented to the payer bank through or by any bank, banker, trust company, Federal

Reserve Bank, post-office, express company, or any collection agency, or by any agency whatsoever; and the legislature of Louisiana made it a misdemeanor punishable by fine or imprisonment for any person to give any notice of the non-payment of any check drawn on any bank in that State after such bank had offered to pay such check without exchange-charge deduction. The North Carolina law made it lawful for all banks and trust companies in that State to charge a fee not in excess of one eighth of one per cent on remittances covering checks, and provided also that all checks drawn on such banks and trust companies

shall, unless specified on the face thereof to the contrary by the maker or makers thereof, be payable at the option of the drawee bank, in exchange drawn on the reserve deposits of said drawee bank when any such check is presented by or through any Federal Reserve Bank, post-office, or express company, or any respective agents thereof.

Following the enactment of this law a number of North Carolina State banks and trust companies obtained an injunction restraining the Federal Reserve Bank of Richmond from refusing to accept in payment, when presented, checks drawn on correspondent banks, and from returning checks to their drawers as dishonored because the drawee banks refused to pay them in cash. The Supreme Court of North Carolina held that this legislation was unconstitutional and dissolved the injunction, but the case was appealed to the Supreme Court of the United States, which in June, 1923, in an opinion rendered by Justice Brandeis (Mr. Justice Sutherland and Mr. Justice Van Devanter dissenting) reversed the opinion of the Supreme Court of North Carolina and upheld the validity of the statute of that State. At the same time, however, the Supreme Court rendered an opinion dismissing a complaint which had been made against the Federal Reserve Bank of Atlanta in which the contention had been made that it was *ultra vires* of Federal Reserve Banks to collect checks on banks which are not members of the

System or affiliated with it through establishing an exchange balance, and which had definitely refused to assent to clearance at par. The Court held that

wherever collection can be made by the Federal Reserve Bank without paying exchange neither the common law nor the Federal Reserve Act precludes their undertaking it; if it can be done consistently with the rights of the country banks already determined in this case. . . . Federal Reserve Banks are thus authorized by Congress to collect, for other reserve banks, for member banks, and for affiliated non-members, checks on any bank within their respective districts, if the check is payable on presentation and can in fact be collected consistently with the legal rights of the drawee without paying an exchange charge. Within these limits Federal Reserve Banks have ordinarily the same right to present a check to the drawee bank for payment over the counter, as any other bank, State or national, would have.

In the North Carolina case the Supreme Court held that

Congress did not in terms confer upon the Federal Reserve Board or the Federal Reserve Banks a duty to establish a universal par clearance and collection of checks; and there is nothing in the original act or in any amendment from which such duty to compel its adoption may be inferred. . . . The Federal Reserve Act does not command or compel these State banks to forego any right they may have under the State laws to make charges in connection with the payment of checks drawn upon them. The act merely offers the clearing and collection facilities of the Federal Reserve Banks upon specified conditions. If the State banks refuse to comply with the conditions by insisting upon making charges against the Federal Reserve Banks, the result will simply be, so far as the Federal Reserve Act is concerned, that since the Federal Reserve Banks cannot pay these charges they cannot clear or collect checks on banks demanding such payments from them.

As a result of the legislation to which reference has been made, and following the opinion of the Supreme Court, Federal Reserve Banks no longer maintain agencies for the presentation of checks to non-member banks which refuse to remit at par. They have revised their par lists omitting the names of such banks and decline to receive on deposit or for collection checks drawn upon them. The result has been merely an abridgment of the par lists, although there has been increasing volume of business. While it is manifestly impossible, in the present circumstances, to establish a universal par clearance system except with the consent of all banks, the system now in operation, incomplete though it be, is efficient and performs a service of great value to the commerce and industry of the country. During my connection with the Board it was pointed out on several occasions that in their origin exchange charges were justified because of the necessity for and the high cost of transporting currency, but that under

existing conditions those charges can be justified upon no scientific or economic principle, since the payment of checks at places other than where the drawee bank is located involves little expense and that is borne by the Federal Reserve Banks. Even the banks which decline to remit at par to the Federal Reserve Banks receive the benefits of the Federal Reserve check clearing facilities by having the checks which they receive collected through a correspondent bank which is a member of the Federal Reserve System, although they contribute nothing to the strength of the System. To the extent that the practice of charging exchange is continued under the operation of the Federal Reserve System, it is an anachronism which permits the charging banks to impose a charge upon commerce and industry after they have ceased to perform the service which in former times justified the imposition of such a charge.[1]

[1] Annual Report, 1920.

CHAPTER VI

CHANGES IN BOARD'S ORGANIZATION'— ACCEPTANCE CREDITS FOR
FOREIGN ACCOUNT — BOARD'S STATEMENT REGARDING
SALES OF BRITISH TREASURY BILLS

THE year 1916 was one of great commercial and industrial activity in the United States and both capital and labor found full and remunerative employment. The country was feeling the stimulus of European demands occasioned by the war, and of the large influx of gold. High prices for agricultural products and a general and well-sustained demand for them brought to the farmers an unprecedented degree of prosperity. Those engaged in all lines of business and industry were unusually strong and independent financially, and, because of the increasing volume of deposits, member banks generally had no occasion to rediscount, and therefore the Federal Reserve Banks were able to maintain very strong reserves.

Before the term of Governor Hamlin as a member of the Board expired on August 9, 1916, he had been nominated by the President, and promptly confirmed by the Senate, for a full term of ten years. There had developed a feeling, however, that the added duties and responsibilities of the governorship of the Board should not be imposed indefinitely upon any one member, but that there should be rotation; and the idea was advanced that each Board member during the last two years of his term should serve as Governor of the Board. The law, however, does not permit the Board to choose its own executive officer; instead, he is designated by, and holds his office at, the pleasure of the President. At the suggestion of the Secretary of the Treasury, I was designated by the President to succeed Mr. Hamlin as Governor, although, if the plan of orderly rotation had been adopted, I should not have been called upon to serve in that position until four years later. At the same time Mr. Warburg was designated Vice-Governor in place of Mr. Delano.

The personnel of the Board remained unchanged and there were no marked changes of policy as a result of the new designations, although there were some modifications in operating methods. During the first two years, the Board had been divided into a number of committees. The practice had been to refer all questions, and various routine matters, to the appropriate committee for consideration and report, before action by the Board was taken. This system worked well in the beginning, but as it was evident that the Federal Reserve System was approaching a period of much greater activity, it was deemed expedient to adopt some plan of organization which would not delay the routine work of the Board. Accordingly, some of the committees were dissolved, and the conduct of purely routine and administrative matters devolved more directly upon the Governor, who under the law is 'the active executive officer' of the Board, and upon the Executive Committee which was composed of the Governor, the Vice-Governor, and, in rotation, a third member of the Board. All the acts of the Governor and of the Executive Committee were, however, reported to the Board for ratification, and no important steps were ever taken without the express authority of the Board. The Board was never under one-man domination.

The Governors of the Federal Reserve Banks had from the beginning been accustomed to hold frequent conferences at which their own administrative problems were considered, and these conferences were of great value in bringing about better and more uniform methods of operation. It had been the custom for these conferences to be held every three or four months upon the initiative of the Federal Reserve Bank Governors themselves, and at places to be selected by them. The Federal Reserve Board would be notified that a conference was to be held in Minneapolis, or Chicago, as the case might be, on a certain date, and would be invited to send one or more members to attend the meeting. Much work of great benefit to the System was accomplished at these meetings, and there was never any intention to have them discontinued. The Federal Reserve Banks are autonomous institutions, each under the control of its own directors, but the law does not give any Federal Reserve Bank or group of Federal Reserve Banks any authority over another. Conferences of Reserve Bank executives, therefore, can only make suggestions, which, if relating to routine matters, are subject to the approval of the directors of the respective banks, and, if bearing upon broader questions of policy, require action by the Federal Reserve Board, which alone is vested by law with supervisory powers over all Reserve Banks. The Board decided that henceforth these conferences should be held in Washington at such times as it should approve. For some years past only two conferences a year have been held; always under the auspices of the Board. This arrangement has brought about a closer contact between the Board and the bank executives, and has expedited the business in hand.

During the autumn of 1916 there was a falling-off in the volume of gold imports which had been very heavy since early in the year 1915, together with a marked increase in the volume of American credits for European account. Some of these were in the form of acceptance credits which involved renewals, and there were also offerings of bonds and other obligations of foreign governments and municipalities. At the same time it seemed more probable from week to week that the United States would be drawn into the European War.

Toward the end of October it was announced that the French Government had arranged with two large trust companies in New York, which at that time were not members of the Federal Reserve System, for an acceptance credit of $100,000,000; the bills to be drawn in such a way as to make them eligible for rediscount at Federal Reserve Banks. Secretary McAdoo was away from Washington at the time on a trip through the West. As he was chairman of the Federal Reserve Board, I felt that he should be advised of this important matter, especially as the Treasury might be interested in the outcome, and I therefore wrote him under date of October 21st, enclosing newspaper clippings, some of which gave emphasis in their headlines to a statement that a credit to France of $100,000,000 could be rediscounted at Federal Reserve Banks. I stated that I thought the Board should make some public announcement of the position of the Federal Reserve Banks in this matter, for should the Board, in view of the great publicity given to the proposed credit, take no notice of statements that the acceptances, renewable for a period of eighteen months, were available for rediscount at Federal Reserve Banks, it would put itself, by its silence, in the attitude of sanctioning such statements. I requested that he telegraph me his views as to the propriety and desirability of a statement by the Board. Mr. McAdoo replied that he thought it would be wise for the Board to authorize a press statement such as was outlined in my letter.

At its meeting on October 23d the Board considered the question of French acceptance credit and by unanimous vote agreed that it should take some action in the matter, particularly as it had learned that circular letters had already been sent out to five or six hundred banks or trust companies throughout the United States. The Board, therefore, directed me to send the following telegram to all Federal Reserve Agents, which telegram was given to the press on the following day:

Board is advised that an acceptance credit approximating one hundred million dollars, drawn on American banks and trust companies, is about to be concluded, on ninety-day drafts, subject to five renewals, the accepting banks committing themselves to advance the money to the foreign borrowers at five and one half per cent per annum, plus acceptance commission of one fourth per cent for each three months. In view of widely circulated press statements that these acceptances will be eligible for rediscount or purchase by Federal Reserve Banks, Board deems it its duty to point out that banking prudence and obligations toward general commercial interests of the country require that Federal Reserve Banks should not acquire acceptances of this character beyond a conservative amount. This view is consistent with the Board's policy in the past, and while it wishes, through all legitimate means, to promote the development of the American acceptance market and to further the growth of our export trade, and while it wishes to avoid any attitude of interference with the powers of member banks in this respect, the Board feels, nevertheless, that it should be clearly understood that these acceptances, which represent obligations, for cash advances aggregating a very large amount, by the acceptors for eighteen months, cannot properly be regarded as paper self-liquidating within a period of ninety days. If offered in excessive amounts, Federal Reserve Banks may be obliged to discriminate against or to exclude entirely acceptances of this character. Board feels that prospective acceptors should have a clear understanding of this.

About the middle of November, Mr. H. P. Davison, a member of the firm of J. P. Morgan & Company, and who had recently returned from a visit to London, came to Washington and conferred with members of the Board at an informal meeting. He outlined the financial position of the British Government. He referred to the large importations of gold which the United States had received from abroad since January, 1915, and expressed the opinion that further importations would prove a source of danger or disturbance to this country. He expressed the view that importations of gold should be discouraged by the extension of credits to those financially sound foreign countries which were large purchasers of supplies in America, and stated that his firm proposed to offer over its counter an indefinite amount of British Treasury bills to the American public, to banks as well as to private investors.

After considering the matter for several days, the Board reached the conclusion that it could not with propriety give its endorsement to this programme, and that, however reluctant it might be to make public a statement of its views, it was necessary to do so. As the matter had been brought to the attention of the Board by a member of the firm which proposed to offer the British Treasury bills, it was felt that, should the Board remain silent, it would put itself in the attitude of tacitly approving the proposition.

The Board was not unmindful, however, of the delicacy of its position, for any statement by it discouraging the purchase of these securities might be embarrassing to our Government in its conduct of foreign relations. As the Secretary of the Treasury was at the time in Arizona, it was not possible through him to ascertain the attitude of the Administration. The Board, therefore, prepared a tentative statement which was sent with an explanatory letter to the President. Not only was approval given to the issuance of a statement by the Board, but certain additions to it were suggested. The Board, therefore, on November 27, 1916, made public the following statement relating to foreign credits. The lines which appear in italics did not appear in the original statement considered by the Board, but were added after correspondence with the President.

In view of contradictory reports which have appeared in the press regarding its attitude toward the purchasing by banks in this country of Treasury bills of foreign governments, the Board deems it a duty to define its position clearly. In making this statement the Board desires to disclaim any intention of discussing the finances or of reflecting upon the financial stability of any nation, but wishes it understood that it seeks to deal only with general principles which affect all alike.

The Board does not share the view frequently expressed of late that further importations of large amounts of gold must of necessity prove a source of danger or disturbance to this country. That danger, the Board believes, will arise only in case the inflowing gold should remain uncontrolled and be permitted to become the basis of undesirable loan expansions and of inflation. There are means, however, of controlling accessions of gold by proper and voluntary coöperation of the banks or if need be by legislative enactment. An important step in this direction would be the anticipation of the final transfer of reserves contemplated by the Federal Reserve Act to become effective on November 16, 1917. This date could be advanced to February or March, 1917. Member banks would then be placed on the permanent basis of their reserve requirements and fictitious reserves would then disappear and the banks have a clearer conception of actual reserve and financial conditions. It will then appear that, while a large increase in the country's gold holdings has taken place, the expansion of loans and deposits has been such that there will not remain any excess of reserves, apart from the important reserve loaning power of the Federal Reserve Banks.

In these circumstances the Board feels that member banks should pursue a policy of keeping themselves liquid; of not loaning down to the legal limit, but of maintaining an excess of reserves — not with reserve agents, where their balances are loaned out and constitute no actual reserve, but in their own vaults or preferably with their Federal Reserve Banks. The Board believes that at this time banks should proceed with much caution in locking up their funds in long-term obligations, or in investments which are short-term in form or name, but which, either by contract or through force of circumstances, may in the aggregate have to be renewed until normal conditions return. The Board does not undertake to forecast probabilities or to specify circumstances which may become important factors in determining future conditions. Its concern and responsibility lie primarily with the banking situation. If, however, our banking institutions have to intervene because foreign securities are offered faster than they can be absorbed by investors — that is, their depositors — an element would be introduced into the situation which, if not kept under control, would tend toward instability, and ultimate injury to the economic development of this country. The natural absorbing power of the investment market supplies an important regulator of the volume of our sales to foreign countries in excess of the goods that they send us. The form which the most recent borrowing is taking, apart from reference to its intrinsic merits, makes it appear particularly attractive as a banking investment. The Board, as a matter of fact, understands that it is expected to place it primarily with banks. In fact, it would appear so attractive that unless a broader and national point of view be adopted, individual banks might easily be tempted to invest in it to such an extent that the banking resources of this country employed in this manner might run into many hundreds of millions of dollars. While the loans may be short in form, and, severally, may be collected at maturity, the object of the borrower must be to attempt to renew them collectively, with the result that the aggregate amount placed here will remain until such time as it may be advantageously converted into a long-term obligation. It would, therefore, seem as a consequence that liquid funds of our banks, which should be available for short credit facilities to our merchants, manufacturers, and farmers, would be exposed to the danger of being absorbed for other purposes to a disproportionate degree, especially in view of the fact that many of our banks and trust companies are already carrying substantial amounts of foreign obligations, and of acceptances which they are under agreement to renew. *The Board deems it, therefore, its duty to caution the member banks that it does not regard it in the interest of the country at this time that they invest in foreign Treasury bills of this character.*

The Board does not consider that it is called upon to advise private investors, but, as the United States is fast becoming the banker of foreign countries in all parts of the world, it takes occasion to suggest that the investor should receive full and authoritative data — particularly in the case of unsecured loans — in order that he may judge the future intelligently in the light of present conditions and in conjunction with the economic developments of the past.

The United States has now attained a position of wealth and of international financial power, which, in the natural course of events, it could not have reached for a generation. We must be careful not to impair this position of strength and independence. While it is true that a slowing down in the process of credit extension may mean some curtailment of our abnormally stimulated export trade to certain countries, we need not fear that our business will fall off precipitately should we become more conservative in the matter of investing in loans, because there are still hundreds of millions of our own and foreign securities held abroad which our investors would be glad to take over, and, moreover, trade can be stimulated in other directions.

In the opinion of the Board, it is the duty of our banks to remain liquid in order that they may be able to continue to respond to our home requirements, the nature and scope of which none can foresee, and in order that our present economic and financial strength may be maintained when, at the end of the war, we shall wish to do our full share in the work of international reconstruction and development which will then lie ahead of us, and when a clearer understanding of economic conditions, as they will then exist, will enable this country more safely and intelligently to do its proper part in the financial rehabilitation of the world.

As was expected, this statement became the subject of much comment, both favorable and unfavorable, in this country. It was received in London with mingled feelings of surprise, resentment, and consternation. Messrs. J. P. Morgan & Company announced that, in view of this statement by a Government Board, 'of which the Secretary of the Treasury and the Comptroller of the Currency are members,' the British Treasury bills would be withdrawn from the American market. In issuing this statement the Board was prompted only by the highest motives. Sentimental considerations had no part in the action taken, for there is no doubt that a majority of the members at the time were pro-Ally in their sympathies. This sentiment became unanimous in April, 1917, when the United States entered the war. Both before and during the war there was no one who rendered more loyal and patriotic service to the country of his adoption than did that member of the Board who happened to have been born in the enemy's country.

CHAPTER VII

BOARD PROPOSES IMPORTANT AMENDMENTS TO ACT RELATING TO RESERVES AND NOTE ISSUES

By January, 1917, it had become almost a foregone conclusion that this country was soon to be drawn into the war. Anticipating this, the Federal Reserve Board had shaped its policies with the view of placing the Federal Reserve Banks in the strongest possible position in order that they might be well prepared to meet the heavy demands which inevitably would be made upon them. The Reserve Banks were advised that they should discontinue the purchase of municipal warrants, and steps were taken in other directions to increase the gold holdings of the banks. To this end the Board requested Congress to amend the Federal Reserve Act in several important particulars. Although the System had been in operation for more than two years, the membership was limited almost entirely to the national banks, which controlled considerably less than half the banking resources of the country. Repeated efforts had been made to induce State banks and trust companies to become members, but only about sixty had responded, and these did not include the larger institutions. At a conference with executives of several large trust companies, the Board called attention to its regulations regarding State bank membership, which had been drawn in the most liberal terms consistent with the law. The bank executives expressed their approval of these regulations, but pointed out that they could not have the effect of a statute, for the Board could at any time rescind or materially alter them, and as the personnel of the Board was subject to change, no assurance could be given against unsatisfactory changes in the regulations at some future time. As the law then stood there was no provision for the voluntary withdrawal of a State bank or trust company which had become a member. While the Board had authority to force such withdrawal for a violation of the law or for non-observance of the regulations, officers of banks operating under State charters were not inclined to effect a voluntary withdrawal by becoming violators of the law.

Another objection raised was that, while State banks were necessarily under the direct supervision of the banking departments of their respective States, they would as members of the Federal Reserve System be to a certain extent also under the supervision of the Comptroller of the Currency. Thus, the State banks and trust companies as members would be supervised by two distinct authorities, while the national bank members would be under the supervision only of the Comptroller of the Currency. It was pointed out also that State bank members must comply with the reserve requirements of the Federal Reserve Act and in addition must carry the reserves specified in the laws of the States in which they were located. Their legal reserves, therefore, would be larger than those of their national bank competitors.

Upon consideration of these objections the Board became convinced that, in order to secure the coöperation as members of any large number of State banks and trust companies, it would be necessary to amend the Act. The Board, therefore, suggested to the Banking and Currency Committees of the Senate and House of Representatives that that section of the Federal Reserve Act which related to membership of State banks and trust companies be amended in order to provide that any such bank or trust company which might desire to withdraw from membership in the Federal Reserve System may do so after six months' written notice to the Federal Reserve Board. At the expiration of that time, upon the surrender and cancellation of all its holdings of capital stock in the Federal Reserve Bank, its membership would lapse. Precaution against excessive withdrawals, which might be embarrassing to a Federal Reserve Bank, was taken by a provision that no Federal Reserve Bank should, unless under express authority of the Federal Reserve Board, cancel within the same calendar year more than twenty-five per cent of its capital stock for the purpose of effecting voluntary withdrawals during that year.

In order to meet the objections made against the dual supervision by the State banking departments and the Comptroller of the Currency, it was suggested that the State banks and trust companies becoming members of the Federal Reserve System, while subject to all provisions of the Act which relate specifically to member banks, should not be subject to examination by the Comptroller of the Currency. It was further suggested that subject to the provisions of the Act and to the regulations of the Board made pursuant thereto, any bank, becoming a member of the Federal Reserve System, should retain its full charter and statutory rights as a State bank or trust company, and continue to exercise all corporate powers granted by the State in which it is created. In order, however, that State banks becoming members should have no greater privileges than were accorded the national banks, it was suggested that the law should require Federal Reserve Banks in discounting for State banks and trust companies to observe the same limitations which the law imposed upon national banks in making loans to their customers. It was not believed that Congress should undertake to regulate the amount which a State bank or trust company might lend to a customer, this being purely a matter for the determination of the respective States, but, as the law did make such a limitation with respect to national banks, it was thought that Federal Reserve Banks should be required to observe the same limitations in its dealings with State bank and trust company members.

The Board proposed also that section 19 of the Act which relates to the reserves of member banks be amended. As originally enacted, this section provided that a bank not in a reserve or central reserve city should hold and maintain reserves equal to twelve per cent of the aggregate amount of its demand deposits and five per cent of its time deposits; that a bank in a reserve city should maintain reserves equal to fifteen per cent of its aggregate demand deposits and five per cent of its time deposits; and that a bank in a central reserve city should maintain a reserve equal to eighteen per cent of the aggregate amount of its demand deposits and five per cent of its time deposits. For a period of thirty-six months after the establishment of the Federal Reserve Banks the original law permitted a bank not in a reserve or central reserve city to carry in its own vaults five twelfths of its required reserve and thereafter four twelfths. A bank in a reserve city was permitted for the same period to carry in its own vaults six fifteenths of its required reserve and thereafter five fifteenths, while a bank in a central reserve city was permitted to retain in its own vaults six eighteenths of its required reserve and was required to carry in the Federal Reserve Bank seven eighteenths, being permitted to carry the balance of its reserve either in its own vaults or in the Federal Reserve Bank, at its option. A bank not in a reserve or central reserve city was obliged for a period of twelve months after the establishment of its Federal Reserve Bank to carry with the Reserve Bank only two twelfths of its required reserve and for each succeeding six months an additional one twelfth until five twelfths had been deposited with the Federal Reserve Bank, which was the amount permanently required. A bank in a reserve city for a period of twelve months after the establishment of its Federal Reserve Bank was obliged to carry with that bank only three fifteenths of its required reserve and for each succeeding month an additional one fifteenth until six fifteenths had been deposited, which was the amount permanently required. In all cases the law permitted the balance of reserves required of a member bank to be held either in its own vaults or in the Federal Reserve Bank or in both, at the option of the member bank. The Board's suggestion was that the reserves on time deposits be reduced with respect to all classes

of banks from five per cent to three per cent; and that the
reserves on demand deposits be reduced in the case of central
reserve city banks from eighteen per cent to thirteen per
cent; for reserve city banks from fifteen per cent to ten
per cent; for banks not in a reserve or central reserve city
from twelve per cent to seven per cent; and that the entire
legal reserves of all member banks should consist of actual
net balances with their respective Federal Reserve Banks.
It was recognized, of course, that member banks must necessarily continue to keep cash on hand, which would not, if the
Board's suggestion were adopted, be counted as reserve, but,
in view of the proposed substantial reductions in reserve requirements it was believed that this would work no hardship on the member banks which would be free to use their
own judgment as to the amount of cash which they should
keep on hand, while the Federal Reserve Banks would be in
stronger position because of the concentration of all reserves
with them even though the percentage of reserve required of
member banks be reduced.

It has been stated by some critics that the Federal Reserve
System has never had any well-defined policy with reference
to gold. With this statement I cannot agree. A discussion
of the gold policy will follow later, but it seems appropriate
here to point out that the first phase of the Board's policy as
to gold was developed in connection with the heavy influx
of that metal which set in shortly after the beginning of the
European War, and which up to the end of the year 1916
had added approximately twelve hundred millions of dollars
to the country's gold holdings. As the Board at this time
had no adequate means of impounding this redundant gold,
the Board in 1916 recommended an amendment which would
give it discretionary power to require member banks to
maintain reserves in excess of those prescribed by law. The
object sought was to prevent, whenever it seemed desirable,
the new gold which was accumulating in the vaults of banks
from becoming the basis of an undesirable expansion of

credit. It was hoped that the leading member banks would appreciate the need of coöperation with the Board in its endeavor to prevent the abnormal increase in our gold stock from providing a basis of inflation, and that they would lend their influence and support to this amendment. This suggestion, however, did not meet with general approval and no action was taken by Congress. The Board then, as stated above, proposed that the law be amended so as to require the entire legal reserves of member banks to be carried with the Federal Reserve Banks. These first phases of the Federal Reserve Board's gold policy were developed as a method of restraining undue and unnecessary expansion of credit at a time when, by reason of abnormal additions to the country's gold supply and a consequent increase in bank deposits, the Federal Reserve Banks were powerless to exercise any effective control by means of discount rates, which, as already explained, had up to 1917 been merely a negligible influence because of the ability of most of the member banks to expand their loans without rediscounting at the Federal Reserve Banks.

Looking ahead, however, it was seen that the time might come when it would be necessary to increase the credit power of the Federal Reserve System. With this end in view the Board suggested that the section of the Act which relates to the issue of Federal Reserve notes be amended so as to permit, in express terms, the issue of Federal Reserve notes, dollar for dollar, against deposits of gold; that all legally acquired paper, bills of exchange and bankers' acceptances bought in the open market, as well as paper rediscounted for member banks, be made available as collateral for Federal Reserve notes, and that the gold held as security by the Federal Reserve Agents be counted as reserve against Federal Reserve notes. As first enacted, the law provided that:

Any Federal Reserve Bank may make application to the local Federal Reserve Agent for such amount of the Federal Reserve notes hereinbefore provided for as it may require. Such application shall be accompanied with a tender . . . of collateral in amount equal to the sum of the Federal Reserve notes thus applied for and issued pursuant to such application. The collateral security thus offered shall be notes and bills, accepted for rediscount under the provisions of section thirteen of this Act. . . . Every Federal Reserve Bank shall maintain reserves in gold . . . of not less than forty per centum against its Federal Reserve notes in actual circulation, and not offset by gold or lawful money deposited with the Federal Reserve Agent. . . . Any Federal Reserve Bank may at any time reduce its liability for outstanding Federal Reserve notes by depositing, with the Federal Reserve Agent, its Federal Reserve notes, gold, gold certificates, or lawful money of the United States.

In the early days of the System the volume of rediscounts was small, and it was found impossible, under a strict construction of the section of the Act above quoted, to issue any large amount of Federal Reserve notes. The theory of the Act appeared to be that Federal Reserve notes would not be required except as a sequence of rediscounting operations, and that Federal Reserve Banks would therefore be in position always to supply currency needs by depositing their rediscounted paper with the Federal Reserve Agent as security for notes. In actual practice, however, it often happens that rediscounts do not create a demand for currency, and again there may be a demand for currency at times when member banks have no occasion to rediscount. In the autumn of 1916, when the large cotton crop of Texas was coming to market, there sprang up in the Dallas district the usual demand for currency incident to the crop-moving period. Cotton buyers throughout Texas would give their local banks demand or sight drafts on concentrating points such as Dallas, Waco, Houston, or Galveston, and the large dealers in those centers would draw sight drafts for large amounts with bills of lading attached on dealers or mill agents in New York and Boston. All such drafts were treated as cash items by the member banks, and it was the practice of the Federal Reserve Bank of Dallas to give member banks credit for them. At that time the law did not permit a Fed-

eral Reserve Bank to rediscount sight drafts, and, although
the Federal Reserve Bank of Dallas was called upon to furnish large amounts of currency against balances created by
these drafts, it could not use them as security for Federal
Reserve notes. Consequently, its reserves were in danger of
depletion at a time when its member banks were borrowing
but little from it, for its note issues were limited to the
amount of rediscounted paper held by it.

It was deemed desirable also to bring under the control of
the Federal Reserve Banks as large a volume as possible of
the gold which was then flowing into the country, and accordingly some of the Federal Reserve Banks, notably the
Federal Reserve Bank of New York, adopted the expedient
of obtaining notes from the Federal Reserve Agent by depositing rediscounted paper, and then immediately cancelling
liability for these notes by depositing gold with the Federal
Reserve Agent; the collateral thus withdrawn would then be
used again as security for additional notes; and this process
would be repeated as many times as desired. This practice
met with a good deal of criticism, and when the Board's
proposition to amend the Act in the manner already described was submitted to the House Committee on Banking
and Currency, objections to this practice were raised by
some members of the Committee who complained that the
Federal Reserve Banks were, without authority of law, issuing and keeping in circulation a large amount of Federal Reserve notes secured by gold, which notes were in effect gold
certificates. The method, indeed, was a cumbersome one,
but the Board was advised by counsel that it was within
the law.

There were outstanding on January 26, 1917, $291,693,000
of Federal Reserve notes, the security for which was
$273,320,000 of gold and $19,115,000 of commercial paper.
Neither contraction nor expansion was occasioned by the
process of accumulating gold with the Federal Reserve
Agents against the issues of like amounts of Federal Reserve

notes, for had the notes not been issued the gold would have remained in circulation. It was not the desire of the Board to force a larger volume of currency into circulation, but its object was to protect the country as far as possible against inflation growing out of large imports of gold, and conversely against the evil consequences of a substantial loss of gold whenever conditions should change so as to render such an outflow advisable or necessary. At that time gold in a bank's vault was legal reserve, while Federal Reserve notes were not. There was no sleight-of-hand about the method employed which was the best that could be devised under the law as it then stood, nor was the method different in principle from the practice that has stood the test of time and experience in other countries. The Board sought merely to be forehanded and to assure itself, as far as it could under the law then existing, that whenever large rediscount operations were followed by withdrawals of gold there should be available the means of supplying Federal Reserve notes in such volume as might be necessary.

The Board explained to the Committee that it was unable to see how deposits of gold against outstanding notes could be prevented without making the issue of notes impracticable, and urged that if any attempt should be made to interfere with the important power which was then exercised in part and held in reserve in part by the Federal Reserve Banks, the usefulness of the Federal Reserve System would be seriously impaired. Any banking system which requires its members to tie up so large a part of their cash resources should be prepared to stand the severest test and to render adequate protection without forcing drastic contraction at a time when such contraction might be most disastrous. Attention was called to the experience of the Federal Reserve Bank of Dallas in the autumn of 1916, which showed clearly that currency requirements do not always synchronize with rediscount operations. One rediscounting bank may require gold or a credit balance, while other member banks in rediscounting may require currency against excess balances caused by remittances of check and drafts.

After prolonged consideration the House Committee on Banking and Currency reported favorably a bill which embodied, with some modifications, the Board's recommendations both as to reserves and note issues. In the bill that section of the Federal Reserve Act which relates to note issues was amended so as to include, in the collateral security to be offered for Federal Reserve notes, gold, gold certificates, notes, drafts, bills of exchange, and acceptances acquired in the open market. The collateral security was in no event to be less than the amount of Federal Reserve notes applied for. The amendment made no change in the provision that each Federal Reserve Bank shall maintain reserves in gold or lawful money of not less than thirty-five per cent against its deposits, and reserves in gold of not less than forty per cent against its Federal Reserve notes in actual circulation; but it provided that when the Federal Reserve Agent held gold or gold certificates as collateral for notes issued to his bank, such gold or gold certificates might be carried as part of the gold reserve which the bank was required to maintain against its Federal Reserve notes in actual circulation.

The Banking and Currency Committee of the Senate also reported the bill favorably. Although little time was left for legislation, the opponents of the par clearance of checks sought to take advantage of the legislative situation by proposing a further amendment designed to allow member banks to make a so-called exchange charge in remitting for checks drawn upon them. This was late in February, and Congress was to adjourn *sine die* on March 4 (1917).

In a last effort to secure action, the Board on February 28th, authorized the transmission of two letters to Senator Owen, who was the Chairman of the Senate Committee on Banking and Currency; one official and the other of a personal character. The official letter was a reiteration of the

importance from the Board's viewpoint of prompt action on
the amendments and the personal letter was as follows:

I have been instructed by the Board to send you the letter enclosed herewith, the idea being that perhaps you might take occasion to read it in whole or in part to-morrow morning, should you
succeed in bringing the bill amending the Federal Reserve Act up
for consideration. It may be proper to state that the Board regrets
exceedingly that there seems to be some danger of vital questions
of national scope and importance — which are covered by some of
the sections of the bill — being complicated by an attempt to involve them with the question of exchange charges on checks drawn
upon country banks. The Board does not feel that this question
of exchange — however Congress may finally decide it — is of sufficient importance to let it obstruct the consideration or passage of
the very important bill that your Committee has reported to the
Senate. Member banks are not getting any exchange as the law
now stands, and the passage or failure of your bill would not affect
their status in this respect.

Would it not be possible to induce those advocating exchange
charges on country checks to let this question go over and be considered on its merits at a later date?

The bill, however, was not brought to a vote in either House
of Congress owing to the legislative jam incident to the closing days of the session, and it was left to the succeeding
Congress to enact the measure into law.

Recently there have been some evidences of a concerted
movement for the repeal of the note issue amendment as a
hastily devised war emergency measure which has outlived
its usefulness. While the necessity for this amendment in
the event of war was foreseen it was not conceived as merely
an emergency measure. It was discussed at Board meetings,
with Treasury officials, in financial journals, and with committees of Congress for at least twelve months before it was
finally enacted. The change made by it was of the greatest
value during the war and in the readjustment period which
followed; and if, as seems likely, we are approaching a time
when other countries will draw more heavily upon our stocks
of gold, it will be indispensable.

In framing measures intended to cover merely war emergencies, it was the practice of Congress to place some limit upon the time during which they should be effective. No such limitation was placed upon this particular amendment, which undoubtedly was intended to be permanent, and should not be disturbed.

CHAPTER VIII

UNITED STATES ENTERS THE WAR — CONGRESS AMENDS FEDERAL
RESERVE ACT — PRESIDENT WILSON URGES STATE BANKS TO
BECOME MEMBERS — DISCUSSION OF THE NEW AMENDMENTS
— FIRST LIBERTY LOAN CAMPAIGN

MOMENTOUS events were taking place, and shortly after he
had entered upon his second term, President Wilson called
an extraordinary session of Congress. On the evening of
April 2, 1917, he delivered his memorable war address before
the two houses in joint session, which was followed on April
6th by the adoption of a joint resolution declaring that there
existed a state of war with Germany.

Bills amending the Federal Reserve Act substantially in
the manner described in the preceding chapter, were introduced in both houses soon after the new Congress convened,
and were reported favorably by the committees; and finally
passed both houses, becoming law on June 21, 1917, upon
the approval of the President. The amendment to section 9
of the Federal Reserve Act which was made at this time was
designed to remove obstacles which had previously existed
in the way of membership of State banks and trust companies. Several applications for membership were received
within a few weeks, but it was evident that a direct appeal
to patriotic impulses should be made in order to secure the
coöperation of a larger number. Believing, however, that an
appeal of this kind should not be made without the knowledge and approval of the President, I was directed by the
Board to submit to him the draft of a letter which it proposed to send to eligible State banks and trust companies
which had not yet applied for membership. As this letter
made an appeal to the patriotism of the banks, the suggestion was made to the President that a statement from him
endorsing it would be of great advantage in securing the response desired. With his usual promptness, the President
replied at once, approving the letter, but suggesting that it

be redrafted for his signature, as a direct appeal over his own signature would be more effective than a mere statement endorsing the Board's letter. The Board gladly complied, and the President's appeal is here given in full, because of its historical value, and continuing applicability in time of peace:

It is manifestly imperative that there should be a complete mobilization of the banking reserves of the United States. All who are familiar with financial operations must appreciate the importance of developing to the maximum our banking power and of providing financial machinery adequate for meeting the very great financial requirements imposed upon our country by reason of the war. A vigorous prosecution and satisfactory termination of the war will depend in no small degree upon the ability of the Government not only to finance itself, but also to aid the Governments associated with it in the war, which must be kept supplied with munitions, fuel, food, and supplies of all kinds. The banking problem involved is one which concerns all banks alike. Its solution does not depend upon the national banks alone, nor upon the State banks. The burden and the privilege must be shared by every banking institution in the country. The important functions of the Federal Reserve Banks in the sale of the Government's securities, in receiving and transferring the billions of dollars involved, in supplying credit facilities, and in protecting the reserves of the country, have become so familiar to all that I am sure it is unnecessary to dwell upon or expound them.

The extent to which our country can withstand the financial strains for which we must be prepared will depend very largely upon the strength and staying power of the Federal Reserve Banks. The Federal Reserve Act is the only constructive financial legislation which we have ever had which was broad enough to accommodate at the same time banks operating under powers granted by the general Government and banks whose charters are granted by the respective States. The unification of our banking system and the complete mobilization of reserves are among the fundamental principles of the Act.

The State banking institutions for some reasons have until recently seemed inclined to hold aloof. Congress a few months ago prescribed very generous terms for the admission of the State banks into the Federal Reserve System which have removed the objections heretofore raised by State banks when considering membership. As the law now stands, it leaves member State banks and trust companies practically undisturbed in the exercise of all the banking powers conferred upon them by the States. The law provides also in definite terms the conditions upon which any State bank or trust company may withdraw from the System. Many of the largest State banks and trust companies are now becoming members, realizing that to win the war we must conserve all of the physical, financial, and moral resources of our country — that our finances must rest on the firmest possible foundation, and that they must be adequately and completely conserved so as to respond instantly to every legitimate demand. How can this necessary condition be brought about and be made permanently effective better than by the concentration of the banking strength of our country in the Federal Reserve System?

May I not, therefore, urge upon the officers and directors of all non-member State banks and trust companies, which have the required amount of capital and surplus to make them eligible for membership, to unite with the Federal Reserve System now and thereby contribute their share to the consolidated gold reserves of the country? I feel sure that as member banks they will aid to a greater degree than is possible otherwise in promoting the national welfare, and that at the same time, by securing for themselves the advantages offered by the Federal Reserve System, they will best serve their own interest and the interest of their customers. I believe that coöperation on the part of the banks is a patriotic duty at this time, and that membership in the Federal Reserve System is a distinct and significant evidence of patriotism.

There are probably eight or nine thousand State banks and trust companies eligible for membership which have not yet united with the system. These institutions have it in their power to add enormously to the resources of the Federal Reserve Banks, thereby broadening and strengthening the foundation upon which our whole financial structure must rest. Permit me to urge that every bank officer and bank director owes a solemn obligation to the country which I am sure they wish to discharge. I, therefore, wish again to impress upon them my solemn conviction that they can best measure up to their duties and responsibilities through membership in the Federal Reserve System.

                    (Signed)   WOODROW WILSON

THE WHITE HOUSE, *October* 13, 1917

This letter was issued in circular form and was sent to several thousand non-member banks and trust companies throughout the country. The effect of the appeal was to bring into the System within a short time State banks and trust companies which, though numerically in a minority, represented a large proportion of the banking resources of the country. Their accession as members greatly increased the strength and prestige of the System, and resulted in giving its membership about seventy per cent of the banking resources of the country. While many banks stated plainly that they were joining purely because of patriotic motives, it is worthy of note that only a comparatively small number of them have withdrawn from the System.

In order to show more clearly the effect of the amendment to section 16, relating to note issues, a table is given below which shows the total of Federal Reserve notes outstanding on November 5, 1920, at a time when rediscounts for member banks were at the peak, the amount of gold available as reserve for note circulation, after deducting the required thirty-five per cent for reserve against deposits, and the free gold — that is, gold above the reserve requirements for these two classes of Federal Reserve Bank liabilities. This table should be compared with the table which immediately follows, which shows how much less the lending power of the Federal Reserve Banks would have been had the Act not been amended.

ACTUAL POSITION — NOVEMBER 5, 1920

Discounts for member banks.....................		$2,826,825,000
Federal Reserve notes in circulation..............		3,354,180,000
Total reserves.................	$2,169,729,000	
Less reserve of 35 per cent against deposits..................	593,224,000	
Gold available as reserve against Federal Reserve notes in circulation........................		1,576,505,000
Required reserve of 40 per cent against Federal Reserve notes in circulation....................		1,341,672,000
Excess reserves (free gold).....................		234,833,000
Additional lending power in form of Federal Reserve notes................................		587,082,000
Reserve ratio...............................		43.0 per cent

From the table below it will be seen that if on November 5, 1920, the Federal Reserve Banks had been operating under section 16 as originally enacted, assuming reserve deposits, loans to member banks, and Federal Reserve note circulation on that date to be the same as they actually were under the amended Act, the reserve ratio of the System would have been 36.3 per cent, while the amount of paper rediscounted for member banks and the amount of Federal Reserve note circulation would have been $203,950,000 in excess of the theoretical maximum if reserves were to be maintained at legal requirements (35 per cent against deposits and 40 per cent against notes).

THEORETICAL POSITION — NOVEMBER 5, 1920
Under original section 16

Discounts for member banks.....................	$2,826,825,000
Federal Reserve notes in circulation..............	3,354,180,000
Excess of Federal Reserve notes over eligible paper	527,355,000
Gold and lawful money......................	2,169,729,000
Total reserves after pledging with Federal Reserve Agent gold and lawful money equal to excess of notes over eligible paper	1,642,374,000
Reserve of 35 per cent against deposits	593,224,000
Gold available as reserve against Federal Reserve notes in circulation	1,049,150,000
Federal Reserve note circulation subject to reserve requirements (amount secured by eligible paper)..	2,826,825,000
Required reserve of 40 per cent against Federal Reserve notes...............................	1,130,730,000
Deficiency in reserves	81,580,000
Reduction in discounts and Federal Reserve note circulation necessary to restore reserves to legal minimum of 40 per cent against notes and 35 per cent against deposits	203,950,000
Reserve ratio.............................	36.3 per cent

Comparison of the two tables shows that under the present law the Federal Reserve Banks had an additional lending power of $587,082,000, while under the original law they would have been over-extended by $203,950,000. In other words, on November 5, 1920, on the basis of maintenance of legal reserves, the Federal Reserve Banks had a lending power of $791,032,000 more than they would have had if the Federal Reserve Act had not been amended. While the Board was authorized by law to reduce reserve requirements, the sentimental effect of such action was feared. The new amendment obviated the necessity for reducing reserves below the normal minimum.

An important effect of the amendment, permitting the issue of Federal Reserve notes directly against gold, which was anticipated by the Board, was to bring into the Federal Reserve Banks much of the gold which had previously been in general circulation. In this way the gold resources of the country were mobilized and the Federal Reserve Banks acquired a credit-giving power which would otherwise have been impossible.

On April 6, 1917, when Congress declared that a state of war existed between this country and the Imperial German Government, reserve deposits of the Federal Reserve Banks were $758,219,000; their holdings of bills rediscounted were $17,928,000; of bills purchased in the open market, $82,735,000; of other investments, $124,878,000; and of gold, including $378,450,000 with Federal Reserve Agents, $943,552,000. Their reserve ratio against combined liabilities for notes and deposits was 75.4 per cent. Had gold with the Federal Reserve Agents been counted at that time as part of the banks' lawful reserves, as was afterwards permitted by the amendment of June 21, 1917, their reserve ratio would have been 84.6 per cent.

Four days before President Wilson delivered his war address to Congress, the Board received a letter from the Secretary of the Treasury saying:

I purpose borrowing for the Government $50,000,000 for ninety (90) days, at two (2) per cent interest per annum, in anticipation of the payment of corporation and individual income taxes due June, 1917. Treasury certificates of indebtedness, authorized by existing law, will be issued in such denominations as may be necessary. This is an excellent opportunity for the Federal Reserve Banks to secure a desirable short-time investment and to demonstrate their usefulness as fiscal agents of the Government. I purpose, therefore, to offer the Federal Reserve Banks, the opportunity to take these certificates. Will you please get in touch with the Federal Reserve Banks and ascertain whether or not they care to take this loan and what amount they respectively desire to take? The funds should be available to the Treasury on or before the 31st instant.

Upon receipt of this, a telegram was sent to the Governor of each Federal Reserve Bank, as follows:

March 27, 1917

Secretary of Treasury informs Board he will offer to Federal Reserve Banks certificates of indebtedness authorized by existing law in suitable denominations aggregating fifty million dollars for ninety days at two per cent interest rate, in anticipation of income taxes due June. Please advise Board promptly if you wish to participate, stating amount desired. Funds should be available to Treasury on or before Saturday next. Secretary of Treasury expresses opinion that this is excellent opportunity for Reserve Banks to secure desirable short-time investment and demonstrate their usefulness fiscal agents of Government.

The opinion of a majority of the members of the Federal Reserve Board, and of all the Federal Reserve Bank Governors, was that the rate proposed, two per cent per annum, was too much below the market, and that it should have been at least two and one half per cent. It was recognized, however, that the country was upon the verge of war and the offer of the Secretary of the Treasury was accepted, each Federal Reserve Bank taking its proper proportion of the issue as allotted by the Federal Reserve Board. This issue was only a beginning, and was followed quickly on April 25th by an offering of $250,000,000 at three per cent, which was promptly distributed by the Federal Reserve Banks among the member and non-member banks of their respective districts. These issues at varying rates have ever since been a part of the Treasury's financial programme. During the war they were made sometimes in anticipation of bond issues and at other times in anticipation of income-tax receipts. After the war they were made in anticipation of tax receipts and more recently have been used in short-time refunding operations.

In May, 1917, distinguished representatives of the English and French Governments came to Washington. Among them were Mr. Balfour, Lord Northcliffe, and Lord Cunliffe, Governor of the Bank of England, M. Viviani, and Marshal Joffre, the hero of the Marne. They were accorded a most enthusiastic reception and evidently impressed upon the authorities a sense of the necessity of making war preparations upon a very large scale and of prompt action. The Federal Reserve Board had a number of interesting conferences with Lord Cunliffe, and one of its members, Mr. Hamlin, former Governor of the Board, accompanied him on a visit to other cities.

Meanwhile the Secretary of the Treasury had taken steps toward providing for the financing of the war. Pending the passage of a revenue bill by Congress, an act was passed (April 24, 1917) which authorized the sale of bonds and Treasury certificates, and the making of loans by the Treasury to Governments with which this country was associated in the war.

The Secretary of the Treasury consulted with the Federal Reserve Board as to the amount of the first bond issue, and he also conferred with the members of the Federal Advisory Council. I recall that he put before the Council the question as to the amount of bonds which might be floated without serious disturbance to the money market. Some of the bankers named $500,000,000 as a maximum figure, while others expressed the view that bids might safely be invited for as much as $1,000,000,000.

Early in April there had been some sentiment expressed in favor of giving the war bonds the circulation privilege. The Comptroller of the Currency for a time at least seemed to be in favor of legislation which would permit national banks to issue circulating notes against their holdings of such bonds with the proviso that the tax on national bank notes thus secured be made equal to the rate of interest borne by the bonds. The Board received letters from various persons advocating this plan, all of which were transmitted to the Secretary of the Treasury, with a strong expression of its own disapproval of the suggestion. The Secretary of the Treasury did not favor the plan and Congress did not give the new bonds the circulation privilege, although it made them fully exempt from income tax. Early in May, Secretary McAdoo announced that he would ask for public subscriptions through the Federal Reserve Banks to an issue of $2,000,000,000 of bonds at three and one half per cent; the bonds to be exempt from all income and other taxes, except inheritance taxes. Secretary McAdoo then made a trip through the country as far north as Minneapolis, as far west as Denver, and as far south as New Orleans, returning to Washington by way of Birmingham, Louisville, Cincinnati, and Pittsburgh, in order to arouse interest in the bond issue to which he had given the name of the First Liberty Loan. At his request I accompanied him on this trip. The First Liberty Loan Campaign was a great success and the issue was largely oversubscribed. Allotments were made through the Federal Reserve Banks, whose Governors had acted as chairmen of the Liberty Loan Committees in their respective districts.

CHAPTER IX

EXECUTIVE ORDERS RESTRICTING GOLD EXPORTS AND REGULAT-
ING TRANSACTIONS IN FOREIGN EXCHANGE — BOARD'S
POLICY IN ISSUING LICENSES

As fiscal agents of the Treasury, the Federal Reserve Banks during the war performed notable and valuable services. They organized member and non-member banks all over the country into bond-distributing agencies, and through the coöperation of these banks, aided by liberal use of the Federal Reserve rediscount facilities, the public was able to subscribe during the period from June, 1917, to October, 1918, for about $17,000,000,000 of bonds. Patriotic impulse was the incentive, but the banks of the country, with the strong support of the Federal Reserve Banks, furnished the means which made possible the translation of impulse into action.

An immediate effect of the entry of the United States into the war and of the large credits given the Allied Governments was an almost complete cessation of the movement of gold to this country, which had been continuous since the early months of the year 1915, although the movement had begun to slacken as early as November, 1916. Foreign Governments had found it convenient to liquidate their obligations due in other countries by purchasing remittances in our own markets, frequently against credits opened by American banks or by the Government. The aggregate trade balance as represented by excess of exports over imports continued during the year 1917 in favor of the United States, although the balances were against us in some cases. There developed a strong tendency on the part of neutrals, as well as by countries associated with us in the war, to withdraw gold from us, and during the months of June, July, and August (1917), the exports of gold exceeded imports by about

$100,000,000. As exports of gold had already been restricted in all belligerent countries, demands for gold in settling international accounts, in adjusting exchange rates, and in strengthening reserves, were naturally made in what was practically the only free market remaining, that is, the American market. As the movement began to assume larger proportions, the President on September 7th issued a proclamation to the effect that:

Except at such time or times, and under such regulations and orders, and subject to such limitations and exceptions as the President shall prescribe, until otherwise ordered by the President or by Congress, the following articles, namely: Coin, bullion, and currency shall not, on and after the 10th day of September, in the year 1917, be exported from or shipped from or taken out of the United States or its territorial possessions . . .

By Executive order of the same date the President directed that:

1. Any individual, firm, or corporation desiring to export from the United States or any of its territorial possessions to any foreign country named in the proclamation dated September 7, 1917, any coin, bullion, or currency, shall first file an application in triplicate with the Federal Reserve Bank of the district in which such individual, firm, or corporation is located, such application to state under oath and in detail the nature of the transaction, the amount involved, the parties directly and indirectly interested, and such other information as may be of assistance to the proper authorities in determining whether the exportation for which a license is desired will be compatible with the public interest.

2. Each Federal Reserve Bank shall keep a record copy of each application filed with it under the provisions of this regulation and shall forward the original application and a duplicate to the Federal Reserve Board at Washington together with such information or suggestions as it may believe proper in the circumstances and shall in addition make a formal recommendation as to whether or not in its opinion the exportation should be permitted.

3. The Federal Reserve Board, subject to the approval of the Secretary of the Treasury, is hereby authorized and empowered upon receipt of such application and the recommendation of the Federal Reserve Bank, to make such ruling as it may deem proper

in the circumstances and if in its opinion the exportation in question be compatible with the public interest, to permit said exportation to be made; otherwise to refuse it.

In pursuance of this order the Federal Reserve Board, with the approval of the Secretary of the Treasury, issued regulations governing the administrative procedure with regard to the exportation of coin, bullion, and currency, and during the remaining months of the war, and for some time thereafter, considered and passed upon all applications for such shipments.

Applications for permission to ship gold to European neutral countries were, except for a few days following the date of the order, invariably declined. A different problem, however, was presented in the case of applications for shipments of gold to the Orient, to Canada, to Mexico, and to South American countries, which had been furnishing necessary raw materials. It was deemed important to continue these trade relationships, while reducing shipments of gold to a minimum. For a short time gold shipments were permitted to go to India, in order to give importers reasonable time to adjust themselves to the new conditions. Silver was permitted to flow freely to the Orient as a means of payment for Asiatic balances. In addition, as a result of negotiations between the Treasury Department and representatives of the Indian Government, provision was made for rupee exchange to the extent of 10,000,000 rupees, which were allotted by Federal Reserve Banks to importers according to their necessities. (Later an additional credit of 10,000,000 rupees was arranged, and after January 1, 1918, an exchange agreement with the Government of Argentina was entered into.) In a few cases shipments of gold were permitted to South American countries.

Applications for shipments of gold into Mexico were granted only for Government account and in cases where such shipments were shown to be essential to effect the importation into the United States of necessary products. The exportations were limited as far as possible and the greater part of the gold which was shipped was for payment of Mexican export duties and for meeting the requirements of Mexican law as to the return into Mexico of the value of the full gold content and twenty-five per cent of silver content of ores and bullion exported from Mexico. Each application was considered upon its own merits, the Board having given notice, in its regulations dated September 21, 1917, that the granting of any specific application would not constitute a precedent. In considering applications the Board adhered strictly to the principle laid down in the Executive order, that if, in its opinion, the exportation applied for was not compatible with the public interest, it should be refused, and it acted also in close coöperation with the State and Treasury Departments and the War Trade Board.

After the flotation of the First Liberty Loan, the organizations which had been effected in the several Federal Reserve districts were continued and strengthened. The Treasury found it more convenient to deal directly with the Federal Reserve Banks in all fiscal agency matters, and the Board had but little to do with the successive Liberty Loan Campaigns which followed the First.

It was not the function of the Federal Reserve Board to determine the financial policy of the Government, nor did the responsibility rest upon it for fixing the rates of interest to be borne by the successive issues of bonds and Treasury certificates. All of these were questions the determination of which rested entirely with the Secretary of the Treasury in his capacity as such, and not as *ex officio* chairman of the Federal Reserve Board.

There were other matters, however, which kept the Board fully occupied during the war. The restrictions placed upon exports of coin, bullion, and currency by the President's proclamation of September 7, 1917, and the duties imposed upon the Federal Reserve Board by the Executive order of the same date, obliged the Board to give close attention to the foreign exchange situation. Much additional work was entailed in passing upon applications for permission to make shipments. As a general rule those whose applications to export gold were refused by the Board accepted the Board's conclusions as final, but, in at least one case, heavy and long-continued pressure was brought to bear to bring about a reversal.

There was an importer of olive oil who had made large purchases in Spain during the season of 1916 through credits arranged by some American banks. For some reason he had not purchased Spanish exchange with which to liquidate these credits, but had preferred to renew them from time to time. Meanwhile the premium on pesetas advanced steadily despite a considerable excess of American exports to Spain over imports from that country. This importer was obsessed with the idea that it was the duty of the Federal Reserve Board to furnish him in some way with Spanish exchange at par or at a nominal premium. For a time he carried full-page advertisements in some of the newspapers stressing the importance and feasibility of maintaining a parity between American, Italian, and Spanish exchange. Then he laid his troubles before Senator Owen, who listened with a sympathetic ear. The restriction of gold exports which followed the President's proclamation of September 7th increased the premium on Spanish exchange and added to the difficulties of this particular importer. For many months both he and Senator Owen were persistent in protesting against the depreciation of the American dollar abroad; and, failing a general leveling of exchange rates, they were insistent that a license should be granted to export to Spain sufficient gold to meet the necessities of this particular case. There were many personal interviews and much correspondence between the Board and the applicant and the Senator, but, as the Federal Reserve Board was unable to see that there was any general public interest which required a license in this case, it adhered to its original position and declined to grant the application. Senator Owen then brought it to the attention of Secretary McAdoo, who, in agreeing with the position taken by the Board, observed that the business carried on by the applicant 'is not an essential industry and serves no useful purpose in the war, and for that, if for no other reason, it is not entitled to special consideration.' Senator Owen then communicated with the President, but for some months was unable to convince the Chief Executive that the license should be granted.

Finally, however, representations were made to the Board by the banks which had been renewing these credits for the importer that, unless the license to export was granted, the applicant would be forced into bankruptcy and his creditor banks would be subjected to substantial losses. It was argued that the public interest would be better served by permitting the export of $1,250,000 of gold rather than face consequences which might affect unfavorably, to some extent at least, the banking situation in Baltimore and Washington where the interested banks were located.

While the Board was deliberating as to whether it might not properly in view of these facts grant the permit, it received an inquiry from the President as to the status of the application. As the Executive order placing an embargo upon shipments of gold had been issued by the President, and as it was in his power at any time to rescind or modify it, the Board felt that it would be relieved from responsibility in this case if the President should indicate a desire that the application be granted. A memorandum covering the case was sent to the White House, and in his letter acknowledging, he said, 'I am very glad to avail myself of the intimation that the Board will act upon my advice in this matter, and my advice is, that the license be granted, all the circumstances being taken into consideration.' The license was accordingly issued (April 15, 1918).

At this time the Federal Reserve Banks had a special deposit of gold in the Bank of England, and the licensee was given the option of withdrawing gold for export in New York or of taking an equivalent amount in British gold sovereigns in London at a stipulated rate. Complaints were made to the Board, to the Secretary of the Treasury, and to the President, who sent me a copy of a telegram signed by Senator Owen protesting against the charge which had been made. I wrote an explanatory letter to the President and in his acknowledgment he said: 'Thank you for your full and satisfactory memorandum under date of June 4 commenting upon the telegram signed by Senator Owen, which I took the liberty of transmitting to you the other day. . . . Your memorandum convinces me that the arrangement for exchange which was proposed is the best that can be obtained. Will you be kind enough to advise him what the arrangement is and what the discount amounts to.'

Realizing the futility of further protest, the licensee authorized his banks to purchase British gold sovereigns through the Federal Reserve Bank of New York at 4.985, which represented an exchange charge for the sovereigns of about $25,000. This was less than transportation and insurance charges would have been on a shipment of gold from New York to London, and in fact was somewhat below current quotations in the London market. My information is that the banks were able to exchange these gold sovereigns for French gold and that this Spanish indebtedness was finally liquidated by a shipment of French gold from Paris, there being no discount in Spain on French gold as was the case with British and American gold.

Meanwhile the Board had established in New York a Division of Foreign Exchange under the immediate direction of Mr. Fred I. Kent. His familiarity with foreign transactions, his thorough knowledge of the intricacies of exchange, his close attention to the work of this division, and the executive ability which he displayed in carrying it on, were of the greatest value to the country.

The original Executive order of the President dated September 7, 1917, placed restrictions upon the exportation of coin, bullion, and currency from the United States and was amplified by Executive orders dated October 12, 1917, and November 3, 1917; which in turn were amended by a new order dated January 26, 1918. In the preamble of this order it was recited that the Executive administration, authority, and power were vested in the Secretary of the Treasury, and that upon the recommendation of the Secretary of the Treasury and in order to vest all necessary authority in the Federal Reserve Board to act as the agency of the Secretary of the Treasury, certain orders, rules, and regulations were prescribed and certain amendments were made to the regulations prescribed by the previous Executive orders.

In the Executive order of January 26, 1918, the terms, 'dealer,' 'foreign exchange,' 'securities,' 'correspondent,' and ' customer ' were defined, and regulations were prescribed covering the following: All transactions in foreign exchange; export or ear-marking of gold or silver coin or bullion or currency; transfers of credit in any form and transfers of evidences of indebtedness or of the ownership of property between the United States and any foreign country or between residents of one or more foreign countries by any person within the United States; transactions in foreign exchange or in securities for or through foreign account, collection dividends, interest, or maturing obligations for foreign account; and licenses from War Trade Board in transactions involving trading with an enemy or ally of enemy.

A committee of the Board met daily to consider and pass upon all applications to export coin, bullion, or currency, and the closest scrutiny was given to the applications, each being treated upon its own merits. During the period from September 7, 1917, to January 1, 1919, licenses were granted permitting gold exportations amounting in all to $45,514,000. In all meritorious cases the Board granted licenses for the exportation of United States currency other than gold and silver certificates; and permits were granted for shipments of more than $86,000,000 of currency for use in Canada, Mexico, Central America, and the West Indies.

The regulations of the Division of Foreign Exchange were necessarily technical and elaborate, but the division was so efficiently conducted that there was little complaint. All cablegrams before delivery or transmission were obliged to pass the scrutiny of the Division of Foreign Exchange. In undertaking to carry through prohibited transactions, attempts were sometimes made to use a private code which had the appearance of a harmless personal telegram. I am told that on one occasion a cable was submitted to be sent to an addressee in Holland, worded as follows: 'Father dead, funeral Thursday.' There was something about the cable which looked suspicious to Mr. Kent, but as he did not feel warranted in stopping its transmission, he changed the language to read: 'Father deceased, interment Thursday'; and thus amended, let it go forward. A few hours later his suspicions were confirmed by a reply reading: 'Is Father dead or deceased? Explain interment'!

With the exception which has already been noted, there was a general disposition manifested to abide by the regulations. A few dealers, perhaps, might not have been unwilling to undertake operations for enemy account, but their knowledge that, if they did so, and were discovered, they would be prohibited from continuing their foreign exchange business for the period of the war, acted as a deterrent. This penalty was one of the important safeguards provided by the Executive order, but on the whole the voluntary and patriotic coöperation of dealers was a constant source of satisfaction. The great banking institutions which transacted the bulk of our foreign exchange business cheerfully subordinated profits to the national interest.

At this point it may be well to consider the purpose of the restrictions which were placed upon the exportations of gold and upon transactions in foreign exchange. The embargo was established as a part of the war policy of the Government. Its purpose was to protect the public interest:

1. By preventing shipments of gold, or remittances of exchange, to destinations where such transfers might be of advantage to the enemy;
2. By conserving the American gold supply for use in connection with the extensive credit operations of the Government.

In passing upon applications for permission to export gold and to allow transactions in exchange, the Board's discrimination was limited to consideration of the question whether the granting of the permit requested would be 'compatible with the public interest.' The Board had no authority to permit such transactions unless it found that they were 'compatible with the public interest,' and it was expressly directed by the Executive order to refuse such applications if, in its opinion, the exportations or transactions in question were not 'compatible with the public interest.' The tests, therefore, that the Board uniformly sought to apply were:

1. Will the transactions be likely to be of benefit directly or indirectly to the enemy? and
2. Will the diminution of our gold supply, resulting from any transaction, be compensated by the addition to our supply of necessary materials resulting from the transaction?

Injury or inconvenience to private interests did not determine the Board's rulings. Public interest was the decisive factor even where the safeguarding of the public interest involved individual injury or loss.

Although exports from the United States during the war period greatly exceeded imports, it is true that in a few countries American exchange was at a discount when under normal conditions it would have been at par or at a premium because of the excess of our exports to those countries. This seeming anomaly is accounted for by the fact that during the war the United States was practically in economic as well as military alliance with Great Britain, France, Italy, and Belgium. It will be remembered that Congress authorized credits to the extent of ten billion dollars to countries which were associated with us in the war, and that these credits were for the most part used by these countries in the purchase of supplies and war material in the United States. Great Britain, for her own account, and for her allies, made larger purchases in the United States than any other country, and these purchases created a corresponding British demand for dollar exchange. During the war the British Government found it expedient to maintain sterling exchange in New York at an arbitrary rate of $4.76⁷⁄₁₆, and in order to maintain this rate it was obliged during the early part of the year 1918 to purchase sterling bills in amounts averaging about $40,000,000 per week. These purchases did not represent the entire volume of sterling bills offered in the New York market, but represented the excess which had to be provided for in order to maintain the rate. The maintenance of sterling at this slight discount was an important factor in the conduct of the war, for it is obvious that, if the British Government had not intervened and had permitted the market to take its course, the large offerings of sterling bills would have depressed the market and forced sterling down to a low point, which would have added greatly to the costs of the supplies and war materials purchased by the Allies. The credits extended by the United States Treasury under authority of Congress were, therefore, more effective for many months — until the American troops in large numbers were ready for action in France — than the military assistance this country was able to give.

In the case of Spain, a neutral country, the trade balance was in favor of the United States, and, even had it been adverse, the dollar could have been maintained at approximately ninety-seven cents by permitting shipments of gold. (American gold was arbitrarily at a discount of three per cent in Spain.) But England and France were both making heavy purchases in Spain and these purchases in each case were far in excess of their exports to Spain. Consequently, British and French exchanges were both at a discount in Spain, and it is therefore plain that as long as the United States coöperated economically as well as in a military sense with these countries, and took no steps to protect the value of the American dollar in Spain, Spanish exchange normally would rise to a point based upon the adverse trade balances of England and France, less the favorable trade balance of the United States. The same observations apply to Switzerland, Holland, Norway, and Sweden, in which countries also American exchange was at a discount. Spain and the Scandinavian countries had at this time a surfeit of gold and practically demonetized it by stopping its coinage and by placing it upon a commodity basis. American exporters to these countries usually drew in sterling, while American importers were required to make payment in terms of the currency of these countries. As the balance of trade was heavy against England in these countries, exchange on London was at a discount, and, conversely, their own exchanges were at a premium. The prices paid for sterling exchange in New York by the British Government made that city the world's highest market for sterling, and therefore holders of sterling bills all over the world sent them to New York for sale. Although shipments of gold from the United States to European neutral countries would under war conditions have been expensive and risky, it would still have been possible, if dollar exchange alone was to be considered, to ship enough gold to restore the parity of the American dollar in neutral countries; but it was neither practicable nor desirable to ship gold in sufficient quantities to restore the parity of the pound sterling or the franc, with which currency the American dollar was associated in the minds of the neutrals, and which under conditions then existing would have to be fully protected before dollar exchange could reach its parity.

Senator Owen in his criticisms to the Board at this time laid particular stress upon the fact that American importers were losing heavily because of the discount on the dollar in these countries despite the trade balance in our favor, and was insistent that steps be taken to correct this condition. In one of his communications he said:

The simplest remedy is to provide that exchange to and from these countries shall be based upon actual merchandise shipments. This can be done by forbidding any exchange or transfer of credits for this purpose, except against actual commodities, until the dollar rises to par, or until foreign exchange is reduced to par.

A second remedy would be to require these countries as a condition of getting our goods to take international securities or our Government bonds to cover their international trade balances. The first remedy is the simplest and the easiest, because stopping arbitrage settlements can be done by our own enactments without the consent of other nations.

He further suggested that the Federal Reserve Board issue a ruling that

No exchange or transfers of credit to meet exchanges shall be permitted by any bank or banker in the United States with any country where the exchange is against the United States, except as against actual merchandise, until the American dollar is brought to gold parity in such country.

Senator Owen was insistent also that Federal Reserve Banks should establish branches in foreign countries for the purpose of stabilizing American exchange, and in a speech in the Senate on February 25, 1918, said:

At first the Federal Reserve Banks contemplated that they would open branches in foreign countries voluntarily, but they did not voluntarily establish these foreign branches and thereupon Congress passed an amendment authorizing the Federal Reserve Board to require them to do this, but the Federal Reserve Board seems not to have found it practicable for some reason to compel any of these banks to establish foreign branches.

Section 14 of the Federal Reserve Act provides that:

Under regulations to be prescribed by the Federal Reserve Board, Federal Reserve Banks shall have power to open and maintain accounts in foreign countries, appoint correspondents, and establish agencies in such countries wheresoever it may deem best for the purpose of purchasing, selling and collecting bills of exchange, and to buy and sell, with or without its endorsement, through some correspondents or agencies, bills of exchange arising out of actual commercial transactions which have not more than ninety days to run, exclusive of days of grace, and which bear the signature of two or more responsible parties, and with the consent of the Federal Reserve Board to open and maintain banking accounts for such foreign correspondents or agencies.

More than a year before this, announcement had been made that an agency agreement had been entered into between the Bank of England and the Federal Reserve Bank of New York, acting on behalf of all the Federal Reserve Banks; and connections had been established also between the Federal Reserve Bank of New York and the Bank of France, the Bank of Italy, the Bank of the Netherlands, and the Bank of Japan.

There is nothing in the Federal Reserve Act which gives Federal Reserve Banks power to establish foreign branches. They are authorized to have only correspondents and agencies. All that these foreign correspondents or agencies could do, exclusive of matters relating to dealing in or ear-marking gold, would be to make cable transfers and buy bills of exchange arising out of commercial transactions. Through these agencies the Federal Reserve Banks would have power, had they desired, to invest in bills payable in sterling, francs, lire or guilders.

The suggestion had been made in 1916 by Secretary McAdoo that Federal Reserve Banks establish agencies in certain South American countries; but neither the Federal Reserve Banks nor the Board, after giving consideration to the question, felt justified during a period of world war in engaging in such transactions. Federal Reserve Banks are trustees of the reserve money of the member banks. They could not during the World War have taken the risk of investing in foreign bills without having assurance that when these bills matured they would be paid in gold; nor could they assume the risk, pending maturity of the bills, of a serious depreciation in exchange rates which would cause a substantial loss. During the war period Russia furnished a striking illustration of the risks that were involved, and after the war Germany and other countries under more conservative governments afforded similar illustrations. During the war exchanges in the United States of all Allied countries declined to some extent and would have declined far more had not the Treasury intervened by granting credits, thus enabling the Allied countries to sustain their exchanges. The Federal Reserve Board felt that Federal Reserve Banks should not during the war period take the risk of heavy loss by purchasing foreign exchange, but that it was the duty of the banks to keep their gold reserves available and as strong as possible for the protection of our own credit situation; nor would the establishment of Federal Reserve foreign branches, even if permitted by law, or the establishment of agencies in neutral countries, have benefited American exchange in countries where the dollar sold at a discount. The restrictions upon exports of gold and upon foreign exchange transactions doubtless caused some inconvenience to importers, and losses in particular cases, but they certainly did not affect the volume of exports. The Executive orders relating to these transactions and the Board's faithful execution of the terms of these orders were undoubtedly important factors in the winning of the war.

CHAPTER X

AT the beginning of the year 1918 the demands made by the war upon the resources of the country were reflected in advancing prices for goods, and personal service, higher rentals, and generally increased costs of living. The financial requirements of the Government, which by common consent were given right of way, made it more and more difficult for private corporations to meet their own requirements, not only for new capital, but for funds with which to pay off maturing obligations.

There was a tendency also on the part of banks throughout the country to increase the rates of interest paid on deposits. This tendency was not confined to the interest paid on savings and time deposits, but in many cities banks increased the rate of interest paid on individual and corporate accounts subject to check, and on balances carried with them by other banks. Some of the banks in the city of New York were bidding as high as three per cent for balances of other banks payable on demand, and the rates offered for time deposits were higher. The reason given by the New York banks was that they were compelled to meet the competition of banks in other cities. This action on the part of some of the large New York City banks led to reprisals by banks in other cities which had not contemplated advances in the rate of interest on deposits, and soon the bidding for business by marking up interest rates on deposits threatened to interfere seriously with the financial operations of the Government. Finally, after a conference between members of the Federal Reserve Board and the Clearing-House Committee in New York, the Clearing-House banks of New York City agreed to fix a rate of two and one half per cent on bank balances payable on demand, with the proviso that the interest rate would be automatically advanced or reduced one quarter of one per cent with each advance or decline of one half of one per cent in the ninety-day rate at the Federal Reserve Bank of New York. This action checked for a time a very dangerous tendency, although the Board realized that it was not a permanent nor altogether satisfactory solution of the problem. It was believed, however, that, because of other steps which were about to be taken toward the rationing of credit, and because of the policy of the Treasury, there would be no advance in Federal Reserve Bank rates during the period of war, and that, therefore, under the New York Clearing-House arrangement there would be no further increase during that time in the rate of interest paid on deposits. The Board had occasion to deal with this question again in January, 1920.

About this time Mr. Warburg and others conferred with the Secretary of the Treasury on the necessity for making some provision for the rationing of credit for essential purposes and its restriction for non-essential uses.

The Federal Reserve Board had created a Capital Issues Committee with Messrs. Warburg, Hamlin, and Delano as members. This committee invited all persons, firms, and corporations who were contemplating unusual expenditures involving the issuance of new securities, as an act of voluntary coöperation to submit their plans to the committee in order that the essential character from the standpoint of public interest, of the proposed expenditures might be determined. While this committee had no authority to prohibit expenditures nor to restrain a corporation from offering its securities on the market, its moral influence in most cases was effective. It was evident, however, that there should be some agency established which could provide for the maturing obligations of corporate enterprises, such as large manufacturing concerns, public utilities, and railroads, whose operations were regarded as essential in the conduct of the war. Ordinarily such enterprises looked to the investment market to absorb securities offered by them, but, owing to the large and continuous offerings of Government obligations, the investment market was no longer able readily to absorb private offerings. Having these conditions in mind, the Secretary of the Treasury developed his plan for the establishment of a War Finance Corporation and for the creation by law of a Capital Issues Committee with larger powers than the Board's Voluntary Committee could exercise. Accordingly a bill was prepared in the Treasury Department, the objects of which were outlined in its caption:

A Bill to provide further for the national security and defense, and for the purpose of assisting in the prosecution of the war, to provide credits for industries and enterprises in the United States necessary or contributory to the prosecution of the war, and for other purposes.

On February 8th the Finance Committee of the Senate, meeting for the purpose of considering this bill, had before it the Secretary of the Treasury, Mr. Warburg, and myself. Mr. Warburg was then Vice-Governor of the Federal Reserve Board and was also Chairman of the Board's Capital Issues Committee. Among the members of the Senate Finance Committee who were present were Senator Simmons, Chairman; and Senators Lodge, Smoot, Stone, McCumber, Gallinger, Gore, Thomas, Townsend, and Jones, of New Mexico. There was a full discussion of the reasons for the establishment of a War Finance Corporation and for the restriction of capital issues. Secretary McAdoo led the discussion and the substance of his remarks was that

the proposed act to incorporate a War Finance Corporation should be regarded primarily as a measure to enable the banks, both national banks and State banks and trust companies, to continue to furnish essential credits for industries and enterprises which are necessary or contributory to the prosecution of the war.

The Government's borrowings, particularly during the period

immediately preceding and following each Liberty Loan, have tended to preëmpt the credit facilities of the banks and often to prevent them from giving needed and customary help to quasi-public and private enterprises. Many instances have been brought to the attention of the Secretary of the Treasury and of the Federal Reserve Board where industrial plants, public utilities, power plants, railroads, and others have found it difficult, if not impossible, to obtain the necessary advances to enable them to perform vital service in connection with the war, because essential credits, ordinarily available to them, are being absorbed by the Government itself.

In Europe central banks are permitted to grant to banks and bankers loans upon stocks and bonds upon certain well-defined terms. The Federal Reserve Act does not provide for these, and the War Finance Corporation is designed as a war emergency to fill this gap. The provisions of the Federal Reserve Act which permit Federal Reserve Banks to rediscount and purchase commercial paper and paper secured by the Government's obligations have had the effect of forcing the banks to discriminate against loans on ineligible paper, even where such loans were vitally necessary for war purposes, in favor of loans on commercial paper even where they represented activities or enterprises not related to the war, and which might well be curtailed during the period of the war. It is believed that the proposed bill has been wisely and conservatively conceived as a war measure to give relief from this condition during the war. The banks of the country would, no doubt, scrutinize with the utmost care both the loans themselves and the security therefor and would exercise their individual judgment upon the borrower's credit before assuming a liability for the amount of the loan, and also because they would be under the necessity of advancing, out of their own resources, twenty-five per cent of the amount loaned. The bill would authorize advances to a bank of only seventy-five per cent of the amount loaned by the bank on the notes or obligations of persons, firms, or corporations whose activities are necessary or contributory to the war.

The bill contemplates that the War Finance Corporation shall lend money to banks, both national and State, which are making loans to enterprises conducted by persons, firms, or corporations producing materials or supplies, or doing anything else which is necessary for or contributory to the war. If a bank, for instance, should loan money, we will say, to a munitions company and take the company's six months' note with the company's bond as collateral security, that note would not be eligible for rediscount in the Federal Reserve Banks; but the War Finance Corporation in such circumstances could advance to the bank against the note of the munitions company, so secured with that bank's endorsement on it, seventy-five per cent of the face of that note. . . .

The provision of the bill permitting direct loans by the Corporation in exceptional cases is intended to provide for those rare instances where it may be made to appear to the Corporation that a meritorious borrower is being unwisely discriminated against by the banks.

As a corollary to the provision for the extension of credits, the bill provides for approval by the Corporation, through a system of licenses, of issues of securities with a view to preventing the use of capital in unnecessary expenditures during the period of the war.

It is important that appropriate provision be made by law, so that, for the duration of the war, funds available for investment in securities shall be effectively and economically used to supply the financial requirements of the Government and of those industries whose operations are necessary or contributory to the war. The ordinary flow of capital, which in normal times is left free to seek its own investment, should during the war be so directed and conserved that these requirements shall be taken care of before funds shall be invested either in new enterprises or for the expansion of such old enterprises as are not necessary or contributory to the prosecution of the war. In these critical times funds available for investment must not be dissipated on miscellaneous capital expenditures which, however useful or desirable in normal times, will not now aid in the success of the war. It is not so much a question of money as a question of labor and materials. It is essential that the demand for labor and materials for industries which are not contributory to the prosecution of the war should be kept within bounds, so that the war needs shall be first provided for. The test must be whether the proposed expenditure will strengthen the industrial and military structure of the country for the purposes of the war. . . .

While patriotic business men and bankers have in many instances voluntarily submitted the question whether the particular security issue then contemplated will be in any way helpful to the prosecution of the war, it is certainly not desirable that matters of such great importance should be left upon a purely voluntary basis. These questions should be dealt with systematically under authority of Congress. The thoughtful and patriotic citizen who voluntarily submits his plans to the Government should not be placed at a disadvantage with his less thoughtful or less scrupulous fellow-citizen who goes ahead with his private affairs without reference to the war needs of his country.

The proposed license system for security issues is in line with the act which established the selective draft in lieu of a voluntary system of creating an army. The sacrifices which must be made if the war is to be won should be made by all alike and not merely by those whose patriotism impels them to volunteer and who would have to carry the entire burden unless the slackers are compelled to do their part.

The bill has been drawn with the double purpose of restricting unnecessary capital expenditures and of providing facilities for aiding those industries whose operations are necessary or contributory to the prosecution of the war. Broadly speaking, all these are 'war industries.' The bill is purely a war measure; designed to conserve the supply of labor and materials for the purposes of the war, and to help supply the war's financial requirements, and to give them a first claim on capital seeking investment in like manner as the war's material requirements have been given a first claim on productions. By the term 'war industries' is meant, not only those industries turning out the actual munitions of war, but also all those supplying any of the other elements of production or distribution in an industrial structure designed to meet the diversified requirements of the war. The bill is not intended to interfere with the continued existence and operation of existing industries, even though not remotely contributory to the prosecution of the war. Such industries should not, however, be permitted to assert a first claim on fresh capital or be considered until the requirements of the Government and of the 'war industries' have been fully met.

The proposed bill creates the War Finance Corporation, to regulate the sale of new issues of securities, and to make loans of its funds or its credit in aid of 'war industries.' It prohibits any person, firm, corporation, or association from selling or offering for sale any securities issued after the date of the approval of the Act unless a license for such sale or offering (if required by the Corporation) shall have been obtained from the Corporation. Through its regulation of security issues the Corporation will be able to keep the field somewhat clear for the borrowing operations of the Government, and at the same time will stand ready and able to aid 'war industries' whose financial requirements may be rendered difficult, if not impossible, to meet in competition with Government loans. This regulation of security issues will also tend to prevent the further diversion of labor and materials into nonessential industries. . . .

The money required for increased facilities for ocean transportation has been provided by Act of Congress. Provision for at least a part of the money required for enlarging railroad transportation facilities is contemplated in legislation now pending in Congress.

The necessary increase, however, in machinery to produce goods which requires the investment of capital in industrial enterprises, not only has not been provided, but a considerable restriction has been imposed upon the usual supply of capital for investment, partly by reason of the investment market having been preëmpted by the Government through the issue of its own bonds and partly because of the natural tendency of investors who, notwithstanding that they have money to invest, hesitate to do so on account of the uncertainties of war.

The situation with which the country is confronted, therefore, seems to require the imposition of reasonable restrictions upon the investment of capital in industries and production not essential for the conduct of the war. It is equally important that there shall be some means of supplying necessary capital to the industries which are essential to the production of war materials and of those things which indirectly contribute to the efficiency of the Nation. The restriction of unnecessary capital expenditures will relieve the market of demands which now interfere, not only with the direct financial requirements of the Government, but which make it difficult for those who are furnishing the Government and the people with essential goods to obtain the capital necessary to increase their production.

The license system proposed is peculiarly applicable to a country of the great size of the United States, where banking and credit transactions are conducted by a vast number of independent banks and private banking firms.

The combined operation of the two functions of the Corporation — that is, the extension of credit and licensing — will make the exercise of supervision and regulation by the Corporation much more effective in putting the productive activities of the country on a war basis than would be the case were the Government simply to make advances without at the same time exercising supervision and control of security issues.

In so far as the Corporation may be called upon to make advances to banks, its first concern would naturally be to aid those for which other instrumentalities of relief have not already been provided; for example, savings banks, and particularly mutual savings banks, which are without capital stock, and which are not operated for the profit of stockholders. As a class these institutions are not members of the Federal Reserve System nor are most of them eligible for membership. Their investments consist for the most part of the securities of the United States and of States and municipalities and of the bonds of industrial, transportation, and utility companies, and also mortgages.

Nothing will tend so greatly to prevent the development of any possible uneasiness among savings bank depositors as the assurance provided by this Act that any solvent savings bank in case of sudden withdrawals can obtain advances upon the security of its investments and promptly liquidate the claims of its depositors. There is considerable apprehension among savings banks as to means of relief if an emergency arises, but I believe that the assurances of support which this War Finance Corporation will provide, will allay all apprehension and probably head off any demand for withdrawals of deposits.

The next concern of the Corporation would be the requirements of commercial banks, which are unable to get required accommodation upon the security of their investments through the Federal Reserve Banks. Many banks which are now called upon to extend large lines of credit to customers which are expanding their businesses to meet the present needs of the Government are obliged to take securities from these customers which are not eligible for rediscount at Federal Reserve Banks. At the same time these banks are being called upon to extend larger lines of credit to their customers than ever before. Their customers are calling upon them, not only for commercial loans to carry their large inventories, but for what are in effect temporary capital loans in order to construct new facilities and add machinery to existing plants for the purpose of filling Government contracts. The burden of these banks is also heavily increased by the financial requirements of the Government which at the same time is calling upon them to lend large sums through sales of Treasury certificates of indebtedness.

In these circumstances the commercial banks are quite naturally discriminating in their loans between those eligible for rediscount by Federal Reserve Banks and those which are not. The proposed Act, however, would remove the ground for any such discrimination, for it provides a means by which such banks may procure accommodation upon certain securities arising out of war conditions which are not eligible at Federal Reserve Banks. The proposed Act would thus free credit pressingly needed at the present time both directly and indirectly for the Government's use. . . .

When Secretary McAdoo had finished, I was called upon. In the course of my remarks I discussed more particularly the banking situation. The observations which follow are a synopsis of my statement to the Committee:

This particular bill has never been sent to the Federal Reserve Board for its consideration, and the Board, therefore, has not taken any stand regarding it, either favorable or otherwise. The Board, however, is interested in the objects which the bill seeks to attain, and is impressed with the importance of some measure of relief for the securities market.

Some time ago the Board adopted a resolution putting itself on record that some governmental intervention was necessary in order to take care of this situation, and it threw out the same idea in its annual report to Congress, which was submitted about two weeks ago. . . .

The Board has been urged repeatedly during the last four or five months to take some step to protect the holders of securities, as well as to liberalize its definition of eligible paper. The savings bank situation has especially been brought to the Board's attention. The savings banks as a rule cannot come into the Federal Reserve System. Mutuals, having no capital, are excluded under the Federal Reserve Act as it stands to-day. Their securities are of such character as to render them ineligible as collateral for loans with Federal Reserve Banks. This applies to a greater or less degree to the investments, not only of savings banks, but to those of State banks, trust companies, and national banks as well.

There has been another development. The Federal Reserve Act defines very clearly what is eligible paper. There are two essential factors which determine the eligibility of paper. One is the time that the paper has to run; in the case of commercial paper, not longer than ninety days, and, in the case of agricultural paper or paper based on live stock, not longer than six months. Time is one factor. The other factor which governs the eligibility of paper is the use to which the proceeds of the paper have been applied. Those two things determine the eligibility of unsecured paper.

The Act goes further, and expressly bars 'merely' investments, such as stocks, bonds, and securities other than United States bonds. As the Federal Reserve System has been developed, and as the banks have found that certain classes of paper are eligible with the Federal Reserve Banks, and that they could go ahead and discount paper of that character very freely, at the same time keeping their portfolios in liquid shape by reason of being able to rediscount this paper with Federal Reserve Banks, a premium, so to speak, has been put upon 'eligible' paper, and the banks more and more have gone into the field of commercial paper and bankers' acceptances. We find that several trust companies which never had bought any paper, never had done any commercial business, in the last six months have gone into the commercial field. There is a distinct preference to-day for eligible commercial paper. Every bank prefers to have a large proportion of bills discounted, eligible for rediscount with a Federal Reserve Bank, thus assuring availability of funds whenever needed.

The new issues of Government bonds have had the effect, naturally, of destroying, to a large extent, the securities market. It follows that when the United States Government has issued a very large amount of four per cent bonds, an amount greater than the investment market can readily absorb, the ordinary securities market is necessarily paralyzed; and the larger the Government issues and the higher the rate, the greater will be the depression of the ordinary investment market. The deposits of savings banks especially go into these Government bonds. Savings banks depositors have invested freely in Government bonds. As these depositors have taken bonds either for investment purposes or from a patriotic sense of duty, their balances are drawn down. Ordinarily, when savings banks deposits decline the banks sell securities, but just now the savings banks have no adequate market in which they can dispose of securities. Regardless of intrinsic values, when banks sell railroad or industrial bonds in the present circumstances, they do so at a ruinous sacrifice, and the larger the offerings are, the worse the situation becomes. So it has been becoming more and more manifest for some time past that there are only two plans to be considered. One is to broaden the base of eligibility and to permit the discount by Federal Reserve Banks of notes secured by ordinary industrial or railroad bonds, and the other is to adopt some plan providing for direct governmental intervention or aid.

Senator Calder some time ago introduced a bill which provided for the rediscount at Federal Reserve Banks of notes secured by bonds as collateral, but the Board has never been in favor of this plan. One of the underlying principles of the Federal Reserve Act is the strictly commercial and purely liquid character of its assets. The Federal Reserve note is secured by gold or by gold plus commercial paper, and the paper pledged to secure the Federal Reserve note ought to be self-liquidating. The injection into the Federal Reserve System of a vast volume of paper secured by miscellaneous industrial and railroad bonds would bring about a radical change in the Federal Reserve System and would alter the character of the Federal Reserve note. The Federal Reserve note at present is an elastic currency. A currency, to be elastic, must have the ability to contract automatically as well as to expand. There can be no elasticity if the movement is all in one direction. It should work both ways in response to the varying requirements of trade and commerce.

With the vast expenditures for war purposes, the great financial operations of the Government, enormous issues of Treasury obligations, and the activity in certain lines of business, it is evident that more currency is needed for purposes of circulation than was the case two or three years ago.

Mr. Warburg, then being called, said:

I am heartily in accord with the objects and aims of this bill and its general plan. There is no doubt but that some organ as here proposed is imperatively required at this time. We have created an emergency machinery for commercial requirements in the Federal Reserve Act; but this is the only important financial country that does not provide any emergency machinery for the purpose of dealing with securities (stocks or bonds). The mere fact that this lack exists creates in times of stress and war a feeling of uncertainty which is a decided weakening of the national strength. What is proposed here is destined to remedy in part this defect and to cope with some of the difficulties and problems caused by the Government's financial operations — the relief will be both actual and in its effect on the general sentiment.

To illustrate: I think there is a great deal of psychology in the situation, so far as savings banks are concerned. When once they know that they can get relief, they probably will not need it so much. I do not believe that we will ever be called upon to issue anything like obligations amounting to $4,000,000,000 of this Corporation, but the power is there, and that is a tremendous benefit and protection for the general situation.

I understood that it is your wish that I should address myself to the question of licensing securities. . . .

Secretary McAdoo at first put out a statement asking everybody to consult with him before issuing securities. The response was so immediate that he found, after a while, that it was more than he himself could well handle without an organization especially created for that purpose, and he asked the Federal Reserve Board whether it would not undertake this for the country. We agreed to do so with a great deal of trepidation. It is a thankless task, and there is a great deal of responsibility connected with it. We finally took it, and the chairmanship of that committee fell to my lot, and that is why I am answering these questions.

We organized an advisory council of three. We asked three men, the ablest and most experienced we could get from the various sections of the country — Mr. Allen B. Forbes, from New York; Mr. F. H. Goff, from Cleveland; and Mr. Henry C. Flower, from Kansas City. These three men came here and served in the capacity of our advisors. We secured Mr. Bradley W. Palmer, of Boston, as our counsel. All these men serve as volunteers without compensation.

What we do at present is simply upon request to express an opinion as to whether or not, after careful examination, securities which are to be offered are compatible with the public interest, and that public interest we consider from two points of view. One is the general public welfare, what is necessary for the health and the strength of the people, and the other is the interest of the Government in the prosecution of the war. We have organized local committees at Federal Reserve Bank points and have invited the most prominent experts to serve in an advisory capacity in their districts. We have taken bankers, public-utility men, and manufacturers — as a rule a mixture of all three — and we have organized out of those a standing committee of five men, which consists of the Chairman of the Federal Reserve Bank, the Governor of the Federal Reserve Bank, and three other men, as described, and to those men we refer, wherever advice is necessary, the application for such local investigation as is necessary. They give us their best opinion. After that our Washington advisory committee passes upon it, and then the committee of three of the Board finally renders its opinion. I have a copy of a letter giving such opinion here. It reads as follows:

'Having inquired into the purpose of the issue above described, we are of opinion that the sale of the said bonds is not incompatible with the interest of the United States.

'This finding constitutes no approval of such issue as regards its merits, security, or legality in any respect.

'In any public offer or advertisement of the said issue, this letter must be incorporated in full.'

That last paragraph was for the purpose of avoiding some houses using our approval as appearing to recommend the security as such. We do not pass, of course, upon the intrinsic merits of any security. . . .

Where it is a question of renewals, as a general principle we feel that we ought to pass those, unless we found that there had been extraordinary profits which might have been used to pay off some of these maturing obligations. But as a general principle we would say they have to be renewed. The same way about refunding of banking debts, where they have been incurred previously, prior to February 1st, we would say yes, they have to be renewed. On the whole, I think a body of this kind would always have the tendency to be very considerate. It involves a terrific responsibility. It is not an easy matter to say to anybody that he should not extend his plant or go on with his regular business.

In reply to an inquiry, Mr. Warburg stated that the total obligations of railroads, public-service, industrial, and municipal corporations maturing for the year 1918 amounted to $799,000,000, as follows: $214,000,000 railroad; $224,000,000 public utilities; $182,000,000 industrials; $120,000,000 State, county, and city; and $58,000,000 companies having domicile in Canada, Cuba, and Mexico.

On the subject of possible inflation, Mr. Warburg said:

We are just now in a terrific process of inflation, the worst that the world has ever seen, taking the world as a whole, not the United States, but the world as a whole. . . . No doubt the process that we are going through or that the whole world is going through is one of terrific inflation. That is to-day expressed by the reduced purchasing power of the dollar. The dollar will buy only fifty per cent of what it bought a few years ago. It is not a question of Federal Reserve note issues. It is a question of the rapid manufacturing of credit. It is because all Governments go ahead and issue billions and billions of dollars of bonds for perishable things of no lasting value and create new credits for them, and do it at such terrific clip that inflation is produced. The mere fact that you take out $100,000,000 of currency is only a very small factor in the case. We have now outstanding about $6,000,000,000 of Government bonds, which all could be taken into Federal Reserve Banks to-day in the same manner as the prospective $4,000,000,000 short-term bonds of the War Finance Corporation. Of these six billions only $300,000,000 have found their way into the Federal Reserve Banks. . . . It stands to reason that with each new issue there will be an increased amount going in, and it must be our object, of course, to keep that down as far as we possibly can. While the Federal Reserve Board and the Federal Reserve Banks may bend their efforts in this direction, the two decisive factors are the scope and speed of the expenditures of the Government, on the one hand, and the saving power of the people, on the other. Whatever the Government spends in excess of the savings of the people will have to be produced by expansion of bank credit. That cannot be entirely avoided, but we have to be careful not to waste our strength too fast. That is why I am so deeply interested in this question of the contraction of unnecessary credit. Credit is just as much a limited thing as any other thing, and we have got to save it, and every individual and every department, State, or municipality, and every corporation has got to save, and unless they do they will have to carry the responsibility for the evil consequences of too rapid inflation. . . . The final result depends upon the expenditures of the Government, on the one hand, and the power of the people and their willingness to save, on the other. In between we can, of course, use our influence to a certain degree, and make it felt within certain limitations, but as long as the war lasts we can put on the brakes only to a degree that will not stop the big wheel of Government from moving as guided by these two factors.

In the course of a few weeks the bill establishing the War Finance Corporation was passed by both Houses of Congress and became law upon approval by the President.

The War Finance Corporation had a capital of $500,000,000 all subscribed by the Treasury of the United States. The Secretary of the Treasury, *ex officio*, was Chairman, and the other directors nominated by the President and confirmed by the Senate were: Eugene Meyer, Jr., of New York; Angus W. McLean, of North Carolina; C. M. Leonard, of Chicago; and myself. I was elected Managing Director for a period of twelve months and retained at the same time my position as Governor of the Federal Reserve Board. The law fixed the sum of $12,000 per annum as compensation for each director with the exception of Secretary McAdoo and myself, who continued to receive salaries only as Secretary of the Treasury and member of the Federal Reserve Board.

Under the terms of the War Finance Corporation Act, the President was charged also with the appointment of seven members of the Capital Issues Committee, subject to confirmation by the Senate. From the Federal Reserve Board he appointed: Charles S. Hamlin, of Massachusetts; Frederick A. Delano, of Illinois; and John Skelton Williams, of Virginia. Mr. Hamlin was made Chairman of the Committee.

The new duties thus imposed upon me kept me fully occupied during the year 1918, and early in 1919 I asked to be relieved of the managing directorship. Mr. Meyer was elected Managing Director in my place. In January, 1920, I resigned as director, and was not connected with the War Finance Corporation when the directors of the Corporation voted to discontinue making new loans. In anticipation of business reaction and financial difficulties at the end of the war, the law was so drawn as to permit the War Finance Corporation to continue to exercise some of its functions for a limited time; but the Treasury burdens were so heavy in 1920 that Secretary Houston deemed it advisable that the War Finance Corporation should suspend active operations. Some critics of the Federal Reserve Board have shown a disposition to censure it for the action of the War Finance Corporation in discontinuing new advances, but it is only fair to say that the members of the Board were not consulted in the matter and knew nothing of the action taken until they read of it in the newspapers. By Act of Congress the War Finance Corporation was required in the early part of 1921 to continue to make advances under the terms of some of the sections of the original War Finance Corporation Act, which enabled it to make new loans until some time in 1923. Additional powers were given the Corporation at the same time. Congress afterward extended the time for making new advances for a period of twelve months, and it was not until late in the year 1924 that the Corporation discontinued its functions as a lending agency, and returned or released to the Treasury the funds employed or set apart for its capital stock. The Corporation, under its enlarged powers, did much to relieve distress in the agricultural sections as it was able to make advances of a character which the law did not permit Federal Reserve Banks to make.

The Capital Issues Committee exercised its functions during the period of the war, but was dissolved shortly after the signing of the Armistice.

In April, 1918, a bill relating to silver coinage passed both Houses of Congress and became a law within a few days from the time it was drafted. This bill is commonly known as the Pittman Act, as it was sponsored by Senator Pittman, of Nevada. In ordinary circumstances the passage of such a bill would have required several years, if indeed it could have been put through at all. The Pittman Act was perhaps the most unique of the war measures, and its passage relieved a situation fraught with the gravest possibilities. The British army was conducting a campaign in Mesopotamia, and India was an important base of supplies for this army. The people in India dislike paper currency and demand gold and silver in commercial transactions. Lord Reading, who had succeeded Sir Cecil Spring-Rice as the British Ambassador at Washington, informed the Secretary of the Treasury that the Treasury of the Indian Government was faced with an utter exhaustion of its stock of silver, and that its inability to maintain silver payments would create an alarming situation throughout India and would have a disastrous effect upon the military operations in Asia Minor. The matter was regarded as being of such extreme delicacy that the information was imparted to only a very few Government officials, Senators and Representatives. It being impracticable to obtain the amount of silver requisite to satisfy the needs of India through market purchases, a bill was prepared in the Treasury Department to authorize the Secretary of the Treasury to break up standard silver dollars to an amount not to exceed $350,000,000 and to sell the silver bullion thus obtained at a minimum price of one dollar per fine ounce. The bill gave the Secretary of the Treasury authority also to purchase silver from American producers at the same price, a maximum of one dollar per fine ounce, up to an amount necessary to replace the silver dollars broken up and sold. In order to provide against any contraction in the circulating medium, the Treasury was authorized to issue one-year notes to be purchased by the Federal Reserve Banks, upon the security of which those banks were authorized to issue Federal Reserve Bank notes in one-dollar and two-dollar denominations, such notes being subject to requirements as to redemption and taxation similar to those imposed upon national bank notes.   Although few members of the House and Senate, outside of those who were on the Banking and Currency Committees, were informed as to the reason for this legislation, both bodies accepted the assurance that avoidance of any discussion of its real purpose was most desirable and that patriotic duty required their support of the measure. The bill was passed very promptly without difficulty. About a year ago the repurchases of silver as provided in this Act were completed and the Federal Reserve Bank notes which were issued to take the place of the silver dollars have all been retired. The urgency of the demand for silver in 1918 was so great that for a short time the market price of silver bullion exceeded its coinage value.

In May, 1918, an Act, commonly known as the Overman Act, was passed authorizing the President 'to coördinate or consolidate executive bureaus, agencies, and offices, and for other purposes, in the interest of economy and the more efficient concentration of the Government.' Under this Act the President was given power, during the period of the war and for six months after the termination of the war by the proclamation of a treaty of peace, or at such earlier time as the President may designate, 'to make such redistribution of functions among executive agencies as he may deem necessary, including any functions, duties, and powers hitherto by law conferred upon any executive department, commission, bureau, agency, office or officer, in such manner as in his judgment shall seem best fitted to carry out the purposes of this Act.' Several Senators expressed a desire to have some of the independent establishments, especially the Interstate Commerce Commission and the Federal Reserve Board, exempted from its provisions, and motions to this effect were lost on a close vote. Although the functions of the Board were never disturbed by the President, the debates in the Senate and House make it clear that, under the authority given him by the Overman Act, he could, had he deemed such action necessary, have transferred to the Secretary of the Treasury or to any other Government official any functions of the Federal Reserve Board, including the power to approve the discount rates of Federal Reserve Banks.[1]

[1] See *Congressional Record*, Sixty-Fifth Congress, vol. 56, pp. 4573, 4579, 4952, 5019, 5605, 5688, 5693–99, 6448, 6452, 6460.

CHAPTER XI

BOARD URGES JUDICIOUS CURTAILMENT OF CREDIT FOR NON-
ESSENTIAL PURPOSES — RETIREMENT OF MESSRS. DELANO
AND WARBURG — AFTER-WAR READJUSTMENT —
VIEWS OF A. C. MILLER

IN June, 1918, the Board mailed a circular letter to banks and trust companies calling their attention to the importance of a judicious curtailment of credit granted for so-called non-essential transactions, and urging the banks to do their utmost in coöperating in a policy looking to a gradual but general curtailment of such credits. This letter will recall to many the domestic conditions — financial and economic — which existed at a critical stage of the war, and was in part as follows:

On June 12th the Secretary of the Treasury addressed a letter to all banks and trust companies announcing his financial programme for the ensuing six months, which involves the sale to and through banks of approximately $6,000,000,000 of Treasury certificates of indebtedness in installments of not less than $750,000,000 every two weeks between June 25th and the 1st of November. In this letter each bank and trust company was requested to invest in these certificates an amount equal to approximately two and one half per cent of its gross resources, or a total of five per cent for each month. Announcement was made at the same time that there was in contemplation an issue of $2,000,000,000 of certificates of appropriate maturities in anticipation of income and excess-profits taxes, for sale more particularly to taxpayers, and that the amount of the regular semi-monthly sales of certificates of indebtedness would be reduced in proportion to the extent to which these tax certificates are taken by the public.

The banking institutions have responded most generously to the appeal of the Secretary of the Treasury. Throughout the country they have pledged themselves without hesitation to subscribe to their allotment, and the result of the initial offering, which has just been closed — a subscription of $838,000,000 in response to a request for not less than $750,000,000 — is evidence of the splendid patriotism of those who direct our national and State banking institutions. . . .

The Board feels in duty bound to reiterate that the banks can render a greater service to the country in this connection, not merely by subscribing their allotments and by using the rediscounting facilities of the Federal Reserve Banks in making payments, but by providing the necessary funds for meeting payments for certificates of indebtedness purchased, by employing for this purpose the accretion of new deposits, and by utilizing the funds that may be made available by a judicious curtailment of credits asked for non-essential purposes.

In order to prosecute the war successfully, the Government is compelled to issue obligations to provide for its large expenditures, which involve waste and destruction rather than a permanent addition to the national wealth. This process in itself tends to inflation, and contributes to a rapid increase in the price of necessities. Abnormal demands by the Government, unavoidable and necessary in the present circumstances, must be counteracted by greater economy on the part of the civilian population, which must decrease, by combined effort, the normal waste incident to domestic life and business pursuits. There is not an unlimited supply of credit, or of goods, or of man power. Wherever possible all such resources should be conserved and set aside for the use of the Government. Credit extended for non-essential purposes involves the use of labor, of transportation, of material, and reserves which ought to be kept free for the use of the Government. Unrestricted credit involves unnecessary competition with the Government and needlessly advances prices, besides impeding and delaying governmental operations.

'Business as usual' and 'life as usual' are impossible at a time when the supreme business of the country is war, and cannot be approximated without interfering with the work of the Government and inflicting serious harm upon the Nation as a whole. The staying power of the country in this emergency depends upon the extent of its resources in men, goods, and gold. An unnecessary use of credit, a needless recourse to the discounting facilities of the Federal Reserve Banks, weakens proportionately the gold reserve of the United States — the financial backbone of the entire Allied group. Whoever wastes the raw material and manufactured products of the country adds to our financial burden by increasing the amount the United States must import from other countries and by decreasing, at the same time, the volume of goods that should be available for export purposes — the best means of paying for the goods acquired from abroad.

Conservation of our commodities and of our gold — preservation of our economic strength — is of the greatest importance in making provision for the period of readjustment which will follow the reëstablishment of peace. . . . The Board wishes to point out also that, by refraining from buying luxuries and by restricting the use of necessities to the actual requirements of health and reasonable comfort, we can create a reserve purchasing power which will be of the greatest value to our industries in bridging over the period of reaction and reconstruction which must follow when war enterprises are transformed into those of peace. An intelligent and prudent use of credit, therefore, will be an important factor in strengthening the national resources during the period of the war, in aiding its successful prosecution, and in maintaining the economic strength of the country for the time of rapidly changing conditions which will come when the war has been won and the millions of men in our armies are returning to the employments of peace.

Thus, by giving your coöperation now in the effort to conserve national resources by the exercise of discriminating judgment in granting credits, you will also do your part in averting the danger of unemployment which is apt to follow a treaty of peace. The Board appreciates the difficulty of laying down a general rule for defining essentials or the degree in which any enterprise is essential, and requests that its remarks on this subject in the April issue of the Bulletin be read again. The Board cannot suggest specific ways in which credit should be conserved or unnecessary expenditures curtailed, as each banker must determine this for himself after conferring with the business men of his community and after a careful study of his local situation. Reasonable discretion should be exercised, and drastic steps calculated to bring about hardships or embarrassments or work injustice should be avoided, but the banks should divert the use of their credit more and more into productive fields, where its employment will result in augmenting the national resources.

About this time, Mr. Frederick A. Delano, who had been a member of the Federal Reserve Board since its organization, and Vice-Governor since August, 1916, tendered his resignation to the President, in order that he might accept service with the American forces in France as a Major in the

United States Army Engineer Corps engaged in the construction and operation of military railways. Mr. Delano was an able civil engineer and experienced railroad executive, and rendered distinguished service in France. When the Armistice was signed, he held the rank of Colonel. As soon as Mr. Delano's colleagues heard of his resignation, the matter was considered formally at a meeting of the Board, and this resolution was passed and entered upon the minutes:

The Board has heard with extreme regret of the proposed resignation of Mr. F. A. Delano. It desires to record its appreciation of Mr. Delano's able and faithful service as a member of the Federal Reserve Board and of those high personal qualities which have made his relation to his colleagues one of unusual mutual confidence and regard. Mr. Delano has served two years as Vice-Governor of the Board and for nearly two years additional as member. During this period of almost four years the Federal Reserve System has attained its growth, while the banking and financial problems of the Nation, in whose solution the Federal Reserve System has necessarily had a large part, have been of unprecedented seriousness. The value of Mr. Delano's contribution to the effective organization of the System and to the successful solution of its problems cannot be overestimated. His departure will be a serious loss to the System and a source of extreme personal regret to his colleagues.

A few weeks later, the Board sustained another serious loss in the retirement of Mr. Warburg, whose term of office expired on August 9th. The resolutions adopted on that day by the Board placed on record the following expression of appreciation of Mr. Warburg's service:

The members of the Board, now that the term of their colleague, Hon. Paul M. Warburg, is about to expire, desire to place upon record this evidence of their high appreciation of the important and valuable services which have been rendered by him in the development and administration of the Federal Reserve System. They wish to express also their sense of personal loss in being deprived of their daily association with him and their feeling that his retirement from the Board is a serious loss to the public service.

Mr. Warburg's thorough knowledge of national and international finance, his indefatigable and untiring industry, his masterly conception and firm grasp of the many important banking problems which have come before the Board, have placed its members under a lasting obligation to him.

The important amendments to the Federal Reserve Act relating to reserves which have enabled the System to meet so fully all the requirements which have been made upon it during the most critical period of the Nation's financial history, and the extension of the use of bankers' and trade acceptances, are among the many important developments which have been due in a great degree to his foresight and untiring efforts.

The Board has received from him also, especially since the entrance of our country into the war, very valuable suggestions regarding the fiscal relations of the banks to the Government, foreign exchange, regulation of gold exports, control of capital issues, and restriction of non-essential credits.

His services can be appreciated best by those who have had the near view of colleagues. The sense of public duty, loyally and ably performed, is after all the chief reward of official life, and whatever the future may have in store for Mr. Warburg, he can feel that he leaves office with the admiration, confidence, and sincere esteem of his colleagues, and with the satisfaction of knowing that he has given valuable assistance to the Board in grasping and solving many of the momentous financial problems, both domestic and international, which have come before it.

The Federal Reserve Bulletin for September, 1918, contained the correspondence between Mr. Warburg and the President on the subject of his further continuance on the Board. Under date of May 27, 1918, Mr. Warburg addressed a letter to the President calling attention to the fact that on August 9th, his term of office as a member of the Federal Reserve Board would expire. He then said:

Certain persons have started an agitation to the effect that a naturalized citizen of German birth, having near relatives prominent in German public life, should not be permitted to hold a position of great trust in the service of the United States. (I have two brothers in Germany who are bankers. They naturally now serve their country to the utmost of their ability, as I serve mine.)

I believe that the number of men who urge this point of view is small at this time. They probably have not a proper appreciation of the sanctity of the oath of allegiance or of the oath of office. As for myself, I did not take them lightly. I waited ten years before determining upon my action, and I did not swear that 'I absolutely and entirely renounce and abjure all allegiance and fidelity to any foreign potentate, and particularly to Wilhelm II, German Emperor,' etc., until I was quite certain that I was willing and anxious to cast my lot unqualifiedly and without reserve with the country of my adoption and to defend its aims and its ideals. . . .

Much to my regret, Mr. President, it has become increasingly evident that should you choose to renominate me this might precipitate a harmful fight which, in the interest of the country, I wish to do anything in my power to avoid and which, even though resulting in my confirmation, would be likely to leave an element of irritation in the minds of many whose anxieties and sufferings may justify their intense feelings. On the other hand, if for reasons of your own, you should decide not to renominate me, it is likely to be construed by many as an acceptance by you of a point of view which I am certain you would not wish to sanction. In these circumstances, I deem it my duty to state to you myself that it is my firm belief that the interest of the country will best be served if my name be not considered by you in this connection. . . .

I have considered it the greatest privilege to serve my country at this time, and I do not abandon lightly a work, half done, in which I am deeply and genuinely interested. But my continuation in office under present conditions might make the Board a target of constant attack by unscrupulous or unreasoning people, and my concern to save any embarrassment to you and to the Board in the accomplishment of its work would make it difficult for me to conserve that independence of mind and freedom of action without which nobody can do justice to himself or his office.

In writing you this letter I have been prompted solely by my sincere conviction that the national welfare must be our only concern. Whatever you may decide to be best for the country will determine my future course. We are at war, and I remain at your orders.

On August 9th the President replied expressing his 'appreciation of the fine personal and patriotic feeling which made that letter one of the most admirable and gratifying I have received during these troubled times,' and said:

Your retirement from the Board is a serious loss to the public service. I consent to it only because I read between the lines of your generous letter that you will yourself feel more at ease if you are left free to serve in other ways. . . .

You carry with you in your retirement from this work to which you have added distinction, my dear Mr. Warburg, my sincere friendship, admiration, and confidence, and I need not add, my cordial good wishes.

On August 14th the resignation of Dr. H. Parker Willis, Secretary of the Board, was accepted, effective September 1, 1918, and Mr. J. A. Broderick was appointed as his successor. Dr. Willis resigned to accept the chair of banking at Columbia University, New York. The Board, however, was not deprived of his services altogether, as he remained until July 1, 1922, as Director of the Division of Analysis and Research, and as editor of the Federal Reserve Bulletin under the supervision as heretofore of the Board's Bulletin Committee, of which Mr. A. C. Miller was Chairman.

The vacancy occasioned by the resignation of Mr. Delano was not filled for more than a year, until September, 1919, when the President appointed Mr. Henry A. Moehlenpah, of Wisconsin, to serve for the remainder of his term, which was to expire on August 9, 1920. For some reason it appeared to be difficult during the last half of 1918 and the first half of 1919 to induce properly qualified men of the Central West to accept membership on the Federal Reserve Board. I am told that a tender of appointment was made to more than a half-dozen men before it was finally accepted by Mr. Moehlenpah.

On a warm afternoon in July, 1919, a gentleman from that section called to see me and, after introducing himself, stated that he had been offered Mr. Delano's place on the Federal Reserve Board. He appeared to have no well-defined idea as to the duties of the Board and inquired if the Board met once a week or twice a month. He seemed astonished when I told him that usually the Board met every day, and said, 'But of course no one ever comes back in the afternoon.' I told him that, on the contrary, few members ever left for the day before five o'clock in the afternoon, and that some of us frequently remained as late as six or seven o'clock. He then wanted to know when we played golf, and I told him that I managed to get along without playing at all. He said that he would not care to give up golf, and was informed that he might be able to arrange for a game two or three times a week. He then inquired as to the patronage that he would have as a member of the Board. I told him that he would have the privilege of appointing his own secretary and stenographer, but that all other appointments in connection with the Board's organization were made by the Board itself. This reply seemed to be rather disappointing, and he asked, 'If I become a member of the Board what will be my prerogatives?' At that time the Treasury had not removed the restrictions regarding entrance to the building which became effective at the beginning of the war, and visitors to the Treasury Department were obliged to use the employees' entrance on Fifteenth Street, and each was required to give his name and address and to state the purpose of his visit. He would then be referred to the Captain of the Watch, who, after further questioning, would admit him. The Secretary of the Treasury had his own private entrance and other Treasury officials as well as Federal Reserve Board members were allowed to use the west entrance which is on the side opposite the White House. My own office overlooked this entrance. In answering his question as to prerogatives, I inquired, 'How did you get into this building?' He said he had a hard time getting in. 'People at the door seemed to think I was a Bolshevik, asked me a lot of questions, and referred me to the Captain of the Watch, who finally let me come up.' I then said, 'As a member of the Federal Reserve Board you would not be obliged to use the Fifteenth Street entrance with the attendant delay, but could come into the building through the entrance here on this side' — (pointing to the west entrance). 'This seems to be about the only prerogative which pertains to membership on the Federal Reserve Board.' The conversation then turned to other topics, and, when he rose to leave, he said, 'I don't think I want the job.'

In October, 1918, the President appointed, as Mr. Warburg's successor for the full term of ten years, Mr. Albert Strauss, of New York, and designated him as Vice-Governor of the Board. Mr. Strauss had been for many years a member of a private banking firm in New York City, and, for a year or more preceding his appointment to the Federal Reserve Board, had represented the Treasury Department on the War Trade Board, and on the Gold Export Committee of the Federal Reserve Board. His familiarity with international finance was of especial value to the Board, and he served until March 15, 1920, when he resigned in order to resume his former banking connections in New York.

In the autumn of 1918 complaints were made by growers of sugar beets in the West that they were unable to obtain requisite credits through ordinary banking channels. The live-stock people in that section had also become nervous over their situation, which afterward became very critical. At that time Federal Reserve Banks were not permitted by law to rediscount any paper having maturity of longer than ninety days, except 'that notes, drafts, and bills drawn or issued for agricultural purposes or based on live stock and having a maturity not exceeding six months,' might be discounted in an amount to be limited 'to a percentage of the assets of the Federal Reserve Bank to be ascertained and fixed by the Federal Reserve Board.' The Federal Reserve Board had long ago ruled that Federal Reserve Banks might rediscount agricultural or live-stock paper to the extent of ninety-nine per cent of their assets, being desirous of extending all possible aid to those engaged in these essential industries. Those engaged in the business of breeding cattle, however, found it necessary to borrow for as long as two years, pending the growth of young calves, and, in fattening matured cattle for the market, credits of at least nine months were often necessary.

In 1923, the law was amended so as to make the maturity limit on agricultural and live-stock paper nine months instead of six months. Before the war a large volume of the live-stock credits was extended by cattle loan companies whose practice was to sell the notes of the ranchmen with their own endorsement to banks throughout the country, and such notes were offered at more attractive interest rates than ordinary commercial paper. The cattle loan companies were able in this way to finance themselves without much difficulty. During the war repeated issues of Government bonds and certificates made such heavy inroads on banking reserves that the cattle loan companies were no longer able to sell their paper in accustomed volume, and the cattle industry felt the pinch. Late in October, 1918, I went West in order to familiarize myself with the situation, visiting Salt Lake City and San Francisco, and conferred with leading bankers in each city. I found that they were extending credit freely to sugar refiners and were caring for the more pressing needs of the cattle men, but that they were reluctant to make advances as freely to growers of sugar beets because of the perishable nature of the product. Sugar beets are not stored in warehouses, but, while awaiting shipment, are piled up in the open and are subject to weather damage. They are grown mainly north of the thirty-sixth parallel of latitude; and in the country west of the Mississippi River, usually on lands having an elevation of one thousand feet or more above the sea. Being left in the open, they are apt to freeze, and if a thaw follows the beets are ruined, although they are not damaged if the cold is continuous and the beets are kept frozen up to the time the refineries are ready for

them. As a rule the cold in the mountain States is continuous and little damage results.

I explained to the bankers in San Francisco that the War
Finance Corporation was not desirous of competing with
them, but that, unless satisfactory assurances were received
that reasonable credits would be extended sugar-growers by
the banks, the War Finance Corporation would feel obliged
to establish agencies for the purpose of making direct loans,
as an adequate supply of sugar was deemed necessary in the
conduct of the war. The bankers agreed to take care of the
situation and no further complaints were made by the beet-
growers. On my return East, I stopped over in Denver,
Omaha, and Kansas City for the purpose of further investigating the cattle situation. On the day of my visit to Kansas City, the premature report of the signing of the Armistice
came over the wires and for several hours the city celebrated
in true Western style. A few days later, I saw in Washington a modified repetition of this celebration on the day the
Armistice was actually signed.

The return of peace, however, did not solve the economic
and financial problems of the country. On the other hand,
it accentuated them, and the Federal Reserve System, in
particular, was brought face to face with a most difficult situation. Many of the war controls were at once discontinued
or relaxed, and agencies, such as the War Industries Board,
the War Trade Board, and the Capital Issues Committee,
were dissolved almost immediately. Europe and America
were, indeed, no longer concerned in the problems incident
to the carrying-on of a bloody and most expensive war, with
which problems they had become familiar, and in meeting
which they were aided by waves of patriotic impulse, but
were now confronted with the novel and hardly less difficult
problems incident to reconstruction and readjustment.

On the evening of December 21, 1918, Mr. A. C. Miller,
of the Federal Reserve Board, delivered an address before
the American Academy of Political and Social Science on the

subject of 'After-War Readjustment.' In the course of this address Mr. Miller said:

Of the eighteen and a half billions of loans thus far put out by the Government, it may be estimated that six billions are being carried by, or in, the banks. To the extent that subscriptions to Government borrowings are paid, not out of cash which the subscriber has actually saved out of his income, but by credit borrowed from his bank, the payment of the subscription must be regarded as having given rise to an expansion of bank credit to approximately an identical amount. Such expansion of credit, unless it sets in motion new forces of saving, results in inflation, first, of credit, then, of currency, and, as a consequence of both, inflation of prices. A bank's deposits and currency are the children of its loans and investments. When the loans and investments, therefore, which occasion an increase of deposits and currency are not definitely tied to the production or saving of goods, they must cause a rise of prices. When the rise of prices resulting from an expansion of credit and currency is not able, or until it is able, to induce a commensurate increase of productive industry to match the increased buying power of the community, the resulting condition is one of inflation, that is one in which there is more purchasing power, in terms of money, afloat in the community than is called for. . . .

Recent events, particularly in the United States and among the northern neutrals of Europe, which like the United States have experienced enormous accessions to their supplies of gold during the period of the war, show that inflation may take place without a suspension of specie payments or the occurrence of a discount on paper. It was the very abundance of gold that helped to advance prices in the United States before our entry into the war. The currency of the United States now, as then, is a gold currency. Prices in the United States are, therefore, gold prices. This fact is incontestable. There is gold enough and more than enough to assure the absolute convertibility of our paper currency in gold. The trouble with our situation is not that the paper dollar is not as good as the gold dollar; just the reverse is true: it is. The trouble with our situation is that neither the paper dollar nor the gold dollar will buy as much as they did before inflation of prices began. At prices as they are, the paper dollar buys as much as the gold dollar. The gold dollar is no better than the paper dollar. The two are interchangeable. Our trouble, therefore, is with dollars, irrespective of their kind. It is one of quantity, not of quality, or, at any rate, not of quality in terms of gold. Our elastic note issue system has enabled us to place the issue of paper dollars on a quantity basis without endangering the integrity of their gold value. The trouble is with the goods value, not with the gold value of the American dollar. Our difficulty is, and therein consists our inflation, that dollars — good financial dollars, 'safe' dollars, gold dollars — have been created in such abundance in comparison with the amount of goods purchasable by them that they have, as a necessary result, lost in their purchasing power — in other words, the supply of money has become disproportionate to the supply of goods with rising prices as the inevitable result.

Mr. Miller then quoted figures showing that between July 1, 1914, and September 1, 1918, the total money in circulation in the United States increased $2,219,000,000, or sixty-five per cent. In reviewing he compared the position of all banks in the United States on June 30, 1914, and their situation on June 29, 1918, and pointed out that their deposits between these dates had increased $11,310,000,000, or fifty-three per cent; their loans and discounts, $6,719,000,000, an increase of forty-four per cent; and their investments (bonds and other securities) $11,058,000,000, an increase of fifty-three per cent. In commenting on these figures, Mr. Miller said:

To the extent that this increase in the supply of the purchasing media of the country has not been offset by a like increase in the production of goods, it must be regarded as unnecessary and superfluous from the economic point of view, whatever may be said in justification of it from the point of view of political and general financial expediency. To the extent that it has been offset by increased production, it presents no difficulty. That there has been an enormous increase in the physical output of goods in the United States during the past four years cannot be questioned. Never before has the country come so near to realizing its full productive capacity; never before has there been so little unemployment or idleness. Some estimates place the increase in the physical products of the country during the past four years as high as twenty-five per cent. If we take a more conservative figure, of twenty per cent, it would suggest the inference that a commensurate proportion of the volume of credit and currency existing in 1914, or some four billions of dollars in the aggregate, was probably legitimately called for by the growth of production in the past four years. . . .

It would appear probable, therefore, that some six billions of credit and currency in the aggregate have been created in the past four and one-half years that cannot be regarded as having been occasioned by the requirements of industrial growth, as measured in terms of physical units. This is also approximately the amount of war securities and war loan paper, as has already been stated, that the banking system of the United States is to-day carrying. To this extent the expansion of banking credit and currency would appear to have been occasioned by the banks having assumed the burden of assisting the placement of Treasury borrowings by the extension, use and lending of their credit. Such use of credit is almost of necessity inflationary in its immediate effects and in its continuing tendencies until corrected.

As to what form the correction should take, he said:

Where there has been inflation, there must follow deflation, as a necessary condition to the restoration of economic health. Contraction of bank deposits and currency, through the liquidation of war loan accounts, is clearly indicated as the next and necessary step in the process of bringing the credit currency and price situation back to normal. . . . The problem of correcting a state of banking inflation is mainly a problem in saving. We must either put more goods behind the outstanding volume of credit and currency — that means production — or we must reduce the volume of credit and currency to suitable proportions — that means saving.

Expenses and spending must be kept down; money must be saved. As it is saved, it must be paid to the banks in liquidation of war loans and other non-productive borrowings. If the money saved is in the form of deposit or checking credits, then the total volume of these in existence and in use will be diminished as they are used to cancel an equivalent amount of loans and thus will the banking structure be contracted and prices be rectified. If in the form of bank notes, the cash holdings of the banks will be built up and they will be enabled to reduce their borrowings from their Reserve Banks and, in this wise, the notes will find their way back to the Reserve Banks, reducing at once the volume of their outstanding note liabilities on the one side and their holdings of bills discounted on the other. Thus will saving effect the reduction in the volume of outstanding currency and credit. The nation must continue to practice thrift.

Looking ahead, Mr. Miller had this to say about the future borrowings of the Government:

The Government's requirements for the remainder of the fiscal year have been stated as likely to be not less than seven billions. This amount, added to the six billions of outstanding war securities which, it is estimated above, have not yet been permanently absorbed, gives us a total of thirteen billions of public securities which must be taken up out of genuine savings if our financial and credit system is to be sterilized of the taint of inflation which at present is upon it. When this is accomplished, prices are likely to be at something that can be regarded as a normal level. Until it is accomplished, there will be an unstable price situation. As it is gradually accomplished, prices will go back to a normal basis in an orderly manner. But if a considerable part of the new borrowings, which the Government must make during the fiscal year and until war accounts are finally closed up, are financed by any considerable expansion of banking credit, we are likely to have more inflation and an aggravation of a price situation which is already sufficiently serious and burdensome.

CHAPTER XII

IN the address from which quotations have just been made,
Mr. Miller took the point of view of an economist and enun-
ciated certain broad economic principles. It should not be
assumed that he intended to convey the impression that the
Federal Reserve Board unaided should undertake to apply
these principles, or that it should put itself in the position of
attempting to dictate prices or of controlling credit with the
view of bringing about such price readjustments which in its
judgment might seem salutary. On the other hand, the
Board had an entirely different view of its duties and functions. The Board's position, stated at a time when prices
had reached still higher levels, will be discussed in a succeeding chapter. There is another point of view which also
must be considered, that of the Treasury, and this, too, will
be discussed later on.

The Congressional elections in November, 1918, resulted
in a substantial Republican majority in the House of Representatives, and in a Republican majority of one in the Senate. The old Congress met for its final session on the first
Monday in December, and was confronted with a large volume of unfinished business. Besides the usual appropriation
bills, it was called upon to consider the Government finances
and the necessity for another bond issue. The Secretary of
the Treasury, the Honorable Carter Glass, who had succeeded Mr. McAdoo upon the latter's resignation in Decem-

ber, 1918, prepared a bill, which he submitted to Congress
soon after the Christmas holidays, to authorize an issue of
four- to five-year notes for the purpose of relieving the Government of the large floating indebtedness it had incurred in
the purchase of supplies and war material for the maintenance and use of the army and navy, and in the construction and operation of war utilities, such as shipyards and
powder plants.

In the meantime President Wilson had gone to France at
the head of a commission to collaborate with similar commissions of the Allied Powers in negotiating a treaty of peace
with Germany and her allies. The decision of the President
to head his own peace commission had been the subject of
much discussion throughout the country, and particularly in
Congress, where the Republican minority voiced its disapproval in common with some members of the Democratic
majority. It soon became evident that it would not be possible to finish the draft of a peace treaty before March 4th,
the date of the expiration of Congress, and, while it was
understood that the President intended to return to the
United States late in February in order to act upon bills
passed by Congress in its closing hours, it was known that
he intended to return to France early in March. Party politics, which, in the language of the President, had been 'adjourned' during the war, were again running high.

It was thought by some that if the regular appropriation
bills, and the bill authorizing the note issue, should fail to
pass, the President would be obliged to call an extra session
of the new Congress, and because of this he would feel compelled to remain in Washington. Much time was consumed
in debates in Congress, and while a few of the appropriation
bills passed both Houses, some important measures, including the Victory note Bill, had not been acted upon as the end
of the session approached. Among these bills was one to
amend the Federal Reserve Act which had been proposed
early in the session by the Federal Reserve Board. While

this was not a bill of first importance, it had no political significance and met with little opposition.

As originally enacted, the Federal Reserve Act provided that, after the Federal Reserve Banks had paid their expenses and dividend claims, 'all the net earnings shall be paid to the United States as a franchise tax, except that one half of such net earnings shall be paid into a surplus fund until it shall amount to forty per centum of the paid-in capital stock of such bank.' The Board believed that provision should be made for a larger surplus fund. No limitation had ever been placed upon the amount of surplus which a national bank or trust company might accumulate, and if the Federal Reserve Banks were to be limited to a maximum surplus fund amounting to only forty per cent of their capital, they would not compare favorably in respect to this element of strength with many of their own member banks. Furthermore, the country was approaching a period of readjustment during which losses might be anticipated. Nor would the Federal Reserve Banks with so small a surplus compare favorably with central banks in many foreign countries. For these reasons the Board suggested, in its annual report for the year 1918, that the law be amended so as to permit each Federal Reserve Bank to accumulate out of net earnings a surplus equal to one hundred per cent of its paid-in capital, and that payments to the Government as franchise tax be suspended in the case of each bank until its surplus reached that amount. In discussing this proposed change with the Banking and Currency Committees of the Senate and House, I referred also to the fact that the Federal Reserve Banks were not provided with permanent quarters; that in most cases the quarters then occupied were utterly inadequate, and that it was impossible to acquire by lease or purchase suitable quarters properly equipped. The banks, therefore, would be obliged to acquire building sites upon which to erect buildings adapted to their needs. I pointed out that it was not advisable that the capital stock of any

Federal Reserve Bank should be represented by its real estate, and that it would be much better to permit the banks to accumulate a surplus large enough at least to counterbalance their investments in land and buildings. All of these considerations seemed to have impressed the committees, for the bill as reported by them and as passed by both Houses of Congress made a far more liberal provision as to surplus than had been suggested by the Federal Reserve Board.

The amendment to section 7 of the Federal Reserve Act as finally passed provided that, after the necessary expenses of a Federal Reserve Bank had been paid and the dividend claims fully met,

the net earnings shall be paid to the United States as a franchise tax except that the whole of such net earnings, including those for the year ending December thirty-first, nineteen hundred and eighteen, shall be paid into a surplus fund until it shall amount to one hundred per centum of the subscribed capital stock of such bank, and that thereafter ten per centum of such net earnings shall be paid into the surplus.

This made available as an immediate addition to the surplus funds of the Federal Reserve Banks their net earnings for the year 1918, which amounted to nearly $27,000,000, and permitted them to accumulate a surplus fund twice as large as the Board had requested, inasmuch as all net earnings could be paid into the surplus fund until that fund equaled the subscribed capital stock of the banks, which was double the actual paid-in capital. In addition the banks were allowed, after they had accumulated surplus equal to one hundred per cent of their subscribed capital to retain each year ten per cent of their net earnings as a further addition to surplus; the remaining ninety per cent to be paid to the Government as franchise tax.

This bill was passed by the Senate in language slightly different from the House bill, although the intent was the same. The House not receding, the bill was sent to a Committee of Conference, which quickly reported an agreement. Ordinarily a Conference report is privileged and can be submitted for adoption at any time. It seems, however, in this case, the Conference Committee inserted a word or two in the bill as reported which did not appear in either the Senate bill or the House bill which had been referred to it. The Conference report was adopted by the House, but when it was submitted to the Senate the point was made that, as it contained new matter, it lost its privileged status and should take its place on the calendar. It was given a place next below the bill to authorize the Victory notes, and almost up to the last minute it looked as though it would fail to receive consideration. However, on Saturday afternoon, March 2d, Republican Senators held a caucus to determine their attitude on the Victory Note Bill, which was then being considered by the Senate. At this caucus it was decided by a majority of one that the defeat of the Victory Note Bill should not be made a party measure. While the Republicans were still in a minority in the Senate, they could easily at that stage defeat any measure by prolonged debate; but as the defeat of the Note Bill had not been made a party measure, few Senators felt disposed to lend their aid in talking it to death. Senator La Follette, Senator Gronna, of North Dakota, and Senator Sherman, of Illinois, however, kept the Senate in session all Saturday night, and took turns in discussing the Note Bill until half-past seven o'clock Sunday morning. At that time they were exhausted and went out for coffee. The Victory Note Bill was then brought to a vote and passed, and immediately thereafter Senator Owen brought up the Conference report on the bill amending the Federal Reserve Act, and this also was passed. The Senate then adjourned until Monday morning, and its final adjournment was taken at noon on that day.

This bill, which was the last one passed by the Sixty-Fifth Congress, amended also section 10 of the Federal Reserve Act by striking out the provision that assistant secretaries of the Treasury should not be eligible to serve as officers of member banks after leaving the Treasury, until after a lapse of two years; and modified the same restriction upon appointive members of the Federal Reserve Board by prescribing that the two-year limitation should apply only to members who might resign, and not to members who had served the full terms for which they were appointed.

The passage of the bill which authorized the issue of notes known as the Victory Loan had a stimulating effect upon business, which had been languishing since the signing of the Armistice. Within a short time it became evident that the renewed activity was not at all justified by underlying conditions, and there was imminent danger that there would be excessive and unhealthy speculation. The price-level was again advancing, and, because of rising commodity prices, the fictitious ease of money, and the general optimistic feeling, there developed a tendency in the agricultural sections to make extensive developments on the farms, in many cases entirely on borrowed money, and to purchase land. In effecting these purchases the frequent practice was to make small cash payments and to give notes secured by mortgage on the land for the balance. In many instances, the land would be resold, and the sellers would receive additional notes for a part of their profits. Manufacturers also showed a disposition to extend their operations and the speculative tendencies in the stock market were pronounced. The officers and directors of the Federal Reserve Banks looked upon all these tendencies with apprehension, and many of them were inclined to advance their discount rates. The law provides that each Federal Reserve Bank shall have power 'to establish from time to time, subject to review and determination of the Federal Reserve Board, rates of discount to be charged by the Federal Reserve Bank for each class of paper which shall be fixed with a view of accommodating commerce and business.' Consequently, no Federal Reserve Bank could change its discount rate except with the consent and approval of the Federal Reserve Board. As the Board did not approve any advance in the discount rate at this time, it seems appropriate to outline here the Board's rate policy.

During the year 1915 and for the greater part of 1916, owing to the abnormal ease of the money market, there was but little resort to the discount facilities of the Federal Reserve Banks. During this period the deposits of member and non-member banks were increasing by leaps and bounds, and the banks as a rule were able to take care of the legitimate needs of customers and to make large purchases of commercial paper without using their credit either with correspondent banks or with the Federal Reserve Banks. In such circumstances it is clear that the Board's influence on credit through discount rates was negligible. Reserve Bank rates were low, in conformity with the general trend of the money market, and open-market operations by Federal Reserve Banks would merely have accentuated the prevailing redundancy of funds available for credits. Higher rates would have brought in even a smaller volume of business. Late in the year 1916, market rates began to stiffen and the volume of discounts with the Federal Reserve Banks showed a tendency to increase, but the banks generally still held a surplus of funds and slight advances in discount rates at some of the Federal Reserve Banks did not materially affect the money market.

After our entrance into the war, the whole situation underwent a radical change. The President, in an address to Congress on April 2, 1917, pledged the entire resources of the Nation to the successful conduct of the war, and war became the paramount business of the country. An issue of Treasury certificates, announced immediately, was followed by the First Liberty Loan campaign, the purpose of which was to secure subscriptions to $2,000,000,000 of bonds bearing three and one half per cent interest. It was apparent that this issue would be followed by others, and in the circumstances it was manifestly the duty of the Board to support the financial plans of the Treasury. Within twelve months about $10,000,000,000 of bonds were sold by the Government, and after April, 1917, there were frequent offerings of Treasury certificates, issued in anticipation of taxes or of the proceeds of bond sales.

Not only with the view of saving to the Government, but mindful also of the effect which high interest rates on Government obligations would have upon investment securities and the money market as a whole, the Secretary of the Treasury determined to hold rates down to the lowest possible level, and he soon announced his purpose to maintain as a maximum a rate of four and one half per cent on Treasury certificates and four and one quarter per cent on Liberty bonds. The Federal Reserve Board felt that it should so direct the policies of the System as to ensure prompt accommodation to banks whose customers might require assistance, either in providing for commercial demands caused by increased business activities, or in making their payments for bonds, as well as to banks which bought bonds for their own account. It was deemed important to prevent disturbances in the money market and to keep interest rates as free from fluctuation as possible. Therefore the Board, before the subscriptions to the first Liberty bond issue were closed, approved a preferential rate of discount for notes offered by member banks secured by Government obligations, whether certificates or bonds, and, in order further to assist the Treasury in disposing of bonds, the Board authorized Federal Reserve Banks to discount, for non-member banks upon the endorsement of a member bank, notes secured by Government obligations, whether made by non-member banks themselves or by their customers, when the proceeds had been or were to be used for the purpose of carrying Treasury certificates or United States bonds. The Board, in this way, distinguished between commercial loans and loans made upon the security of Government obligations, by approving a preferential rate in favor of the latter. The policy of the Board during the war was justified by results. The war was won. The bonds were widely distributed, and each new issue showed a larger number of subscribers than the preceding one, the number of subscribers to the third Liberty loan being more than seventeen million and to the fourth more than twenty-one million. As the rates on Government obligations were advanced, the preferential rates on paper secured by these obligations were increased correspondingly at the Federal Reserve Banks. So that instead of a rate of from three to three and one half per cent as first established, rates at the Reserve Banks after the early months of the war ranged from four to four and one quarter per cent on paper secured by Government issues, with a maximum rate of five and one quarter per cent on ninety-day commercial paper and five and one half per cent on six-month agricultural paper.

The Board did not believe, during the war period, that marked advances in rates would be advisable in view of the obvious necessity of avoiding any policy likely to disturb the financial operations of the Treasury. The needs of those industries and commercial enterprises which were directly contributory to the conduct of the war had to be supplied at all hazards, and a drastic advance in discount rates would not have reduced the financial requirements of such concerns, but would merely have imposed an added cost upon the people.

In its letter of July 6, 1918, to which reference has already been made, the Board called attention to the importance of a wise discrimination between essential and non-essential credits. It believed that the exercise of discriminating judgment on the part of the banks throughout the country in making their loans would be more effective in counteracting any tendency toward undue credit expansion than an advance in rates would be. The suggestion was made by the Board that the Federal Reserve Banks organize, each in its own district, local groups comprising leading bankers and business men, in order to discuss ways and means of bringing about the result desired.

In April, 1919, the Board gave serious consideration to the suggestions made by several of the Federal Reserve Banks that the discount rates be advanced. It had already, during the period of business hesitation which immediately followed the Armistice, approved their action in modifying differential rates, as it no longer saw any reason for giving holders of Government securities advantage in the way of interest over those who desired to borrow money for use in agriculture, commerce, and industry. The Treasury authorities, however, were opposed to an increase in the discount rate at this time. They pointed out that they were then organizing the Victory Loan Campaign to sell $4,500,000,000 of four-year notes, and that, in justice to those who had subscribed to the war issues, the Secretary of the Treasury believed that the rate of interest should not be substantially higher than that borne by the third and fourth Liberty loans, and that he had therefore determined to fix the rate of interest on the notes at four and three quarters per cent. As he could no longer invoke the patriotic impulses which had been so effective in stimulating subscriptions to the wartime issues, the Secretary of the Treasury felt that in placing the Victory Loan he was confronted with an undertaking difficult enough at best. Unless he could rely upon the same measure of support by the Federal Reserve System that had been accorded Secretary McAdoo, the success of the loan would be imperiled, and it was obvious that its failure would be disastrous to the country. The Board, therefore, did not approve any advance in rates. The Federal Reserve Banks and the Board urged the public to respond liberally to the needs of the Treasury, and the Liberty loan organizations throughout the country were revived and functioned admirably. The success of the Victory Loan, oversubscribed by sixteen per cent, by more than twelve million subscribers, under such difficult conditions, was the crowning achievement of a series of financial operations unparalleled in the history of the country. The success of the loan, however, accentuated the dangerous tendencies to which allusion has already been made. The volume of exports continued large, but many overlooked the fact that the buying power of Europe was overestimated, and that our exports to European countries in large part were being paid for out of the unused portion of the credits of $10,000,000,000 which had previously been authorized by Congress to countries associated with us in the war. These unused credits at the beginning of the year 1919 amounted to about $2,500,000,000. The Board repeated its warnings, and did all it could, short of approving higher rates, to discourage the excessive use of credit for non-essential purposes.

It was thought that the removal by the President of all the war-time restrictions upon the export of gold, June 7, 1919, with the resulting large exports of gold from the country, would exert a sobering influence and cool the ardor for overtrading and speculation. During the first thirty days nearly $100,000,000 of gold was exported, and the total exports of gold up to the end of the year amounted to $346,000,000. The excess of gold exports over imports during the year was $279,333,000.[1] Net exports of silver amounted to $140,000,000. The removal of the gold embargo, however, had no sobering effect. The continued advance in prices brought about a general advance in wages, and, as wages increased, the price-level would rise again. A vicious circle had been created, ever widening as prices and wages sought to overtake each other. H.C.L. (not Senator Lodge, but the High Cost of Living) had become a very grave economic problem, and indeed bade fair to develop into a political issue. The President took occasion to communicate with Congress on the

---

[1] This was offset in part by the receipt of $173,400,000 of gold from the Reichsbank in payment of foodstuffs sold to the German Government. For several months this gold was held by the Bank of England for account of the Federal Reserve Banks, but it was eventually transferred to New York.

subject, and some members of that body, who eighteen months later were most extreme in denouncing the Federal Reserve Board because of the decline in prices which by that time had taken place, were now violent in their criticisms of the Board for having brought about inflation and high prices. Early in August the Senate, at the instance of Senator Myers, of Montana, adopted a resolution (S.R. 142), directing the Banking and Currency Committee to investigate and report on the advisability of legislation to provide for the gradual reduction of the volume of currency in circulation. The Chairman of the Committee addressed a communication on this subject to the Federal Reserve Board, which on August 8, 1919, replied in a letter in part as follows:

The Federal Reserve Board acknowledges receipt of your letter of the 5th instant asking for an expression of its views as to the advisability of legislation providing for the gradual reduction of the currency in circulation as proposed by Senate Resolution 142.

The Board would suggest that, in determining whether or not legislation is necessary or desirable to regulate the volume of currency in circulation, consideration be given to the various forms of money which make up the sum total of our volume of currency. A distinction should also be drawn between the stock of money in the country and the amount actually in circulation.

With respect to gold coin, gold certificates, standard silver dollars, silver certificates, subsidiary silver, and Treasury notes of 1890, the Board assumes that it is recognized that no legislation is necessary.

The United States notes, or legal tenders, which have remained at the fixed amount of $346,681,016 since March 31, 1878, have not been a disturbing factor since the passage of the Act of March 14, 1900. An adequate gold reserve of more than forty-five per cent is now held against these notes, most of which are in the form of small bills of $1, $2, and $5 denominations. Notes of these denominations are needed in the daily transactions of the public, and were the United States notes to be retired, the issue of an equal volume of small bills in some other form of currency would be necessary. To effect the retirement of the United States notes, funds would have to be withdrawn from the Treasury to be supplied either by taxation or by the sale of interest-bearing obligations. The Board does not believe that any legislation with respect to United States notes is necessary or desirable at this time.

The national bank notes outstanding on August 1, 1919, amounted to $658,118,855, a reduction of nearly $60,000,000 since July 1, 1914. The greater part of these notes is secured by United States two per cent bonds, and provision has already been made in section 18 of the Federal Reserve Act for their gradual retirement.

Federal Reserve Bank notes, which are secured by United States obligations and are taxed just as national bank notes are, have been issued only to replace in part national bank notes retired and standard silver dollars melted or broken up and sold as bullion under authority of the Act of April 23, 1918, known as the Pittman Act. The issue of these notes has, therefore, brought about no increase in the circulation medium.

The amount of Federal Reserve notes outstanding has increased from $357,239,000 on April 1, 1917, to $2,504,753,000 on August 1, 1919. It appears, therefore, that those who see in the larger volume of circulation in the United States the prime cause of increased costs of living and who seek a remedy by a forced contraction of the currency must have in mind the Federal Reserve note and section 16 of the Federal Reserve Act as amended June 21, 1917, which provides for its issue and redemption.

In analyzing our present monetary situation, and in considering the causes which have led to the expansion of credits and note issues during the war, we should not lose sight of some of the developments of the pre-war period and of their effect upon credits and prices. Very heavy purchases of supplies of all kinds were made in this country by European belligerents during the years 1915 and 1916, payment for which involved the shipment to us of large amounts of gold. The stock of gold in the United States on July 1, 1914, was $1,890,678,304. This amount increased steadily until April, 1917, the date of our own entry into the war, when it reached $3,088,904,808, an increase of about $1,200,000,000. Bank deposits likewise show a large increase, the net deposits of national banks having risen from $7,495,149,000 on June 30, 1914, to $10,489,217,000 on March 5, 1917, while the net deposits of all banks in the United States increased from $17,996,150,000 in June, 1914, to $24,891,218,000 in June, 1917. Net deposits of national banks had further increased up to May 12, 1919, to $11,718,095,000, and those of all banks in June, 1918 (the latest

date for which figures are available), to $26,769,546,000. Shortly
after April 6, 1917, when the Congress declared war, the Treasury
began to sell bonds, notes, and certificates in large amounts, resulting in a net increase in the public debt to August 1, 1919, of
$24,518,064,840.

On July 1, 1914, the total stock of money in the United States,
exclusive of that held by the United States Treasury, was
$3,419,168,368. On April 1, 1917, the stock of money, esti-
mated on the same basis, was $4,702,130,941, an increase of
$1,282,962,573, of which increase $883,481,028 was in gold.

On July 1, 1914, there were no Federal Reserve notes in existence, while on April 1, 1917, there were outstanding $357,239,000.

The amendment to the Federal Reserve Act approved June 21,
1917, changed substantially the original reserve requirements for
member banks and provided that their entire lawful reserve should
be carried with the Federal Reserve Banks. This same amendment authorized the Federal Reserve Banks to exchange Federal
Reserve notes for gold. The result of these two changes in the law
was to transfer immediately large sums of gold from the vaults of
the member and non-member banks and from general circulation
to the Federal Reserve Banks, and this caused a change in the
methods of accounting for gold by the Federal Reserve Banks and
Federal Reserve Agents.

In order to avoid confusion in determining the volume of money
in actual circulation, it is necessary to distinguish between tables
showing the total stock of money in the country and tables showing the circulation outside of the Treasury and Federal Reserve
Agents' vaults, and to limit our view to amounts held by member
and non-member banks and the public, which are exclusive of
amounts on hand at Federal Reserve Banks, held by Federal
Reserve Agents, and held in the Treasury.

The Reserve money held by or for the Federal Reserve Banks
serves, of course, as a basis for credit, but it forms no part of the
currency in circulation. Upon this basis the amount of money in
circulation on July 1, 1914 (there being no Federal Reserve Banks
in operation at that time), was $3,419,168,368, made up as follows:
Gold coin and certificates, $1,649,775,803; silver dollars and silver
certificates, including Treasury notes of 1890, $552,203,610; all
other currency, $1,217,188,955, being circulation per capita, $34.53.

The corresponding amounts of money in circulation on April 1,
1917, December 1, 1918, and August 1, 1919, are shown in the
following table:

AMOUNT OF MONEY OUTSIDE THE TREASURY AND FEDERAL RESERVE BANKS

	April 1, 1917	December 1, 1918	August 1, 1919
Gold coin and certificates	$1,989,152,000	$861,245,000	$728,046,000
Silver dollars and silver certificates (including Treasury notes of 1890)	532,700,000	372,489,000	241,505,000
Federal Reserve notes....	357,239,000	2,607,445,000	2,504,753,000
Federal Reserve Bank notes................	3,170,000	87,737,000	166,289,000
All other currency........	1,218,715,000	1,201,069,000	1,156,297,000
Total........	$4,100,976,000	$5,129,985,000	$4,796,890,000
Amount per capita outside the Treasury and the Federal Reserve Banks..............	$37.88	$48.13	$45.16

Assuming that the date, December 1, 1918, marks the beginning of the post-war period, the table shows changes during this period up to August 1, 1919, as follows: Gold coin and certificates in circulation decreased $133,199,000; silver dollars and silver certificates, including Treasury notes of 1890, decreased $130,984,000; Federal Reserve notes decreased $102,692,000; Federal Reserve Bank notes increased $78,552,000; all other currency decreased $44,772,000, being a net decrease in circulation for the post-war period of $333,095,000, or $2.97 per capita.

In considering the question of currency in circulation, there should be taken into account the various factors which have entered into the demand for currency, among which are: the gradual enlargement of payrolls, both as to the number of workers and amount paid to each; the effect of higher wages upon deposits in banks and upon the amounts of money carried by shopkeepers in their tills and by individuals in their pockets; the amounts of money locked up or carried on their persons by workmen who have been receiving high wages, and who, especially in the case of ignorant foreigners, are unwilling to deposit their savings in banks or to invest in Government bonds; the amount of money carried away by workmen returning to their homes in foreign countries; and the fact that the circulating media of the Philippine Islands, Hawaii, Cuba, Porto Rico, Santo Domingo, Haiti, Honduras, Panama, and in part, Mexico, include United States paper cur-

rency and subsidiary silver. The amounts required in these countries, most of which are very prosperous, have greatly increased
in the last few years.

The total foreign circulation of United States currency cannot
be stated accurately, but is estimated to be at least $150,000,000.

The difficulty, indeed the impossibility, of keeping in circulation
an excessive volume of Federal Reserve notes should be understood. The issue of these notes has been carefully safeguarded by
the Federal Reserve Act, and ample provision has been made for
their redemption. Federal Reserve notes are redeemable in gold;
they cannot be forced into circulation in payment of the expenses
of the Government, or for any other purpose, as they can be issued
only in exchange for gold or against a deposit of negotiable paper
growing out of a legitimate commercial transaction, plus the required gold reserve of not less than forty per cent. Upon payment
of commercial paper which has been deposited to secure Federal
Reserve notes, there results either an immediate return of an
equal amount of notes to the bank, or an automatic increase in the
percentage of gold reserve available for their redemption. Federal
Reserve notes are not legal tender, nor do they count as reserve
money for member banks. They are issued only as a need for them
develops, and as they become redundant in any locality they are
returned to the Treasury at Washington, or to a Federal Reserve
Bank for redemption. Thus there cannot at any time be more
Federal Reserve notes in circulation than the needs of the country
at the present level of prices require, and as the need abates, the
volume of notes outstanding will be correspondingly reduced
through redemption. The increased volume of Federal Reserve
notes in circulation during the past three years, in so far as it is
not the result of direct exchanges for gold and gold certificates
which have been withdrawn from circulation, is the effect of
advancing wages and prices, and not their cause.

There has undoubtedly taken place during the last two years
a certain amount of credit expansion which, under the circumstances
connected with our war financing, was inevitable, but this will be
corrected as the securities issued by the United States Government for war purposes are gradually absorbed by investors. . . .

The principal cause of the advance of prices before and during
the war was the urgent need of the Governments of the allied
world for goods of all kinds for quick delivery in large volume, and
the competition of this buying by Governments with purchases by
private individuals who failed to contract their expenditures at a

rate commensurate with the growing expenditures of these Governments. In the post-war period, through which we are now passing, the country has experienced rising prices owing, in part, to a general relaxation of the war-time régime of personal economy, resulting in an increased demand for commodities by individuals who restricted their purchases during the war, but who are now buying in competition with export demand. In addition, accrued incomes and increased wages have led to heavy demands for commodities not of prime necessity, which have resulted in diverting labor and material from essentials to non-essentials.

The Federal Reserve Board believes that any currency legislation at this time is unnecessary and undesirable, and would suggest that, whether viewed from an economic or financial standpoint, the remedy for the present situation is the same, namely, to work and to save; to work regularly and efficiently in order to produce and distribute the largest possible volume of commodities; and to exercise reasonable economies in order that money, goods, and services may be devoted primarily to the liquidation of debt and to the satisfaction of the demand for necessities, rather than to indulgence in extravagances or the gratification of a desire for luxuries.

CHAPTER XIII

A Period of Readjustment Foreshadowed — Discount
Rates Advanced — Attitude of the Treasury —
The Progressive Rate

ALTHOUGH the Board did not believe that the large volume
of Federal Reserve notes in circulation was in itself responsible for the high cost of living and for the wave of reckless
extravagance which was sweeping over the country, some of
its members did believe very strongly that immediate steps
should be taken to correct the conditions growing out of the
artificially low discount rates which seemed to promote,
rather than to check, the undue extension of credit by banks
in general. These members now looked with favor upon a
substantial advance in the discount rates, having in mind a
maximum of six per cent. At this time the rate on fifteen-
day paper, including member banks' collateral notes, secured by Liberty bonds and Victory notes, was four per cent
at eight of the Federal Reserve Banks, and four and a quarter per cent at Richmond, Chicago, Kansas City, and San
Francisco; and on fifteen-day paper secured by United States
certificates of indebtedness the rate was four per cent at all
the banks, with the exception of the San Francisco Bank,
where the rate was four and a quarter per cent. As an argument against an advance of rates, it was pointed out that
the market value of Government bonds would be depressed
and that the burden upon those who had borrowed money
to meet their subscriptions would be increased, as banks
undoubtedly would raise their customers' rates.

While Treasury officials were opposed to an advance in
rates at this time, they did not raise this objection. In an
address delivered in April, 1920, the Assistant Secretary of
the Treasury, Mr. Russell C. Leffingwell, after explaining
the considerations which determined the rates of interest

borne by the Liberty bonds and Victory notes, and referring
to the fact that four and three quarters per cent Victory
notes were then selling on an interest basis of about six and
a quarter per cent, said:

A year ago it was freely predicted by financial authorities that
Victory notes would shortly go to a premium, and the Liberty
bonds would be selling at or near par within a year or two. Every
one knows why these sanguine expectations have not been realized. With the Armistice, and still more after the Victory loan, our
people underwent a great reaction. Those who had bought Liberty
bonds as a matter of patriotism, but not as investors, began to
treat their bonds as so much spending money. Those who had
obeyed the injunction to borrow and buy Liberty bonds ignored
the complementary injunction to save and pay for them. . . .
This was the first and immediate cause of the depreciation of
Liberty bonds, affecting them particularly. . . . Liberty bonds
have depreciated because they [the people] are treating their
Liberty bonds as spending money.

Personally, I was anxious in August, 1919, to have the
discount rates advanced, and had frequent conversations
with Assistant Secretary Leffingwell on the subject of rates.
I assumed that the views he expressed coincided with those
of the Secretary of the Treasury. While he was not strongly
opposed to an advance in commercial rates, he protested
particularly against an advance at this time in rates on collateral notes secured by Treasury certificates of indebtedness. He pointed out that the total Government indebtedness — bonds, notes, and certificates — had about reached
its peak (the maximum was $26,595,000,000 on August 30,
1919), and that gradual reductions from this time on were
anticipated. He stated that Treasury certificates were being
issued in part as an outright borrowing by the Government,
as well as in anticipation of the quarterly payments of income and excess profits taxes. By January, 1920, he expected to be able to retire a substantial amount of the certificates, and after that date they would be issued only in
anticipation of revenue coming in from income and profits

taxes. The Treasury was unwilling to offer certificates at a rate which would make them salable on the market without the artificially low rate maintained by the Federal Reserve Banks, and he said that an advance in the rate on paper secured by certificates would seriously embarrass the Treasury.

Early in September the Federal Advisory Council met, and at its morning session decided to recommend that all discount rates be advanced. Mr. Leffingwell, however, appeared before the Council in the afternoon, and, raising the objections above outlined, stated that after January 1st the Treasury would interpose no objection to an advance in rates, and induced the Council to withhold the recommendation which it had decided to make.

Although the United States had again become a free gold market, the central banks of other countries, which still maintained rigid restrictions upon the export of gold, had discount rates much higher than those of the Federal Reserve Banks. These conditions increased greatly the demands upon the American money market, and during the autumn commercial paper ranged from six to eight per cent, and on several occasions call-money rates in New York were from twelve to thirty per cent. The low discount rates of the Federal Reserve Banks, coupled with stringent conditions in the market, invited heavy offerings of paper, and the loans of the Federal Reserve Banks rapidly increased while the reserves declined in a corresponding degree. During the month of November all Federal Reserve Banks advanced their rates one quarter of one per cent and these advances were approved by the Federal Reserve Board. This moderate increase, however, had no appreciable effect upon the general situation.

Notwithstanding the high prices prevailing, the staple crops of the year 1919 were not marketed as rapidly or as freely as was normally the case. The inability of the railroads to furnish adequate transportation facilities was probably responsible in part, but there was a disposition on the part of many producers and middlemen to hold for still higher prices. Meanwhile stocks of goods were accumulating on the shelves of the merchants and in the warehouses and factories, all of which added to the strain on the banks. In order to maintain their required reserve, several of the Federal Reserve Banks had been obliged at various times during the year, and some of them almost continuously, to rediscount with other Federal Reserve Banks. Normally during the month of January there is a large return flow of currency to the financial centers from the country districts, extending sometimes well into March. This would be accompanied by a reduction in the loans of the banks and by lower interest rates on commercial paper. Hitherto the liquidation following the marketing of crops had been reflected in substantial reductions in the loan accounts of the Federal Reserve Banks, but their holdings of discounted paper on the last Friday of December, 1919, were only about $19,000,000 less than on the last Friday of November, and nearly $500,000,000 larger than on the corresponding date in December, 1918. The total loans and advances made by all Federal Reserve Banks to member banks, which on January 2, 1920, amounted to $2,231,000,000, had been reduced by January 30th to $2,174,000,000, but by February 20th they had increased to $2,358,000,000. On January 2, 1920, the banks had outstanding, in actual circulation, Federal Reserve notes amounting to $2,998,992,000. On January 23d this amount had been reduced to $2,844,227,000, but by February 20th it had risen to $2,977,124,000. These figures reflected the negligible relief afforded by the marketing of crops, and also the abnormally large portion of the crops still held back. To the failure of the producers to market their crops in an orderly way in the season of 1919–20 must be attributed to a large degree their troubles in the fall of 1920, when the new crops were ready for market. Not only was it burdensome to carry over these unsold stocks, but their volume, adding materially to the supplies which sought buyers in the fall, was an important factor in the demoralization of prices. This was especially true in the case of cotton.

During the month of January the Federal Reserve Board approved for all the Federal Reserve Banks substantial advances in discount rates. While it was deemed expedient to continue preferential rates on paper secured by Government obligations, the rates at all Federal Reserve Banks were made uniform. On discounted bills maturing within ninety days, secured by Treasury certificates of indebtedness, the rate at all banks was four and three quarters per cent; on paper secured by Liberty bonds and Victory notes, five and a half per cent; on commercial paper maturing within ninety days, six per cent; and on agricultural and live-stock paper maturing within six months, six per cent. A further change was made during the month of February by advancing the rate on paper secured by Treasury certificates to five per cent at all the banks except those of St. Louis, Minneapolis, and San Francisco.

After the death of Senator Martin, of Virginia, in November, 1919, the Governor of Virginia appointed the Honorable Carter Glass, the Secretary of the Treasury, to succeed him *ad interim*, pending the next regular election. Mr. Glass having decided to accept this appointment, his resignation as Secretary of the Treasury was accepted by the President, who appointed to succeed him in that office the Honorable David F. Houston, who, since March 5, 1913, had been Secretary of Agriculture. The resignation of Mr. Glass became effective on February 2, 1920, on which day Secretary Houston took the oath of office. During his administration of the Treasury the rates of interest on Treasury certificates issued were considerably higher than the rates borne by previous issues. The new rates conformed more closely to market conditions and made it possible for the certificates to be sold without the preferential and artificially low rates which had been maintained in previous years by the Federal Reserve Banks.

THE FEDERAL RESERVE BOARD AS CONSTITUTED IN DECEMBER, 1919

Left to right: W. P. G. Harding, W. T. Chapman (Secretary), Adolph C. Miller, H. A. Moehlenpah, Carter Glass, Albert Strauss, Charles S. Hamlin, John Skelton Williams

For some months call-money rates in the New York market had been high and were subject to frequent fluctuations. On March 8, 1920, the Senate adopted a resolution directing the Federal Reserve Board 'to advise the Senate what is the cause and justification for the usurious rates of interest on collateral call loans in the financial centers, under what law authorized, and what steps if any are required to abate this condition.' In its reply the Board called attention to tables showing discount and interest rates prevailing in various centers in all Federal Reserve districts during the previous sixty days, and pointed out that these tables showed that the maximum and minimum rates on demand loans secured by collateral had been approximately the same as commercial-paper rates in all cities except New York and Boston. While the legal rate of interest in Massachusetts is six per cent, higher rates by contract are authorized, and consequently the limitation to six per cent is occasionally exceeded, and a rate higher than six per cent is not necessarily usurious. The Board called attention also to the fact that the only financial center in this country in which there is maintained a call-money market of national importance is New York City, and that while the rates charged there on call loans may frequently exceed the legal rates allowed for commercial paper, they are not usurious under the laws of the State of New York, which specifically exempt collateral demand loans of not less than five thousand dollars from the six per cent limitation which lenders must observe on other loans on pain of incurring the penalty prescribed for usury.

The national banking law provides that national banks may receive and charge, on any loan or discount, interest at the rate allowed by the law of the State, territory, or district where the bank is located. As to the 'causes and justification' of the high rates of interest which may legally be charged on collateral call loans in New York, and as to the 'steps . . . required to abate this condition,' the Board stated that there existed a wide difference of opinion among persons who had given thought and study to the question. Indeed, broad and fundamental questions of general economic and social policy are involved — in the last analysis, the whole question of the utility of speculative dealings in securities and commodities on organized exchanges is involved; and more immediately, the question of the methods and practices of the leading speculative markets of the country, margining, stock manipulation, and kindred matters also susceptible of abuse. As to these the Board has never had occasion officially to form an opinion; the Federal Reserve Act specifically precludes the purchase or discount by Federal Reserve Banks of 'notes, drafts, or bills covering merely investments or issued or drawn for the purpose of carrying or trading in stocks, bonds, or other investment securities, except bonds and notes of the Government of the United States.' The Board could not undertake to form a judgment upon the matters above referred to without study and investigation of such a comprehensive nature as would seriously interfere with the conduct of its regular work, and which, had the Board the requisite authority, would require the services of experts and assistants for the employment of which the Board does not feel authorized to expend funds accruing from statutory assessments on the Federal Reserve Banks for the purpose of defraying the ordinary expenses contemplated by the Federal Reserve Act.

With its reply the Board transmitted a memorandum which had been prepared by the Federal Reserve Agent in New York explaining at length the nature and operation of the New York call-money market and the causes of high and fluctuating rates for call money in that center. It was pointed out that the New York Stock Exchange loans had for several weeks reached the highest point in the history of the Exchange and that the rates on call money depended upon the demand and upon the supply of loanable funds. Extracts from this memorandum, which will be of special interest to those who desire to know something of the operations of the call-money market in New York, will be found in the Appendix.[1]

About this time there were indications that a reaction in

[1] See Appendix B, page 280.

business was at hand. Commodity prices throughout the world had risen to a point where consumption was checked because of the inability or unwillingness of people to pay the prices demanded. The event which foreshadowed the beginning of the readjustment period took place, not in the United States, but in the Far East, in Japan. For many months during a time of fatuous optimism and of reckless extravagance, there had been a heavy demand for silks. The exports of silk from Japan to the United States and other countries had been very heavy. The demand seemed to be insatiable, and prices underwent frequent changes always on an ascending scale. Suddenly the demand fell off. A drastic price reaction followed. Japanese banks began to call loans or to require additional collateral, and during the closing days of March there ensued in Japan a veritable panic. The crash swept down many Japanese banks and commercial houses, and while it produced no immediate repercussions in this country, the Board was, I believe, unanimous in the belief that the time had come to make further preparations for weathering an economic crisis here.

While only about sixty-five per cent of the member banks were borrowing at Federal Reserve Banks, many of them were borrowing very heavily, and reports showed that practically all banks were fully loaned up. The gold reserves of the Federal Reserve Banks amounted to but little more than $2,000,000,000, and the average reserve percentage of the banks had declined to about forty-two per cent. As the entire legal reserves of all member banks were required by law to be carried with the Federal Reserve Banks, it was evident that they were maintaining actual gold reserves only when the gold reserves of the Federal Reserve Banks reached one hundred per cent, and that, as the Reserve Banks had a reserve of only forty-two per cent, the actual gold reserves of the member banks were weakened correspondingly. Acceptances made by member banks, as permitted by law, against exports and imports did not find a ready market even at the high rates then prevailing, and were being purchased for the greater part by the Federal Reserve Banks, mainly by the Federal Reserve Bank of New York for its own account and for that of a few other Reserve Banks which had surplus reserves. Many of the Federal Reserve Banks would have had reserves far below the legal minimum but for rediscounts made with other Reserve Banks. Nevertheless, a good deal of pressure was exerted by Senator Owen and others to bring about lower discount rates, and some critics have averred repeatedly that the fall in prices which took place later in the year could have been averted, or at least materially modified, had the Federal Reserve Banks reduced their rates of discount. Especially violent was the criticism against the so-called progressive rate, which was in force for several months at four of the Federal Reserve Banks. In order to bring about a more uniform distribution of the financial burden among all member banks, Congress had early in the year, at the suggestion of the Federal Reserve Board, amended the Federal Reserve Act so as to permit Federal Reserve Banks to adopt a graduated scale of rates based upon the amount of borrowings by any given member bank. These graduated rates were not mandatory, but were merely optional. The four banks which adopted the plan allotted to each member bank an amount which it could rediscount at the normal or regular rate. This amount was determined:

1. Upon the assumption that all member banks would borrow.

2. In such circumstances, upon the amount of accommodation that the Federal Reserve Bank could extend to each member bank out of its own resources, without rediscounting with other Federal Reserve Banks, and without going below its required reserve.

If a member bank had borrowed the amount allotted to it in this way, it would pay, in addition to the normal rate, one per cent more on the excess borrowed up to a certain sum, after which it would pay an additional one per cent on the further excess. In the Kansas City district the effect was to distribute the burden and to increase the number of borrowing banks. In most of the States of that district contract rates as high as ten per cent were permissible by law, and when a bank which was a heavy borrower at the Federal Reserve Bank would be asked by a customer for an additional loan, the rate it would usually charge would be higher than the rate at which some bank which was not a borrower, or only a moderate borrower, would be willing to lend. The application of the progressive rate was intended as a corrective or deterrent to overextended banks, and as a means of avoiding higher rates to all banks. In another district the adoption of the progressive rate had no marked effect, and in still another it did not work well and the plan was soon discontinued. The progressive rate was abolished in all districts early in 1921, and in 1923 Congress repealed the amendment authorizing it. The difficulty with the progressive rate lay, not in the law itself, but in its administration by one or two of the banks which had adopted it. While a maximum rate on excessive borrowings of ten or twelve per cent would have accomplished the purpose intended, and probably have aroused but little criticism, no limitation was imposed at first by the banks which had adopted the plan, and one member bank paid for a few days, on an advance of a few thousand dollars, a rate equal to eighty-five per cent per annum. While the actual amount paid was small, and while the Federal Reserve Banks afterward refunded to borrowing banks all interest paid in excess of a maximum rate of twelve per cent, prejudiced critics made much of this particular case and brought upon the Federal Reserve Board and upon the System in general much undeserved criticism.

Adverting to the contention that Federal Reserve Bank rates should have been substantially lowered in April or May, 1920, I wish to point out that, even if this course had been adopted, it is by no means certain that the drastic price reactions would not, nevertheless, have taken place.

They did occur in all other countries, and had there been no corresponding fall of prices in this country the demands upon our banks would have been all the heavier. The United States was a free gold market, and had it remained at the same time the cheapest money market in the world, our financial structure would have been subject to the severest strain. The Board in that event would have been forced to suspend the reserve requirements, which would probably have resulted in the presentation of large amounts of Federal Reserve notes for redemption in gold for hoarding, which would have reduced reserves still further. In such circumstances prices could have been sustained only in terms of irredeemable paper money. Continuous credit inflation inevitably leads to currency inflation, and currency inflation is always progressive, making necessary time and again recourse to the printing-press. To prevent a catastrophe a halt has to be called at some point. It is not denied that the halting of inflation causes hardship and distress, but no one can truthfully assert that in Europe the distress has been greater in those countries whose currencies maintained some value than in countries like Russia, Austria, and Germany, whose currencies finally came to be utterly worthless. The Board was never in favor of a policy of deflation; it sought merely to prevent further inflation. In its Annual Report for the year 1919, it said:

The expansion of credit set in motion by the war must be checked. Credit must be brought under effective control and its flow be once more regulated and governed with careful regard to the economic welfare of the country and the needs of its producing industries.

Deflation, however, merely for the sake of deflation and a speedy return to 'normal' — deflation merely for the sake of restoring security values and commodity prices to their pre-war levels without regard to other consequences, would be an insensate proceeding in the existing posture of national and world affairs. . . .

Too rapid or too drastic deflation would defeat the very purpose of a well-regulated credit system by the needless unsettlement of mind it would produce and the disastrous reaction that such unsettlement would have upon productive industry.

Radical and drastic deflation is not, therefore, in contemplation, nor is a policy of further expansion. Either course would in the end lead only to disaster and must not be permitted to develop. . . . There need be no occasion for apprehension as to our ability to effect the transition from war-time to peace-time conditions if reasonable safeguards against the abuse of credit are respected. There is, however, no need for precipitate action or extreme measures. Extremes must be avoided, the process of adjusting the volume of credit to a normal basis should be effected in an orderly manner, and its rapidity must be governed by conditions and circumstances as they develop. Much will depend upon the coöperation of the business and general community. Indeed, without such coöperation progress can be neither rapid nor substantial. Much will depend also upon the rapidity with which the unabsorbed portion of the outstanding issues of war securities passes into the hands of permanent holders. As the national debt is thus absorbed and as it is reduced through the operation of the sinking fund, the loan accounts of the banks should be reduced correspondingly, until the proper balance between the volume of credit and the volume of concrete things, which credit helps to produce and which are the normal basis of credit, is restored. This equilibrium, it cannot be too frequently or too emphatically stated, can be restored only by speeding up the processes of production, by the orderly distribution of goods, by the avoidance of wasteful consumption, and by the increased accumulation of savings. These are the fundamental economic processes upon which the proper functioning of the Federal Reserve Banks must depend. The Federal Reserve System can do much to assist these processes, but it cannot of itself and alone compel them. Efficacious action along these lines involves the intelligent and earnest coöperation of the business and general community. While the Federal Reserve Board will always be mindful of the interdependence of credit and industry and of the influence exerted on prices by the general volume of credit, the Board nevertheless cannot assume to be an arbiter of industry or prices. Its primary duty, as the guardian of the Nation's ultimate banking reserve, is to see that the banks under its supervision function effectively and properly as reserve banks.

CHAPTER XIV

FEDERAL RESERVE CONFERENCE ON MAY 18, 1920 — REDIS-
COUNTING BETWEEN FEDERAL RESERVE BANKS — DE-
CLINE IN COMMODITY PRICES NOT SYNCHRONOUS
WITH ADVANCE IN DISCOUNT RATES

SECRETARY GLASS, a short time before his retirement from
the Treasury, transmitted a letter to the Board in which he
expressed the hope that the Federal Reserve Banks would
not rely wholly or too heavily for the prevention of the abuse
of the facilities of the Federal Reserve System upon the increased rates which had been established, which, as he stated,
he himself had joined in approving. He said:

I believe it to be of prime importance that the Federal Reserve
Board should insist upon, and that the Governors of the banks
should exercise, a firm discrimination in making new loans to prevent abuse of the facilities of the Federal Reserve System in
support of the reckless speculation in stocks, land, cotton,
clothing, foodstuffs, and commodities generally. . . . I need not
say that such steps should be taken not only firmly, but with
discretion, and in such a way as not to involve grave hardship to
individuals or injury to the general welfare. . . . I need scarcely
add that this letter is written in no spirit of criticism. The Governors of the Federal Reserve Banks have served their country with
devotion, courage, and wisdom during the trying period that is
past. It would be difficult for me to give adequate praise to the
patriotic spirit of self-sacrifice which has actuated them or adequate appreciation of the skill and sagacity with which they have
performed their duties. During the war they have naturally
turned for leadership to the Treasury, since its operations were
the dominating factor in the financial situation. It would, however, be a great misfortune if, now that the Treasury operations
are on a diminishing scale, the Governors of the Federal Reserve
Banks are allowed to feel that the problems of the future were for
them to solve each according to his own best judgment. The need
of leadership is no less great, the need of examining the situation
from a broad national and international point of view is no less

imperative. I look to see the Federal Reserve Board, not critically nor aggressively, but patiently and persistently, provide this leadership.

On January 6, 1920, the Board held a conference with bankers representing twenty-five clearing-house associations throughout the country. At this time there was a renewed tendency among banks to increase rates of interest paid on deposits and bank balances. The same thing had occurred in 1918, and reference has already been made to the action which was taken by the New York Clearing-House. In opening the conference, I called the attention of those present to the great expansion which had taken place in our credit structure, and urged the importance of discouraging non-essential loans and putting the banks back into a position where they could expand or contract their loans according to the industrial and commercial requirements of the country. I reminded the bankers present that if the Federal Reserve Banks, as a reflection of the condition of the member banks of the country, whose reserves are kept entirely with the Federal Reserve Banks, should be permitted to expand to the very limit of their resources, and if the country should then be confronted with an emergency, we should be obliged to meet that emergency just as though there were no Federal Reserve System. This significant statement was made, which had been duly considered and approved by the Board, 'It is going to be necessary, perhaps, to raise rates beyond their present level. I am not here to make a prophecy, but you should all bear in mind that a further rate increase is a contingency which must be reckoned with.' Reference was then made to the rules regarding interest on deposits and bank balances which had been adopted two years before in New York and some other cities, which provided for a sliding scale on bank balances ranging between a minimum of one per cent and the maximum of three per cent based upon the ninety-day discount rate for commercial paper at the Federal Reserve Bank. I stated that it should be thoroughly understood by bankers throughout the country that the Board could not be hampered in its approval of discount rates for Federal Reserve Banks by any arrangement made by banks, or associations of banks, as to rates of interest which were made dependent upon Federal Reserve Bank discount rates. In other words, the Board would exercise its statutory rights and would be absolutely and entirely free to approve such rates as might in its opinion be demanded by the interests of the country without reference to any competition for deposits which might result.

In April, 1920, a movement began in the South, which soon spread to other parts of the country, to induce men to wear overalls. This movement was intended as a protest against the high price of men's clothing, and it was argued that a decrease in the demand for ordinary suits of clothes would effect a reduction in the price. An immediate effect was to increase materially the price of denims, of which material overalls are made. Perhaps this agitation had some influence also in precipitating the decline in the price of wool which followed a few weeks later. The movement was of short duration, but its significance lay in the fact that people were complaining of the decreased purchasing power of the dollar and that high prices were tending to reduce both consumption and production. About the first of May a large department store in New York advertised a horizontal reduction of twenty per cent on many of the articles carried in stock. This indicated that the retail trade was beginning to find it difficult to dispose of goods at prevailing prices.

On April 30th the loans of the Federal Reserve Banks, together with bankers' acceptances bought, amounted to $2,942,000,000; the Federal Reserve notes in actual circulation amounted to $3,074,555,000; the gold reserves held by the banks aggregated $1,936,720,000. These figures showed that not only was the gold reserve lower than in January, but that since that time there had been an increase in loans and in Federal Reserve notes outstanding. The summer was ahead of us, and then would come the crop-moving season for which provision must be made. The discount rates at Federal Reserve Banks ranged from five to five and a half per cent on notes secured by Government obligations, and at all banks the rate on commercial paper, and on agricultural and live-stock paper, was six per cent. Several of the banks advised the Board that their rediscount rates were out of line with current rates and were asking for a further increase. One or two of the others, having determined to give the new progressive rate a trial, were not asking for an increase in normal rates. The Board was very reluctant to approve for any Federal Reserve Bank a discount rate higher than six per cent. While recognizing the force of the arguments made by the banks which had asked for a higher rate, the Board hoped that the exercise of a wise discretion on the part of the member banks in making loans would make further advances in the Federal Reserve Bank rates unnecessary.

The Federal Advisory Council had notified the Board that it would hold its regular quarterly meeting in Washington on May 17th, and the Board deemed the occasion opportune for a discussion and analysis of the credit situation throughout the country. In order to ascertain the views of a larger number of dispensers of credit than were represented by the twelve members of the Federal Advisory Council, the Board extended an invitation to the three 'Class A' or banker directors of each Federal Reserve Bank to meet the Council and the Board in Washington on Tuesday, May 18, 1920. This conference has often been referred to by extreme critics as 'the great conspiracy' or 'the crime of 1920.' It had been known for several days in advance of the meeting that this conference would be held, and the fact that it had been held was immediately given to the press, which gave the public an outline of the proceedings. A comprehensive account of the conference appeared a few days later in the 'Federal Reserve Bulletin' for June.

In my opening address, which was a general review of the situation, I pointed out that since June 30, 1914, there had been an expansion of banking credit in the United States, probably attributable to the war, of about $11,000,000,000, with an increase of money in actual circulation of about $1,900,000,000; and went on to say:

The expansion of national bank credits was sixteen per cent, or at the rate of ten and a half per cent a year, during the nineteen months of the war. From April 1, 1919, to April 1, 1920, the increase in bank loans was approximately twenty-five per cent. . . .

It is evident that the country cannot continue to advance prices and wages, to curtail production, to expand credits, and to attempt to enrich itself by non-productive operations and transactions without fostering discontent and radicalism, and that such a course, if persisted in, will eventually bring on a real crisis.

There is a world-wide lack of capital, and with calls upon the investment market which cannot be met, there is an unprecedented demand for bank credits. The fact must be recognized that, however desirable on general principles continued expansion of trade and industry may be, such developments must accommodate themselves to the actual supply of capital and credit available.

Official bank rates now in force in the leading countries are higher than at any time during the present century, except during the war panic week at the beginning of August, 1914. . . .

Our problem, therefore, is to check further expansion and to bring about a normal and healthy liquidation without curtailing essential production and without shock to industry, and, as far as possible, without disturbance of legitimate commerce and business.

As a rule there is a substantial reduction in the volume of commercial loans during the first quarter of the year. This liquidation is entirely natural and healthy, and is necessary in order that the banks may be prepared to meet the demands made upon them during the crop-making and harvesting seasons. There has been no such liquidation during the present year; on the contrary, commercial loans have steadily increased. Thus the public has anticipated demands for banking credit which are usually made later on in the year. The average reserves of the Federal Reserve Banks are now about forty-two per cent, as against forty-five per cent at the beginning of the year, and about fifty-one per cent twelve months ago.

The solution of the problems confronting us will require the coöperation of all banks and the public. Whatever personal sacrifices may be necessary for the general economic good should be made. The war-time spirit to do things that are worth while must be revived, and there should be the fullest coöperation in an effort to produce more, save more, and consume less. The banks should lean less heavily upon the Federal Reserve Banks, and rely more upon their own resources. Unnecessary and habitual borrowings should be discouraged, and the liquidation of long-standing non-essential loans should proceed. Drastic steps, however, should be avoided and the methods adopted should be orderly. Gradual liquidation will result in improvement, while too rapid deflation would be injurious and must be avoided. . . .

With respect to credits, the problems of the Federal Reserve Board, the Federal Reserve Banks, and the member banks, while interrelated, are distinctive. The Federal Reserve Board has but little direct contact with the member banks; it deals with general conditions and principles rather than with individual cases and details. The Federal Reserve Banks, on the other hand, are in daily contact with their member banks and have constant dealings with them. Between the Federal Reserve Banks and the Federal Reserve Board, as the supervisory and coördinating body, there is necessarily a close and intimate relationship. The member banks transact the greater part of the primary banking business of the country. They receive the deposits of the public and are the media through which ordinary commercial credits are extended. . . .

Regardless of the extent of its legal powers, it would be a most difficult task for the Federal Reserve Board, sitting in Washington, to attempt, by general rule of country-wide application, to distinguish between 'essential' and 'non-essential' loans. During the war there was a broad underlying principle that essentials must be 'necessary or contributory to the conduct of the war,' but, notwithstanding the sharp outline of this principle, much difficulty was experienced by the various war boards in defining essentials and non-essentials. All the more difficult would it be for the Federal Reserve Board to make such a general definition now when there is no longer that purpose as a guide. . . .

In the Federal Reserve Act no express condition is made regarding the essential or non-essential character of the transaction giving rise to a note which may be offered for discount, and the Federal Reserve Board is not required and properly could not be expected generally to adopt such a criterion of eligibility. It is too much a matter of local conditions and local knowledge to justify at this time any general country-wide ruling by the Board even if such a ruling were deemed helpful.

On the other hand, there is nothing in the Federal Reserve Act which requires a Federal Reserve Bank to make any investment or to rediscount any particular paper or class of paper. . . . The Federal Reserve Act, however, requires the directors of a Federal Reserve Bank to administer its affairs 'fairly and impartially and without discrimination in favor of or against any member bank,' and subject to the provisions of law and the orders of the Federal Reserve Board to extend 'to each member bank such discounts, advancements, and accommodations as may be safely and reasonably made with due regard for the claims and demands of other member banks.' Thus, the directors of a Federal Reserve Bank have the power to limit the volume and character of loans which in their judgment may be safely and reasonably made to any member bank. . . .

It is the view of the Board, however, that, while Federal Reserve Banks may properly undertake in their transactions with member banks to discriminate between essential and non-essential loans, nevertheless, that discrimination might much better be made at the source by the member banks themselves. The individual banker comes in direct contact with his customers; he is better qualified than any one else to advise the customer because of his familiarity, not only with the customer's business, but with the general business conditions and needs in his immediate locality. In making loans he is bound by no general rule of law as to the character of the purpose for which a loan is being asked. He is entirely free to exercise discretion and can make one loan and decline another as his judgment may dictate. He can estimate with a fair degree of accuracy the legitimate demands for credit which are liable to be made upon him, as well as the fluctuations in the volume of his deposits. He knows what industries sustain his community, and is thus qualified to pass upon the essential or non-essential character of loans offered him. He knows, or should know, what rediscount line he may reasonably expect of his Federal Reserve Bank, and he ought not to regard this line as a permanent addition to his capital. With knowledge of the limitations or penalties put upon his borrowings from the Federal Reserve Bank, the banker may be depended upon to use a more discriminating judgment in granting credit accommodations to customers, and that judgment he must exercise if the present situation is to be remedied fundamentally.

It is true that under existing conditions the volume of credit required in any transaction is much greater than was the case in pre-war times, but it is also true that the resources of the member and non-member banks would be ample to take care of the essential business of the country and to a large extent of non-essentials as well if there were a freer flow of goods and credit. If 'frozen loans' were liquefied, and if commodities which are held back either for speculative purposes or because of lack of transportation facilities should go to the markets, and if large stocks of merchandise should be reduced, the resultant release of credit would have a most beneficial effect upon the general situation. . . .

While the problem of credit regulation and control is national and even international in its scope, yet in the last analysis it is merely an aggregation of individual problems, and the proper working-out of the situation must depend upon the public and upon the banks which deal with the public. The public must be made to realize the necessity of economy in expenditures and in consequent demands for banking credit.

The banks themselves are best able to impress the importance of this policy upon the public. The Federal Reserve Banks may be depended upon to do their duty to the member banks and the public, but to accomplish results the banks and the public must do their part in accelerating the processes of production and distribution and in restricting waste and extravagance.

In the discussion which followed, the directors of the Federal Reserve Banks described conditions in their respective districts. After the bank directors had concluded their remarks, other members of the Board, including Mr. Miller and Mr. Williams, expressed their views. Mr. Miller said in part:

Sometimes on occasions of this kind you want a word or a phrase upon which to hang things, and I was struck in the course of deliberations this morning with the frequent occurrence of the word 'discrimination.' I think the country will accept that as on the whole indicating a temperate and responsible attitude on the part of the Federal Reserve System and member banks of the country in dealing with this problem, and on the whole that is the one thing that would seem to me worth specifying as a general objective in any report a committee of this conference might make in the way of a recommendation to the Federal Reserve Board as to what in its opinion must be done to handle conditions successfully in this country so as not to dampen the ardor of enterprise, not to throw any chill over industry, but also with the constant suggestion that banks are to use such influence as they have to restrain the unproductive use of credit, applying the test of unproductiveness under existing conditions and not under normal conditions, and to restrain the reign of extravagance.

I have no hesitation in saying for myself that I do not feel at all optimistic about the outlook. I do not for a moment expect that we are going to deflate in this country, and I think we are only deceiving ourselves if we talk about deflation. We must, however, arrest the rate of growth of credit, and we must expect that, with the swell in the productive activities of the country that come with the approaching crop season, there will be a natural swell in the volume of credit, which need not alarm us. . . .

As I see it, beyond that the problem is to present this in such a way to the bankers of the country as will secure their coöperation, and with their aid also to present it to the user of credit. After all, credit is given only as somebody wants credit, and to a certain extent our problem is to restrict the appetite for credit, and it is not the banker that borrows credit, or, if he borrows it from the Reserve Banks, he borrows it only as the first step in the process of lending credit to somebody else. Eventually, it is the user of credit that has got to be brought into a more or less responsive and acquiescent attitude in this policy of control. . . .

I come back to the word 'discrimination' in the extension of credit, as on the whole pointing the way toward the road that we have got to travel, and perhaps in some parts of the country even blaze, in order to get back to the situation that the Governor very happily described this morning as the restoring of a more normal relationship between the total volume of credit in existence and the total volume of production. I would amend it only in one particular, the production of those things that people who care for the country, who are sensitive to the requirements of the times, and who are willing to coöperate in a great national endeavor will not quarrel with the production of things that immediately are more important, and the postponement of things that for the moment are less important.

The following extracts are from remarks made by Mr. Williams:

Mr. Chairman, and gentlemen, I do not know that I have anything special to add to the very excellent presentation of the whole subject which you gave this morning, which was supplemented by the various speakers who have preceded me.

There are one or two aspects of the situation, however, to which I think I would like to direct your attention especially. You have been speaking of extravagance and the production of non-essentials and luxuries. It seems to me it would be very helpful if every bank in the country should constitute itself a missionary for thrift and saving and try to urge upon the workers, upon the laboring people, and upon those whose incomes have been swollen, the importance of laying up for the rainy day and for old age. It seems to me, with the large wages that are being paid now in industrial establishments, that it offers a splendid opportunity for you to increase and build up the savings deposits in your banks. I was very much disgusted the other day to hear of my chauffeur buying about three silk shirts at ten dollars apiece. . . .

I think that, when these individual cases of extravagance and luxury come to our attention, if we should call the attention of the spendthrifts to the importance of starting a savings account, it would be helpful. It seems to me that the banks could very well afford to do some little additional advertising in behalf of thrift and saving, and appeal to the laborers, who are getting more now in their daily wages than they ever dreamed of in the years gone by.

One difficulty of the present situation is that the conditions of which we complain in this country are world-wide. We have not simply to remedy things within our four borders, but they are overlapping in all the civilized and uncivilized countries. . . .

I do think it is tremendously important that every individual bank, besides being a missionary for thrift, should each admonish and warn and hold the strings of their money-bags with a very discriminating hand, and should bring about a proper and reasonable degree of contraction. I think my friend, Doctor Miller, expressed the view of the meeting yesterday, that he was not very hopeful of our ability to bring about much contraction — about as far as he went was to desire and hope that we should not inflate any further. I think, though, that we should go further; I think we should, and must, bring about a reasonable degree of deflation or contraction. . . .

My parting word is to urge that the member banks keep themselves in solid condition and lean as little as possible upon the Federal Reserve Banks, and that the member banks do not undertake to make their loans year in and year out, or month in and month out, except on unusual calls and in emergency cases, from the Federal Reserve System. I am reminded, in conclusion, of the hopeful and reassuring lines of the old hymn:

'Ye fearful saints fresh courage take;
The clouds ye so much dread
Are rich in mercies and shall fall
In blessings on your head.'

There was a general agreement with the views expressed in my address, and a resolution was adopted approving the sentiments expressed by me as representing the views of the Federal Reserve Board. It was further resolved, 'that the bankers here assembled believe that the widest publicity should be given the address, and that they hereby agree to abide by the spirit of the address in the conduct of their own affairs, and that they will encourage its general adoption by the bankers and people of our country.'

The effect of the transportation situation upon the credit situation was generally remarked, and there was a disposition to attribute much of the continued heavy demand for credit to unsettled conditions in transportation. A resolution was adopted stressing the need for increasing transportation facilities, and this resolution was presented by a committee of five directors on May 19th to the Interstate Commerce Commission and to the Shipping Board.

Toward the close of the conference there was some discussion of the possibility of a further advance in discount rates and of the effect which might be expected. It had always been the policy of the Federal Reserve Board, and has continued to be up to the present time, to discourage any

public discussion by Federal Reserve Bank officers and directors of possible changes in discount rates, and, as the conference was about to adjourn, I cautioned those present to re-
frain from making any statements which might give the impression that a further advance in rates was in contemplation. It was not certain that the rates would be advanced,
and it was obvious that any public discussion of the possibility by any member of the conference would have a dis-
quieting effect without producing any good result. The records show that, exclusive of members of the Federal Reserve
Board, there were forty-nine persons present at the conference, representing every Federal Reserve District. The suggestion made in my concluding remarks that nothing be said
about possible changes in discount rates has been seized upon
by one of the Board's most irreconcilable critics as conclu-
sive evidence of a design that those present at the meeting
should profit from advance information which was to be
withheld from the general public. As a matter of fact,
no one at the conference was in a position to know that
any changes whatever would be made. Changes in discount rates must first be proposed by the directors of a
Federal Reserve Bank, and to become effective must be approved by the Federal Reserve Board. It was manifestly
desirable that the impressions created upon the public mind
by the conference should be reassuring rather than alarming,
and, as it had always been the policy of the Board not to
discuss discount rates with representatives of the press, it
seemed to me advisable to call the attention of the bankers
present to this fact. My remarks at this conference, which
were unanimously endorsed by those present, did not suggest or indicate any change in the policy which the Federal
Reserve Board had followed consistently for several months.
In fact, my remarks were based upon and followed closely
a statement made by me in opening the conference which
was held by the Board on January 6, 1920, with bankers representing twenty-five clearing-house associations through-

out the country. This statement, which was given to the press on that day, outlined clearly the policy of the Board and appeared in leading newspapers throughout the country.

As an evidence of the state of the public mind at this time, mention should be made of a resolution offered by Senator McCormick, of Illinois, and adopted by the Senate of the United States on May 17, 1920 (the day before the conference was held), which reads as follows:

Resolved: that the Federal Reserve Board be directed to advise the Senate what steps it purposes to take or to recommend to the member banks of the Federal Reserve System to meet the existing inflation of currency and credits, and consequent high prices; and what steps it purposes to take or recommend to mobilize credits in order to move the 1920 crop.

In offering this resolution, Senator McCormick no doubt was influenced by complaints which were then coming in from all quarters regarding the high cost of living.

Some months later, after commodity prices had declined as a result of world-wide reaction, he was reproached by some for having, through the resolution which the Senate adopted at his instance, incited the Board to put into effect 'a murderous deflation policy.' The Board did not put such a policy into effect and never considered doing so, but, in justice to the memory of the late Senator McCormick, it is only fair to state that his resolution had no bearing upon the policies of the Board, which had already been developed, and its adoption by the Senate on the day before the conference with the Federal Advisory Council and the 'Class A' directors was merely a coincidence. The Board in response to this resolution called attention to the conference which had been held and incorporated the substance of my address to the conference. In this letter to the Senate the Board went on to say:

The Board feels assured that the banks of the country now realize the necessity of more conservatism in extending credits and of a reasonable reduction in the volume of credits now outstanding. The Board will not hesitate, so far as it may be necessary, to bring to bear all its statutory powers in regulating the volume of credit, but wishes to point out that the more vital problems relating to the movement of the 1920 crop are physical rather than financial.

This was the unanimous view of those present at the conference on the 18th instant, at which the following resolution was adopted:

The whole country is suffering from inflation of prices with the consequent inflation of credit. From reports made by the members of this conference, representing every section of the country, it is obvious that great sums are tied up in products which if marketed would relieve necessity, tend to reduce the price-level, and relieve the strain on our credit system.

This congestion of freight is found in practically all of the large railroad centers and shipping ports. It arises chiefly from inadequate transportation facilities available at this time and is seriously crippling business. We are informed that the per-ton-mile of freight increased in three years — 1916, 1917, and 1918 — 47 per cent, while the freight cars in service during the same period increased 1.9 per cent.

A striking necessity exists which can only be relieved through the upbuilding of the credit of the railroads. This must come through adequate and prompt increase in freight rates. Any delay means the paying of greater cost directly and indirectly, and places a burden on the credit system which in the approaching time for seasonal expansion may cause abnormal strain. Even under the load of war inflation, high price-level, and extravagances the bank reserves would probably be sufficient if quick transportation could be assured during the time of the greatest strain.

Therefore be it resolved: That this conference urge as the most important remedies that the Interstate Commerce Commission and the United States Shipping Board give increased rates and adequate facilities such immediate effect as may be warranted under their authority, and that a committee of five, representing the various sections of the country, be appointed by the Chairman to present this resolution to the Interstate Commerce Commission and the United States Shipping Board with such verbal presentation as may seem appropriate to the committee.

On May 10th, President Wilson sent to the Senate the name of the Honorable Edmund Platt, of New York, Chairman of the House Banking and Currency Committee, to be a member of the Federal Reserve Board, and the nomination was confirmed on May 28th. Mr. Platt who was designated by the President as Vice-Governor of the Board, was appointed to fill the unexpired term of Mr. Albert Strauss, of New York, who had resigned on March 15th.

In order to approximate market conditions more nearly, the directors of some of the Federal Reserve Banks voted during the latter part of May to increase their discount rates. These increases as approved by the Board brought the rate on paper secured by Treasury certificates of indebtedness up to five and a half per cent at eight of the banks, while on such paper Boston, Kansas City, and Dallas still maintained a five per cent rate, and San Francisco a rate of five and a quarter per cent. The rate on paper secured by Liberty bonds and Victory notes was advanced to six per cent at New York, Richmond, Chicago, and Minneapolis, to five and three quarters per cent at Cleveland and San Francisco, and the other banks maintained a rate of five and a half per cent. The rate on commercial paper, and on agricultural and live-stock paper, was advanced at this time to seven per cent at New York, Chicago, and Minneapolis; and soon afterwards the rate at the Federal Reserve Bank of Boston was advanced to seven per cent on commercial and agricultural paper. A few changes were made in the rates on paper secured by Treasury certificates of indebtedness and by Liberty bonds and Victory notes, bringing them up to a maximum of six per cent at six of the banks. These rates were the highest ever maintained by the Federal Reserve Banks, but compare with a minimum rate of eight per cent in effect at the Bank of England during this period.

Because of the low reserve percentage of the banks and of the constant tendency of balances to shift from one Federal Reserve District to another, it had become necessary in 1919 to resort to large and frequent rediscount transactions between the Federal Reserve Banks themselves. Such transactions increased both in frequency and in volume during the year 1920 and continued in a smaller degree for several months in 1921. During the year 1920 the total of the rediscount transactions and sales of bills between Federal Reserve Banks amounted to $3,672,792,000. By far the larger part of the accommodation given in this way to other Federal Reserve Banks during the year was extended by the Federal Reserve Bank of Boston ($1,000,557,000) by the Federal Reserve Bank of Philadelphia ($758,875,000) and by the Federal Reserve Bank of Cleveland ($1,478,882,000). The banks to which the larger part of this accommodation was extended were: Richmond, $700,000,000; Atlanta, $307,997,000; Chicago, $283,178,000; St. Louis, $315,499,000; Minneapolis, $293,500,000; Kansas City, $411,636,000; and Dallas, $436,013,000.

The net balances due lending Federal Reserve Banks by borrowing Federal Reserve Banks on account of notes and bills rediscounted at the close of each calendar month during the year were as follows:

January	$114,460,000	July	$148,704,000
February	106,156,000	August	215,455,000
March	96,480,000	September	250,296,000
April	163,084,000	October	260,440,000
May	148,552,000	November	168,435,000
June	126,167,000	December	122,174,000

Rediscounts between Federal Reserve Banks can be made only by consent of the Federal Reserve Board, which is authorized by law to permit, or, upon the affirmative vote of five members, to compel, a Federal Reserve Bank to rediscount for another. The banks, however, showed such a spirit of coöperation that no compulsion was ever necessary, although there were times when at least one of the banks (Cleveland) was rediscounting larger amounts for other Federal Reserve Banks than it was for its own member banks. No application of a Federal Reserve Bank for rediscount accommodation was ever declined.

Much has been said in the halls of Congress and elsewhere of the 'murderous deflation' alleged to have taken place during the year 1920. As far as the Federal Reserve System was concerned, there was no contraction of credit or currency during that year. On the contrary, there was a substantial increase during the year both in the amount of bills discounted and of Federal Reserve notes in circulation, as will be shown by the following table:

FEDERAL RESERVE NOTE CIRCULATION AND BILL HOLDINGS OF THE TWELVE FEDERAL RESERVE BANKS COMBINED

(In thousands of dollars — ooo omitted)

DATE, 1920	FEDERAL RESERVE NOTE CIRCULATION	BILLS DISCOUNTED	BILLS BOUGHT IN OPEN MARKET
January 30.............	$2,850,944	$2,174,357	$561,313
February 27............	3,019,984	2,453,511	531,367
March 26..............	3,048,039	2,449,230	451,879
April 30...............	3,074,555	2,535,071	407,247
May 28................	3,107,021	2,519,431	418,600
June 25...............	3,116,718	2,431,794	399,185
July 30................	3,120,138	2,491,630	345,305
August 27.............	3,203,637	2,667,127	321,965
September 24..........	3,279,996	2,704,464	307,624
October 29............	3,351,303	2,801,297	298,375
November 26..........	3,325,538	2,735,400	247,703
December 30..........	3,344,686	2,719,134	255,702

It has been shown in the preceding pages that all advances in Federal Reserve discount rates took place before July 1st, and that the most marked advances were made before March 1st. It is interesting, therefore, in considering the effect of these advances upon prices, to note the price trend throughout the year of the three great agricultural staples, wheat, corn, and cotton. Accordingly, there is inserted here a table giving quotations upon these commodities on or about the 15th and the last day of each month throughout the year.

It will be seen that material advances in all three of these staples occurred after the discount rates had been advanced in February, and that there were no substantial or continued declines in the prices of any of them until the new crops began to come upon the market. On October 31st, wheat was

Quotations on Wheat, Corn, and Cotton on or about the Fifteenth and the Last Day of Each Month in 1920

Date	Wheat — No. 1 Northern Minneapolis (cash)			Corn — No. 3 Chicago (cash)			Cotton Middling — New Orleans (spot)
January 15..		*2.215		1.48	to	1.50	.40.25
31..		*2.215			1.515		.39.88
February 15..		*2.215		1.475	to	1.49	.39.25
29..		*2.215		1.48	to	1.49	.40.25
March 15..		*2.215		1.55	to	1.575	.41.00
31..	2.85	to	3.00	1.65	to	1.66	.41.00
April 15..	2.95	to	3.05		1.68		.41.50
30..	3.05	to	3.15	1.80	to	1.83	.41.25
May 15..	3.15	to	3.20	2.14	to	2.16	.40.25
31..	2.95	to	3.10	1.88	to	1.90	.40.00
June 15..	2.90	to	3.00	1.825	to	1.85	.40.75
30..	2.80	to	2.85	1.76	to	1.77	.39.50
July 15..	2.90	to	3.00	1.53	to	1.55	.39.00
31..	2.35	to	2.40	1.45	to	1.455	.38.75
August 15..	2.65	to	2.75	1.595	to	1.60	.35.00
31..	2.45	to	2.52		1.50		.29.50
September 15..	2.53625	to	2.60625		1.3675		.28.50
30..	2.255	to	2.355	1.255	to	1.28	.23.00
October 15..	2.2525	to	2.2825	.94	to	.945	.20.25
31..	2.0825	to	2.1325	.885	to	.895	.20.50
November 15..	1.775	to	1.825		.84		.18.25
30..	1.46875	to	1.50875	.725	to	.73	.15.25
December 15..	1.57125	to	1.61125	.73	to	.74	.14.75
31..	1.7025	to	1.7425	.73	to	.74	.13.50

* Government price.

still above $2.00 a bushel. On August 31st, corn was still around $1.50 a bushel, and did not fall below $1.00 until October. Cotton was 40¾ cents a pound as late as June 15th; 35 cents on August 15th; 28½ cents on September 15th, and did not fall below 20 cents until after October 31st. The large volume of unsold stocks of these commodities carried over from 1919 had much to do with the drastic decline which followed the harvesting of crops in 1920. In the case of cotton, on July 31st, the end of the cotton year, the carry-over was about 5,000,000 bales, and the new American crop, 13,400,000 bales, was the second largest ever produced. This amount of American cotton was too much for the world market and a drastic decline in price was inevitable.

On September 20th, Mr. D. C. Wills, Federal Reserve Agent at the Cleveland Bank, was given a recess appointment as a member of the Board by President Wilson to fill the vacancy occasioned by the retirement of Mr. Henry A. Moehlenpah, whose term had expired on August 9th. This appointment was made under section 10 of the Federal Reserve Act, which provided that 'the President shall have power to fill all vacancies that may happen on the Federal Reserve Board during the recess of the Senate by granting commissions which shall expire thirty days after the next session of the Senate convenes.' The commission which the President first gave to Mr. Wills limited his tenure of office to conform to this requirement. As the Senate was to convene on December 4th, this would have made the term of Mr. Wills expire on January 3, 1921. While Mr. Wills was unwilling to accept an appointment for the full term of ten years, he had expressed his willingness to serve until a permanent appointment could be made. The paragraph from section 10 of the Federal Reserve Act which has just been quoted does not conform to the Constitution of the United States, which provides that, in filling vacancies which may occur during the recess of the Senate, the President may grant commissions which shall expire with the next session of the Senate. Upon being apprised of this fact, President Wilson sent Mr. Wills a new commission which extended his term until March 4th. The Act of June 3, 1922, amended the Federal Reserve Act in this particular to conform to the constitutional provision.

CHAPTER XV

DURING the summer of 1920, the Presidential election campaign was in progress. Members of the Board were urged by some political leaders to bring about a reduction in discount rates, and the suggestion was made to me that a rate as low as three per cent would be popular and therefore desirable. The Board, however, not being influenced by purely political considerations, agreed with the view of Reserve Bank directors that conditions warranted no reduction.

Because of my residence in a Southern State, there were many in the South who felt that I should do something to protect the price of cotton. Some of my correspondents, apparently overlooking the fact that I was not the entire Federal Reserve Board, and was not omnipotent, urged me to issue a statement calling attention to the intrinsic value of cotton, to its importance as an article of export, to the high cost of producing it, and to urge upon banks generally that they should make liberal advances on warehouse receipts for cotton, with the assurance that the Federal Reserve Banks would discount freely such paper when offered by member banks. At a conference which the Board held in Washington in September with representatives of cotton producers, it was pointed out that should the Board issue such a statement it would be called upon to issue a similar statement respecting wool, wheat, corn, and other commodities, to say nothing of manufactured products. Such a statement would be likely to defeat its purpose because it would advertise the weakness of the market position of the commodity affected. Comparatively few banks would be influenced by such a suggestion. Prudent bankers always consider their liability as endorsers of rediscounted paper, and in making loans have regard to their own safety. All bankers knew that the Federal Reserve Board had nothing to do with the actual rediscounting of paper, and it was a matter of public knowledge that the Federal Reserve Banks in the South were already heavy borrowers from other Federal Reserve Banks. It was my belief, in the circumstances then existing, that any attempt to enlist banking support for any particular commodity by a statement to the press would be unwise, and that any advances made would be on a very low basis of valuation. This would tend to lower the market price so that it would approximate the loan valuation; a result which followed the formation of the cotton loan pool in the autumn of 1914. I suggested that it would be much better to let the situation, unpromising as the outlook seemed to be, work itself out in a natural way, as I was assured that the Federal Reserve Banks were doing, and would continue to do, everything in their power to aid, and I expressed the belief that the member banks would be in position to function more effectively if nothing were done which might create a panicky feeling. Unfortunately, no stenographic record was made of the proceedings of this conference, but those who participated in it expressed themselves at the time as being satisfied with the position taken by the Board, and some of them in newspaper interviews so expressed themselves. However, within a few months I was charged with having brought about the drastic decline in the price of cotton which had occurred, and with causing the ruin of thousands of cotton farmers and merchants throughout the South. One chronic senatorial fault-finder charged me with being a traitor to my section, and to substantiate the charge said that I had it in my power to prevent the price of cotton from falling below thirty cents. He stated that I could have advised member banks to loan at this figure and could have compelled Federal Reserve Banks to rediscount the notes, and that had I done this the market could not have declined

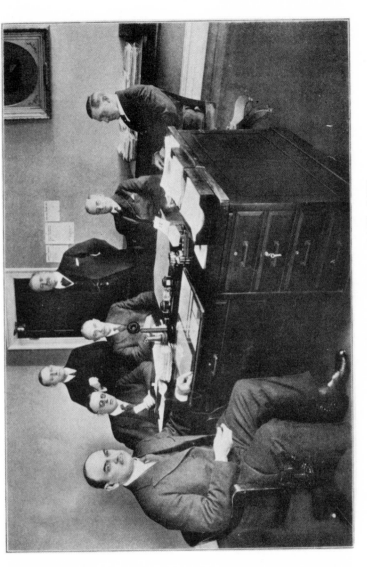

THE FEDERAL RESERVE BOARD, 1920

Left to right: David F. Houston, W. P. G. Harding, Charles S. Hamlin, Edmund Platt, John Skelton Williams, D. C. Wills, A. C. Miller

below thirty cents; for who would sell his cotton for less when he could borrow at that figure? The cotton mills, thus, not being able to buy cotton below thirty cents, would have been compelled to pay that price or more for their cotton, and in this way the market price would have been stabilized!

On December 7th at the invitation of the officers of the American Farm Bureau Federation, I addressed the annual meeting of that organization at Indianapolis. In my remarks there I reviewed the banking situation and incorporated the substance of some of the statements I had made at the Washington Cotton Conference in September. This address to farmers will be found in Appendix C, page 284.

During the autumn of 1920 some rather insistent requests were made of the Board for a ruling defining as eligible for rediscount certain classes of paper which, in the opinion of the Board's counsel, could not be admitted under the terms of section 13 of the Federal Reserve Act. Representatives of firms engaged in the cotton factorage business appeared before the Board in October, and urged that the Board rescind the ruling which it had made twelve months before under advice of counsel, that notes of cotton factors, when issued or drawn for the purpose of obtaining funds to lend to others, were not eligible under the terms of the Federal Reserve Act for rediscount by a Federal Reserve Bank. In issuing that ruling, however, the Board stated also that the mere fact that the maker of the note was a cotton factor did not of itself render the note ineligible; and that in cases where a cotton factor had the status of a merchant, and had borrowed money to make payments for cotton actually purchased by him, his note was eligible, because the proceeds were used for a commercial purpose. At a later date the Board had pointed out also that, where a cotton factor took a note from a customer to whom he was making advances, such note would be eligible for rediscount if the proceeds were used by the customer for a commercial or agricultural purpose. The

Board with two dissenting votes declined to rescind or modify this ruling, and the charge has been made that its refusal to do so forced upon the market hundreds of thousands of bales of cotton which otherwise could have been carried over. It has never been shown, however, that any appreciable amount of cotton was affected by the Board's ruling. The Federal Reserve Banks had never held at any one time previous to the Board's ruling in October, 1919, more than fifty thousand dollars of cotton factors' paper of the kind declared ineligible by that ruling, and no evidence was ever presented to the Board to show that the ruling affected the ability of cotton factors to obtain credit. Fifty years ago the cotton factorage business was far more extensive than it is to-day. The development of local transportation facilities, the establishment of banks in practically all towns in the cotton belt, and the direct dealings of local merchants with the farmers, have operated to reduce to a very great extent the business of cotton factors and to circumscribe their field of operations. At the present time the larger part of the cotton factorage business is transacted in New Orleans, Memphis, Savannah, and Augusta.

In a conversation with Senator McKellar, of Tennessee, whose home is in Memphis, I suggested that, in order to meet the wishes of the Memphis cotton factors that their notes be declared eligible for rediscount, it would be necessary to amend the law; and at his request I drafted for him a bill which provided that 'the notes, drafts, and bills of exchange of factors issued as such making advances exclusively to producers of staple agricultural products in their raw state shall be eligible for such discount.' In January, 1922, Senator McKellar offered this bill from the floor of the Senate on a day when several other bills amending the Federal Reserve Act, and offered in the same way, were adopted; but at that time he failed to secure a majority vote for his bill. It was, however, adopted later on in the session, following a favorable recommendation by the Committee on Banking and Currency, and is now a part of section 13 of the Federal Reserve Act.

When the Sixty-Sixth Congress reconvened in December, 1920, for its final session, the effect upon its temper of the marked decline in commodity prices which had taken place was at once apparent. The Federal Reserve Board which in May had been blamed for having permitted inflation and high prices, was now denounced for having caused deflation and falling prices. The activities of Congress were immediately directed to the consideration of measures designed to relieve the credit situation in general, and agricultural conditions particularly.

In his annual report, the Secretary of the Treasury, in referring to discontinuance of the activities of the War Finance Corporation, said:

... Producers whose products could not be satisfactorily marketed and whose prices were falling demanded that the Treasury intervene. They asked either that it deposit money in certain sections or that the activities of the War Finance Corporation be resumed. Neither of these things was feasible. The Treasury had no money to lend and no money to deposit except for Government purposes. It is not in the banking business and should not be. It is borrowing money periodically to meet current obligations at a cost of about six per cent. ... Furthermore, the War Finance Corporation was a war agency and was created to help win the war. It was clearly desirable that war agencies should cease to function as quickly as possible. The only power of the Corporation which had any possible bearing on the situation is one which was inserted after the Armistice with a particular possible state of facts in view. Fearing that, with the cessation of exports for military purposes after the Armistice, exports might not go forward, Congress empowered the Corporation, in order to promote commerce with foreign nations, to make advances under certain conditions. The War Finance Corporation had no money of its own. It or the Treasury would have had to borrow the money and borrow it at a cost of about six per cent.

In a hearing before the Joint Committee on Agriculture shortly before Congress reassembled, Secretary Houston reiterated and amplified this statement. Nevertheless, during the first two weeks of the session a resolution was adopted by both Houses of Congress authorizing and directing the War Finance Corporation to resume its activities. This resolution was vetoed by the President, but was passed again, over his veto, and thus became law. At the same time, in response to demands for a general relaxation of credit, a bill was introduced in the Senate to fix the maximum rate of interest or discount which Federal Reserve Banks could charge at five per cent per annum. This bill was referred to the Banking and Currency Committee of the Senate, and a copy was sent by the Chairman of that committee to the Federal Reserve Board with a request for an expression of its opinion. In its reply dated December 16th, the Board referred to the fact that, prior to the year 1834, a similar limitation had been imposed upon the Bank of England with disastrous consequences, which had compelled the removal of the limitation; and went on to say:

The Federal Reserve Board desires to put itself on record as unalterably opposed to this bill or to any bill which in any way attempts to limit the power now vested in it and in the Federal Reserve Banks to regulate the rates of discount which those banks may charge. . . . In conclusion, and by way of summary, if this bill should become a law it is the Board's firm belief that the Federal Reserve Banks would find it impossible while functioning in a normal way to protect their gold reserves, that the Federal Reserve System would within a very short time cease to be in any sense a reserve system, and would become a mere instrument for the acceleration and perpetuation of expansion, and that a wholesale scramble for the funds of the Federal Reserve Banks would ensue which would leave those banks only two alternatives — one, to lend their funds at the rate prescribed until the exhaustion of their reserves had been completed, and the other to fix a definite limit upon their total volume of loans, thus adopting a rigid system of credit rationing. In the one case they would reach a point where they would be unable to make further rediscounts, no matter how insistent or meritorious the demands might be, and in the other they would find it necessary to place all applications for discount accommodations on a waiting list until repayment of prior loans made new funds available.

This bill failed to pass, and a similar bill was defeated in the succeeding Congress.

Meanwhile, pressure was being brought to bear upon the Board for a reduction in discount rates. Perhaps the directors of the respective Federal Reserve Banks were likewise urged to submit lower rates to the Federal Reserve Board for its approval, but as to this I have no knowledge. No Federal Reserve Bank, however, during the final months of 1920 and the early months of 1921, requested the Federal Reserve Board to approve a downward revision of its rates. On the contrary, all Reserve Banks took the position that the maintenance of existing rates was necessary. During the month of December current open-market rates for prime commercial paper, running from thirty days to six months, were generally, at all financial centers, eight per cent, with occasional quotations ranging from six and a half to seven and three quarters per cent. At the same time commercial banks in the larger cities in all districts reported on customers' paper, maturing from thirty to ninety days, minimum rates of six per cent and maximum rates of eight per cent, except in two Western cities where maximum rates of nine and ten per cent were reported. A few cities located in States which had rigid usury laws reported maximum and minimum rates of six per cent.

The accompanying table (see page 194) taken from consolidated statements of the twelve Federal Reserve Banks shows the position of the Federal Reserve Banks on December 30, 1920, as compared with their position on December 26, 1919.

These figures show conclusively that there was no contraction of currency during the year 1920. On the other hand, there was an increase of $188,000,000 in the amount of money in actual circulation. The total loans and advances of the Federal Reserve Banks also showed a substan-

PRINCIPAL ITEMS IN CONSOLIDATED STATEMENT OF
FEDERAL RESERVE BANKS [1]

(In thousands of dollars — 000 omitted)

	December 26, 1919	December 30, 1920
Total gold reserves....................	$2,078,342	$2,059,333
Total gross deposits.	2,779,570	2,321,417
Federal Reserve notes in actual circulation	3,057,646	3,344,686
Rediscounts with other Federal Reserve Banks.............................	40,615	115,257
Bankers' acceptances sold other Federal Reserve Banks	69,899	6,917
Bills discounted, secured by Government obligations........................	1,510,364	1,141,036
All other.............................	684,514	1,578,098
Bills bought in open market............	585,212	255,702
Investments:		
United States Government bonds......	26,834	26,859
United States Victory notes...........	64,000	69,000
United States certificates of indebtedness.............................	273,507	261,263

	January 1, 1920	January 1, 1921
General stock of money in the United States	$7,961,320,139	$8,372,970,904
of which there was held outside the United States Treasury and Federal Reserve System	5,312,009,003	5,500,702,153
Per capita	$49.81	$51.29

[1] From United States Treasury statements.

tial increase during the year. The reduction of $330,000,000 in the amount of bills bought in the open market was attributable mainly to the decline in the volume of foreign trade. The reduction of $360,000,000 in the amount of advances made by Federal Reserve Banks on notes secured by Government obligations indicates that Government securities were being absorbed by permanent investors. These reductions were more than offset by an increase of more than $893,000,000 of commercial and agricultural paper rediscounted by the banks. The decrease of $458,000,000 in the total gross deposits reflects, of course, a much greater decrease in the deposits of member banks, whose increased borrowings, however, show that their loans had not been reduced in proportion to the decline in deposits.

During the month of January, 1921, it appeared to the Board — or at least to a majority of its members — that there were some signs of improvement in the situation. The crops were moving with greater freedom, the borrowings of Federal Reserve Banks were being reduced, and the cash reserves of the Federal Reserve Banks were increasing. It seemed an opportune time to stress the favorable factors in the situation with a view of developing a more confident and optimistic spirit. Attention was called to the fact that the banks of the country generally had responded to the urgent needs of those dependent upon them for credit accommodations, and, while exercising care and discretion in making new loans, had not resorted to precipitate or drastic means of forcing collections. It was pointed out that there had been no deflation for the sake of deflation, but that, with the passing of the era of reckless extravagance, undue expansion had been checked. The Federal Reserve System, which had shown its ability to assimilate credits in ever-increasing volume in order to meet the requirements of a great producing country in time of war, had during the past year shown its ability to absorb the shock of sudden reaction and had prevented a money panic such as hitherto had always occurred after periods of extraordinary expansion. It was pointed out that the reserve position, the inherent strength of the Federal Reserve Banks, had so much improved that no apprehension need be felt that the Federal Reserve System could not continue to render effective aid in stabilizing the general banking situation.

There were some, however, who felt that the most pressing need was a lower rate at the Federal Reserve Banks, without which there could be no improvement, and with which they seemed to think there would be an immediate revival.

Senator Owen, who had early in the year 1920 written two

letters to the Board protesting against an advance in rates, wrote again on November 18th a letter to which wide publicity was given. As Chairman of the Senate Committee on Banking and Currency, he had taken a prominent part in the framing and passage of the Federal Reserve Act, and because of this fact the views expressed in his letters to the Board were given more consideration and publicity than would have been accorded similar views from a less prominent source! There was certainly a wide difference of opinion between Senator Owen and a majority of the members of the Federal Reserve Board as to the relation of the Board to the Federal Reserve Banks, and as to the functions of the Federal Reserve Banks, which under the law can have no direct dealings with the public, but can only make loans and advances to their member banks in the manner prescribed in section 13 of the Federal Reserve Act. The Board was not inclined to accept as correct many of the dicta in the Senator's letter, nor did it regard as logical the conclusions drawn from them.

Senator Owen began his letter by saying:

I wish to again appeal to you and to the Federal Reserve Board to lower the rates of interest charged by the Federal Reserve Banks, and expand the loans of the Federal Reserve Banks to the extent which may be required for purposes of legitimate production and distribution. American banks are justified in charging six and seven per cent, because they pay two and three per cent for deposits, and they are entitled to make a profit of two and three per cent above their overhead charges on the deposits which they handle as merchants of credit. . . . The Federal Reserve Banks under these high interest rates are measurably destabilizing credits and promoting industrial depression under the arbitrary high interest rates which the Reserve Banks are charging. If the Reserve Banks would be content with the same margin of profit in interest rates which the average bank of the country obtains, they would be charging a rate of between three and four per cent.

Senator Owen protested against the Board's alleged policy of indiscriminate deflation and the refusal of credit to legitimate industries, which, he said, 'the Reserve Banks can well afford to make to whatever extent required by the country.' In order to demonstrate this he pointed out that:

The Bank of England has outstanding 139,920,000 pounds sterling in Bank of England notes secured by 121,420,010 pounds of gold held in trust by the Issue Department of the Bank of England for the benefit of the noteholders, together with 18,500,000 pounds of Government debt, and other securities so that the Bank of England notes, though not underwritten by the British Government, are secured up to one hundred per cent. However, under the need for the economical use of gold, public opinion and the Government of Great Britain sustains the Bank of England in refusing to redeem its notes in gold just as the Bradbury notes are not redeemed in gold. England is not on a gold basis. Last Saturday gold was selling in London per ounce at 121 shillings and 11 pence (par value 85 shillings per ounce). In other words, gold was at a premium of forty-five per cent in London, while selling at par in New York. This explains why the paper pound sterling in New York is selling on the Exchange around $3.35 per pound.

The Treasury notes of the British Government issued for currency have behind them thirteen per cent of gold, and are not redeemable in gold.

The Bank of England notes are not redeemable in gold, as a matter of fact. . . .

The deposits of the Bank of England have a cash reserve running from ten to fourteen per cent in Bank of England notes, including about one per cent of actual gold. The Bank of England can command gold, nevertheless, and is not *alarmed*. . . .

If the Federal Reserve notes were issued up to the thirteen per cent reserve of the Bradbury notes, the $2,100,000,000 of gold would sustain Federal Reserve notes equal to $16,155,000,000, or an expansion of credit equal to over $12,000,000,000.

The Board had never sought to interfere with or to influence the Federal Reserve Banks in the proper exercise of those statutory powers which were conferred solely upon them, and the discount rates in effect had been approved by the Board after they had been proposed by the directors of the Federal Reserve Banks. The demands made upon the banks for accommodations were so heavy that many of them, in order to maintain their required reserves, were redis-counting with other Federal Reserve Banks. It is true, as Senator Owen said in his letter, that the law made provision for a reduction of these reserves below the normal minimum, and it is probable, had the war continued another year, that the Board might have been obliged to avail itself of this pro-vision. It is probable also that it would have been necessary to do so had the discount rates not been advanced early in 1920. The banking conditions in England, as described in Senator Owen's letter, were not brought about as a deliber-ate choice of the British Government and the Bank of Eng-land, but were the result of war-time necessities. While pro-testing against the Federal Reserve Bank rates of six to seven per cent, Senator Owen took no exception to the eight per cent rate of the Bank of England which bank he held up to us as an example. During recent years we have seen in various European countries that there is such a thing as the flight of capital. This has taken place in Germany, in France, and at times even in England; and as long as certain unfavorable conditions, such as currency inflation, unbalanced budgets, unscientific income taxation, and agitation for a capital levy, continue, the flight of capital cannot be checked merely by oratory, nor by appeals to the people to have confidence in their country, in its money, and in its govern-ment. The United States had been maintaining a free gold market since June, 1919. Reference has already been made to the large volume of gold exports during the months which immediately followed the removal of the gold embargo, and while in November, 1920, it seemed that other nations were no longer in a position to draw gold from the United States, there was still a possibility that we might experience in this country a flight of capital, not to other countries, but to strong boxes and to various hiding-places. Lack of confi-dence in banks causes depositors to withdraw funds and to put their money in hoarding. There were indications, as an analysis of bank statements will show, that large amounts were being hoarded during the period under review. As long as the money hoarded was in the form of paper currency, the stability of the Federal Reserve Banks was not materially affected; but what would have been the result had the hoarded money been gold or gold certificates? Senator Owen in his letter, although commenting favorably upon the British banking situation, stated that Bank of England notes were no longer being redeemed in gold, and that although the British banks were abundantly protected by public opinion and by the support of the British Government behind the Bradbury notes, and that while public opinion and the British Government sustained the Bank of England in refusing to redeem its notes in gold, there was a premium on gold in London of forty-five per cent, while it was selling at par in New York.

The Federal Reserve Banks had outstanding at this time more than $3,300,000,000 of Federal Reserve notes. The law requires that these notes be redeemed on demand in gold or lawful money at any Federal Reserve Bank, and in gold at the Treasury in Washington. The banks and the Treasury were complying with the law and were redeeming Federal Reserve notes in gold whenever called upon to do so. Had the reserves of the Federal Reserve Banks, in the pursuance of the cheaper credit policy advocated by Senator Owen, fallen below the legal minimum, what assurance was there that holders of Federal Reserve notes might not have become alarmed, and generally have begun to demand their redemption in gold? Such redemptions would have reduced the reserves still further, and, as the total volume of Federal Reserve notes outstanding was already more than a billion dollars in excess of the total gold reserves held by the Federal Reserve Banks, repeated demands might have compelled the banks to suspend the redemption of the notes. Without redemptions it would have been impossible to maintain the parity of the notes with gold, and they would have gone to a discount. Assuming that this would have brought about an advance in prices and a return of activity, an increased volume of notes would have been necessary which would have caused a still greater discount. Prices, although rising, would have been quoted in terms of irredeemable paper money. The Board may have been overcautious, but those who profess to see no danger in permitting reserves to fall below a prescribed minimum, arbitrary though it be, should remember the predicament of the second Cleveland Administration, when the Treasury's gold reserve fell below the traditional $100,000,000. The courageous steps taken by President Cleveland, with Congress refusing to aid, to restore the gold reserve, alone enabled the Treasury to continue redemptions of legal-tender notes in gold, and saved the country from a silver basis. At the end of the year 1920, Federal Reserve notes outstanding amounted to nearly ten times as much as the legal-tender notes which caused Mr. Cleveland so much trouble, and the national debt, represented by United States bonds and Treasury notes and certificates, was about twenty times as large as in 1894. With all these considerations in mind, the Board did not feel justified in suggesting to directors of Federal Reserve Banks that discount rates be lowered without regard to current market rates; nor did it feel that it would be prudent, in defending its policy, to refer to the possible effect of a renewed credit expansion upon the ability of the banks and the Treasury to maintain Federal Reserve notes on a parity with gold.

In its reply to Senator Owen the Board therefore refrained from touching upon this point, although tempted to suggest that, if the situation warranted steps which might result in placing the country upon a paper money basis, the responsibility for such action should be assumed by Congress.

CHAPTER XVI

CORRESPONDENCE WITH COMPTROLLER WILLIAMS — HE BECOMES A CRITIC OF THE BOARD

THE statutory five-year term of the Comptroller of the Currency, Mr. Williams, expired on February 2, 1919. He had been nominated by President Wilson for another term, and, if I remember correctly, the Senate Committee on Banking and Currency reported his name favorably to the Senate. However, Senators who were opposed to Mr. Williams blocked action upon his nomination, and the Senate adjourned on March 4, 1919, without having confirmed it. A law was enacted about thirty years ago, which permitted heads of departments to retain in office bureau chiefs whose statutory terms had expired, pending the appointment and qualification of their successors. Under authority of this law, Mr. Williams was permitted to hold over as Comptroller of the Currency by Secretary Glass, and later by Secretary Houston. Upon the assembling of the Sixty-Sixth Congress, President Wilson again sent to the Senate the nomination of Mr. Williams to be Comptroller of the Currency, and over this nomination a remarkable contest developed which extended over a period of about eighteen months. Strong support for Mr. Williams was enlisted, and some Republican Senators indicated their intention of voting to confirm him. It is probable that, had his nomination been reported by the Senate Committee on Banking and Currency, it would have been confirmed by a majority vote of the Senate, even though the majority report of the committee had been unfavorable; but several members of the committee, including its chairman, were opposed to the confirmation of Mr. Williams, and, after some meetings at which no action was taken, the chairman declined to call the committee together for further consideration of the nomination.

Toward the end of the year 1920, Mr. Williams became convinced that the committee would make no report to the Senate, and he accordingly made his arrangements to retire from office early in March, at the end of President Wilson's term. About the time he reached this conclusion, on December 28, 1920, he addressed a letter to the Board in which he took an extremely pessimistic view of existing conditions, and in which he stated that 'it is my strong belief that it is within the power of the Federal Reserve Board at this time, by the adoption of new, wise, liberal, and sound policies, and the announcement of such policies, to instill a feeling of confidence and hope and to check the spirit of demoralization which, unless arrested in time, may lead to disaster.' While he suggested that 'definite and energetic action, even if precedent must be disregarded, accepted rules suspended or waived, and new plans and methods devised,' the policies which he specifically recommended were:

1. The suspension or modification of the progressive interest rate in the two or three districts where it had been adopted.
2. The reduction of the rate of interest charged by Federal Reserve Banks on loans of member banks secured by Liberty Bonds, to a uniform rate of four and a half per cent.
3. A stipulation by the Federal Reserve Board that banks borrowing from Reserve Banks should 'not exact from customers interest in excess of some rate or margin to be determined, which will leave not more than a reasonable profit to the member bank.'

And by inference:

4. The establishment of a uniform Federal Reserve Bank rate of six per cent on commercial and agricultural paper; 'six per cent interest is enough to charge under present conditions.'

The core of his letter, however, was contained in the following paragraphs:

While there appears to be this scarcity of money, and of credit in the great agricultural and producing sections of the West and

Northwest and in the South and Southwest, we find that individual banks in New York City are borrowing from the Reserve System, in a number of cases, more than 100 million dollars *each;* and sometimes as much as 145 million dollars is loaned there to a single bank — twice as much as the total loans some of the Reserve Banks have been lending recently to *all* the member banks in their districts.

The records show that at the time of the last call for reports of condition of the banks, about the middle of November, one bank in New York was borrowing over 134 million dollars, or about 20 million dollars in excess of what the Federal Reserve Bank of Kansas City was advancing to the 1091 member banks in the Tenth Federal Reserve District covering the States of Kansas, Nebraska, Colorado, Wyoming, and parts of Missouri, Oklahoma, and New Mexico.

Another banking institution in New York was borrowing at the same time from the Federal Reserve Bank about 40 million dollars more than the aggregate which the Federal Reserve Bank of Minneapolis was lending to its 1000 member banks in the great States of Minnesota, North and South Dakota, Montana, and part of Wisconsin.

Another individual bank in New York was borrowing from the Reserve Bank at the time of the last call about 30 million dollars more than the Federal Reserve Bank of Dallas was lending to all the national banks in that district, including the State of Texas, and parts of Louisiana, Oklahoma, New Mexico, and Arizona; while still another banking institution in New York had gotten loans from the New York Reserve Bank which approximated in amount the total of the loans made by the Federal Reserve Bank of St. Louis to the 569 member banks in that particularly important district, including the whole State of Arkansas, parts of Illinois, Indiana, Kentucky, Tennessee, and Mississippi, and the larger part of the State of Missouri.

The Federal Reserve Bank of New York was also lending to one of its member banks at the same time 20 million dollars more than the Federal Reserve Bank of Richmond was lending to all the member banks in the Fifth Reserve District, including the States of Maryland, Virginia, North and South Carolina, and the larger part of West Virginia. . . .

Briefly, the official figures tell us that *four* banking institutions in New York City, at the time of the last call, were borrowing from the Reserve System an average of over 118 million dollars each — or practically as much money as the Federal Reserve Banks of St. Louis, Kansas City, Minneapolis, Dallas, and Richmond all combined were lending to the more than 4000 member banks in twenty-one (21) States in the Union, comprising more than one half of the entire area of the United States. If our Reserve System has the funds to lend in such huge sums to the banks in New York, for such uses, is it not difficult to understand why money should be so scarce in the interior where the real wealth of the country is being so largely provided, and where money is so distressingly needed? . . .

A copy of this letter was sent by Mr. Williams to every member of the Board, and it was afterwards ascertained that he had sent copies to various other persons, including some Senators and Representatives; but he persistently declined to give the names of those to whom copies had been sent. The Comptroller's office was located adjoining those of other members of the Board, and he could easily have made known his views to them informally or expressed them orally at any meeting of the Board. It appeared that his purpose was to bring outside pressure to bear upon the Board. A few days after the receipt of this letter, Senator Glass called at my office and stated that he had received a copy. He was much disturbed by some of the statements made in the letter until I went over them with him, and made the explanations which will presently appear in this text. Mr. Williams continued at frequent intervals until his retirement from office to write letters to the Board, sometimes sending two a day. Much of this correspondence has been printed in a report of a Congressional Joint Commission in the summer of 1921, and there is no occasion to reprint much of it here. However, in order to give the reader an idea of the Board's point of view, extracts from its reply dated January 13, 1921, to Mr. Williams's letter of December 28th, are presented below:

. . . It is our confident belief that but for the precautionary measures taken several months ago, general conditions to-day would be far worse than they are and that the prospects of stabilization and revival would be much more remote. We wish to emphasize the fact that this process of drastic readjustment has been world-wide and that the effects have been most severe in those countries where the inflation of bank credit and currency has been most pronounced. We believe that as far as this country is concerned the crisis has been passed, and we are of the opinion that the policies which were carried into effect by the Federal Reserve Board have prevented one of the greatest financial cataclysms of modern times.

We do not agree with you that, in order to relieve existing conditions, 'precedents must be disregarded, accepted rules suspended or waived, and new plans and methods devised,' particularly if those new plans and methods are fundamentally unsound. We believe your suggestion that the Federal Reserve Board reduce the rate of interest charged by Federal Reserve Banks on loans of member banks secured by Liberty bonds to a uniform rate of four and a half per cent is essentially unsound. You say that 'The owners of those bonds do not ask the Government to buy their bonds to save the holders from loss, and it hardly seems right under present conditions to tax these borrowers for interest on money borrowed from the Reserve Banks one and three quarters per cent or two and three quarters per cent more than the bonds yield, especially when this interest so collected goes to the Government indirectly.' Entirely apart from the question whether these bonds were sold to a patriotic public at rates of interest lower than they should have borne, the Federal Reserve Banks are certainly under no moral or legal obligation to protect the bondholders from loss of interest, and the discount policy of the Federal Reserve System cannot be adjusted to suit the convenience or relieve the necessities of individual holders.

Many billions of these bonds have been paid for in full and the effect, in the present circumstances, of a Federal Reserve Bank discount rate of four and a half per cent on paper secured by Liberty bonds would be to induce a temporary and artificial ease in the money market, which could not be sustained, because the lending power of the Federal Reserve Banks has its limitations, and which might result in a temporary revival of the speculative spirit which was so strongly in evidence fourteen months ago and which had such an unhappy effect upon the commerce and business of the country. . . .

Apparently you hold the view that the decline in prices has been caused by restriction of credit on the part of the Federal Reserve

Banks and by the member and non-member banks of the country. Your own reports show that there was a marked increase in the loans of all national banks between September, 1919, and November, 1920, and the rediscounts of Federal Reserve Banks for member banks increased steadily until November 5, 1920, when they reached the highest point in the history of the System. Since that date there has been a moderate reduction in the loans and discounts of Federal Reserve Banks, due mainly to seasonal liquidation. It is significant, however, that the most rapid decline in prices took place before November 5th, while the loans and advances made by the Federal Reserve Banks were constantly increasing and the volume of Federal Reserve notes outstanding was still expanding. It seems clear to us, therefore, that the decline in prices was due to economic causes and cannot be ascribed to restriction of credit or to contraction of currency. . . .

We are surprised at the references you make to the dealings of individual banks in New York City with the Federal Reserve Bank there, and particularly at your attempt to show that a few large banks in that city have been receiving undue favors at the hands of the Federal Reserve Bank. Your statements are calculated to mislead the uninformed, for you say that, about the middle of November, one bank in New York was borrowing about 20 million dollars more than the amount the Federal Reserve Bank of Kansas City was advancing to 1091 member banks in the seven States or parts of States embraced in its district; that another New York bank was borrowing at the same time about 40 million dollars more than the amount which the Federal Reserve Bank of Minneapolis was lending to its 1000 member banks, and that another bank in New York City was borrowing 30 million dollars more than the Federal Reserve Bank of Dallas was lending to all national banks in its district (making no reference to advances to State member banks). You say also that another New York bank had received advances from the Federal Reserve Bank of New York equal approximately to the total loans made by the Federal Reserve Bank of St. Louis to its 569 member banks, and again that the Federal Reserve Bank of New York was lending to one of its member banks 20 million dollars more than the Federal Reserve Bank of Richmond was lending to all member banks in the Fifth Federal Reserve District.

These statements, if made public, would lead, no doubt, to much unjust criticism of the Federal Reserve Bank of New York which had made the loans, and of the Federal Reserve Board which had not prohibited them, but they are far from giving all the facts in the case. In the first place, you take no account of the banking power of the Federal Reserve Bank of New York as compared with the Federal Reserve Banks of Richmond, St. Louis, Minneapolis, Kansas City, and Dallas, nor do you think it worth while to state the amount of the capital and surplus of the five banks referred to and what their reserve balances are. You probably know that all Federal Reserve Banks have a theoretical basic or normal discount line, which is based upon the reserve balances carried by the member banks plus the member banks' stock-holding in the Federal Reserve Bank. You do not state, what you doubtless know, that there are many member banks in the Federal Reserve Districts of Richmond, St. Louis, Minneapolis, Kansas City, and Dallas which have rediscount lines at their Federal Reserve Banks many times in excess of their basic lines and relatively greater than any line ever given by the Federal Reserve Bank of New York to any of its member banks. In order to correct any wrong impressions which you may have or which may be received by any who may read your letter, we call attention to the following table which shows the basic lines, borrowings from the Federal Reserve Bank, and ratio of such borrowings to basic lines of five large New York City banks and all member banks in six Federal Reserve Districts, as of November 15, 1920. The five New York City banks named in the table are undoubtedly the banks referred to in your letter.

	BASIC LINE	BORROWINGS FROM FEDERAL RESERVE BANK	PER CENT OF BORROWINGS TO BASIC LINE
(New York City)			
Bank A...............	$104,966,000	$123,818,000	118
Bank B...............	89,838,000	118,125,000	131
Bank C...............	62,058,000	97,150,000	157
Bank D...............	59,174,000	102,746,000	174
Bank E...............	41,884,000	65,000,000	155
Total.............	$357,920,000	$506,839,000	142
All members in the Federal Reserve District of			
Richmond.............	$102,188,000	$123,555,000	121
Atlanta...............	81,913,000	172,658,000	211
St. Louis.............	121,648,000	142,927,000	117
Minneapolis...........	85,145,000	107,520,000	126
Kansas City...........	128,355,000	147,118,000	115
Dallas.	91,763,000	101,057,000	110
Total.............	$611,012,000	$794,835,000	130

You will notice that in the Atlanta District the percentage of borrowings of all member banks to their basic line is 211, which is greater than that of the New York City bank which shows the largest percentage of borrowings to basic line. You will observe, furthermore, that the average percentage of borrowings to basic lines of the five New York City banks on November 15th was 142, while the average percentage of borrowings of all member banks in the six Federal Reserve Districts of Richmond, Atlanta, St. Louis, Minneapolis, Kansas City, and Dallas on the same date was 130. It should be borne in mind that the borrowing banks in these districts constitute probably not more than sixty per cent of the total members, so if only borrowing banks are considered their percentage of borrowings to basic line would be much greater than that shown in the table, which relates to all member banks. . . .

Normally the discount rate of a Federal Reserve Bank should not control the rates at which member banks loan money to their customers. In many States the Federal Reserve Bank discount rate is so much lower than the contract rate permitted by law that the Federal Reserve discount rate, as a matter of fact, does not control the rates at which customers are accommodated by member banks. No Federal Reserve Bank has a flat rate or an average rate higher than seven per cent for any class of paper. In six States the legal rate of interest is eight per cent and in eight States that rate is permitted by contract; in eleven States a contract rate of ten per cent is allowed, and in ten States a twelve per cent rate is legal by contract. Four States — California, Maine, Massachusetts, and Rhode Island — permit any rate to be charged under contract, and in New York any rate agreed upon in writing is legal on collateral demand loans of five thousand dollars and over. We believe that the theory that discount transactions should yield a profit to the member banks is a fallacy which owes its wide credence in part to the fact that the Federal Reserve Banking System, which has some of the attributes of a central banking system, is comparatively new, and partly to the abnormal times through which we have passed, the inevitable effects of which are now being experienced. . . .

We do not agree with you that it would be wise to encourage further expansion by reducing rates, and it should always be remembered that there are about twenty-four billion dollars of Government obligations available to member banks as collateral for loans eligible for rediscount by Federal Reserve Banks. Based upon the experience of other countries, it is evident that if the

limit of expansion should be reached in this country, a condition
of depression infinitely more serious and more widespread than
that now existing would follow. . . .

After the retirement of Mr. Williams from office, his attacks upon the Board became more and more violent, and
continued until the expiration of my term of office in August,
1922. In general his criticisms did not impress me as being
constructive, but seemed to appeal to passion and prejudice
rather than to calm judgment. In public addresses, reprints,
and posters, he denounced the Federal Reserve Board and
the Federal Reserve Banks for their alleged extravagance
and inefficiency, and it appears from the 'Congressional
Record' that he prepared at least one speech which was delivered by Senator Heflin on the floor of the Senate in which
the Board was charged with a deliberate attempt to destroy
the industrial and agricultural interests of the country and
with responsibility for wrecking the prosperity of the Nation. It has already been pointed out that his attempts to
discredit the Board began with his letter of December 28,
1920. The climax of his invective against the Board was
reached in an address which he made at Augusta, Georgia,
in July, 1921. This address was widely circulated throughout the country, and the local newspaper which reported it
demanded in flaming headlines that the members of the
Board be immediately removed for their malfeasance and
incompetence. Yet there appears to be nothing in the official
reports of Mr. Williams, as Comptroller of the Currency,
which coincides with the statements made in his letter of
December 28th, or with the personal views he expressed after his retirement from office. The last annual report which
Mr. Williams made as Comptroller of the Currency was sent
to Congress in page-proof form on February 7, 1921. In it
there is nothing which reflects in any way upon the administration of the Federal Reserve System, nor is there any
suggestion that the drastic decline in prices and the general
depression which set in during the last half of 1920 was due

in any respect to the policies or operating methods of the Federal Reserve System. On the contrary, several pages are devoted to a discussion of the world-wide economic causes which brought about the drastic reaction, and there are several passages which refer in complimentary terms to the Federal Reserve System. The following quotations are made from this report:

The story of Japan's industrial and financial experience is largely similar to the experience of South American and European countries — some of them our allies, and others neutral. Some of these countries are now going through a business cataclysm similar to that through which Japan has so recently passed. In our own country we have been thus far fortunate enough — thanks largely to the splendid efficiency and stabilizing influence of the Federal Reserve System — to avoid the financial crises and complete disorganization which have made havoc elsewhere. We have passed with comparative safety through exceedingly troubled and nerve-racking times; but difficult and dangerous problems remain to be solved, the solution of which will demand clear heads and steady nerves. . . .

The deflation which at that time (1919) was obviously inevitable has come, and the country is now in many respects on a sounder basis, economically, than it has been for years. . . .

Largely through the aid and excellent functioning of the Federal Reserve System, the business and banking interests of the country have passed successfully through the perils of inflation and the strain and losses of deflation without panic and without the demoralization which has been produced in the past at various times from far less serious and racking causes. Those banking and other interests which at the outset so vigorously opposed the Federal Reserve System are now among its warmest advocates. . . .

The past seven years have been, in numbers of persons and extent of interests involved, the most momentous and critical in the history of this Republic. We have had to face and solve gigantic and unprecedented problems, and the banking and financial machinery of the country has been subjected to a test and strain unparalleled. It has been the duty of our country very largely to finance the world, and in carrying out the program which fate imposed upon us we have overcome successfully difficulties that at times seemed almost insurmountable and we have met every righteous demand made upon us. Our Federal Reserve financial and banking system, inaugurated in 1914, has been of inestimable value; and without its aid, tasks which we have so successfully accomplished would have been impossible.

On the occasion of my birthday anniversary in May, 1920, Mr. Williams wrote me a very cordial letter in which he said:

I share the pride and satisfaction which the people of your State and section feel in your well-deserved success in public life. The qualities which won for you a high place and position in civil life have enabled you to hold with credit and distinction the very important office you now occupy, and in which you have rendered signal service to the country in the particularly trying and difficult times through which we have been passing.

I am sure that your record in Washington will always be a source of pride and thankfulness to yourself and to your posterity in the years to come.

I trust that you may live to enjoy many more years of usefulness and honor.

Shortly before his retirement, Mr. Williams invited all the Federal Reserve Board members to be his guests over the week-end at his country estate near Richmond, and the invitation was accepted by three of them. Mr. Williams is an admirable host, and upon this occasion he arranged an unusually delightful programme for the entertainment of his guests. In describing the arrangements he had made, in a letter to me under date of February 10, 1921, he said:

I am looking forward with great pleasure to having my colleagues with me in my home city and am glad that my friends there are to have the opportunity of making the acquaintance of the members of the Board who have performed such very valuable services to our country in the critical and serious times through which we have been passing.

Mr. Williams was undoubtedly sincere in his belief that the discount rates of the Federal Reserve Banks should have been reduced in January, 1921, without regard to actual conditions in the money market. But other members of the

Board, equally sincere, recalling the effect of artificial rates, believed that Reserve Bank rates should be related to market rates, and that improvement in the position of the banks, increasing confidence in them, and the redepositing of hoarded money, would most speedily and surely result in a general relaxation of interest rates. This opinion was in accord with that of the officers and directors of the Federal Reserve Banks, and of the members of the Federal Advisory Council. They were all reluctant to adopt a policy which might tend either to check the development of a stronger banking position, or to impress the public as merely a gesture. The Federal Reserve Banks could not make direct loans to individuals, firms, and corporations, and the interest rates to such borrowers depended upon the strength of their names, the value of their collateral, and the supply of loanable funds, rather than upon the Federal Reserve Bank rate. The improvement in the banking situation, noted in January, continued in a moderate degree, and beginning in April the rates were reduced, and continued to be reduced throughout the year as changing conditions appeared fully to warrant them. Perhaps with the perspective gained after the lapse of years there may be some who, although thinking differently at the time, are now satisfied that the rates might safely have been reduced in January, 1921; although it is not clear that a moderate reduction would have had any marked beneficial effect, and a slashing cut might, as has been explained in comments on Senator Owen's letter, have been distinctly dangerous. As a matter of fact, Mr. Williams up to the day of his retirement had never suggested that the rate on commercial and agricultural paper be lower than six per cent. Six of the Federal Reserve Banks had never exceeded that rate, although of these six, two with the progressive rate schedule were charging higher rates on borrowings in excess of the so-called normal line. I have always been at a loss to understand what occurred between February and July, 1921, to change the good opinion which Mr. Williams had so generously expressed of the work of his colleagues on the Federal Reserve Board.

The improvement in the reserve position of the banks which was noted in January continued during the month of February, and it is probable that there would have been a downward revision of rates during that month but for one important factor — Treasury financing. With its large outstanding indebtedness represented by short-term notes and certificates, the operations of the Treasury had a most important bearing upon the money market, as in fact they have to-day and will continue to have for many years to come. A new administration was about to come into power, and it was the feeling of the Federal Reserve Banks, in which a majority of the Board concurred, that consideration of rate changes should be deferred until the incoming Secretary of the Treasury had an opportunity to determine and announce his policy. Under Secretary Houston's policy of issuing Treasury certificates bearing rates of interest at which they would normally sell on the market, much pressure on the Federal Reserve Banks had been avoided, and it was generally hoped and expected that his successor would continue this policy. This expectation was realized.

Two days before the expiration of President Wilson's term of office, I wrote him a brief note expressing my appreciation of the uniform consideration he had always accorded me, and, while I indicated that no acknowledgment was expected, I received on the next day a cordial note from him in which he said:

Your generous letter of March first gives me an opportunity to say how glad I have been to show my confidence in you, which has been very great, and to express my admiration for the way in which you have administered the very difficult duties assigned you.

I had only three personal interviews with President Wilson during the whole time he was in the White House. The fact that the Secretary of the Treasury was Chairman *ex officio* of the Federal Reserve Board made it unnecessary as a rule for me to ask for an appointment with the President, but several times I had occasion to communicate with him in writing. He always replied to my letters on the day of their receipt, except once, when he wrote the following day and began his letter with an expression of regret for his delay in making acknowledgment.

CHAPTER XVII

THE NEW ADMINISTRATION — THE FARM BLOC-JOINT COMMIS-
SION OF AGRICULTURAL INQUIRY — CORRESPONDENCE
WITH GOVERNOR OF NEBRASKA

PRESIDENT HARDING, after his inauguration at noon on March 4, 1921, immediately sent to the Senate the names of those he had selected for his Cabinet. Confirmation followed at once, and the Honorable Andrew W. Mellon took the oath of office as Secretary of the Treasury, thus succeeding the Honorable David F. Houston. The resignation of the Comptroller of the Currency, Mr. Williams, had become effective at the close of business March 2d, and the interim appointment, made in September, 1920, of D. C. Wills as a member of the Federal Reserve Board lapsed on March 4th. About the middle of March, President Harding appointed D. R. Crissinger, of Marion, Ohio, to be Comptroller of the Currency, and in May, he appointed as a member of the Board, to succeed Mr. Wills, John R. Mitchell, of St. Paul, Minnesota.

Money rates remained steady during the month of March, and there were practically no fluctuations in the rate for commercial paper. In the stock market during the first half of the month there was a slightly increased demand for funds, which was related probably to preparations for the payment of income taxes. Immediately following the income tax payments, there was the usual temporary relaxation which generally occurs after the quarterly tax payments are made. Call-money rates in New York declined from seven per cent to six on several successive days, although the ruling rate remained at six and a half to seven per cent. The demand for investment funds as well as for bank loans continued active, and offerings were promptly taken without satisfying the demand. Not only was there continued domestic demand, but many foreign corporations were arranging their affairs with the view of obtaining accommodations in the United States. The situation still appeared to warrant careful nursing and the avoidance of any policy which would result in an unwise use of credit. The new Secretary of the Treasury, Mr. Mellon, in his first statement to the banks said that 'the Nation cannot afford extravagance, and, so far as is possible, it must avoid entering upon new fields of expenditure. . . . The people generally must become more interested in saving the Government's money than in spending it.'

On April 15th, the Federal Reserve Bank of Boston reduced its rate on commercial and agricultural paper from seven to six per cent, and this action was soon followed by a reduction in the rate of the Federal Reserve Bank of New York to six and a half per cent. During the month of May, readjustments were made by other Federal Reserve Banks so that, by the first of June, eight of the banks were maintaining a six per cent rate on commercial and agricultural paper, while four, those of New York, Chicago, Minneapolis, and Dallas, had a rate of six and a half per cent. At the same time the Federal Reserve Bank of Philadelphia had a rate of five and a half per cent on notes secured by Liberty bonds and Victory notes, while at all other banks the rate on this class of paper was six per cent. The rate on notes secured by Treasury certificates of indebtedness was six per cent at all the banks.

Meanwhile, the progressive rate had been discontinued by the Federal Reserve Banks of Atlanta and Dallas, and the application of that rate had been modified by the Federal Reserve Banks of St. Louis and Kansas City. At the St. Louis bank the average borrowings in excess of the basic line were subject to one half per cent progressive increase for each twenty-five per cent, while at the Kansas City bank, the rate on discounts in excess of the basic line was subject to a progressive increase of one half per cent for each twenty-

THE FEDERAL RESERVE BOARD, 1921–22

Left to right: Andrew W. Mellon, W. P. G. Harding, Edmund Platt, Charles S. Hamlin, A. C. Miller,
D. R. Crissinger, John R. Mitchell

five per cent by which the amount of loans exceeded the basic line, with a maximum rate of twelve per cent.

At the end of May the consolidated statement of the Federal Reserve Banks showed a marked improvement over their condition at the end of May, 1920. Their gold holdings had increased about $448,000,000, their loans had declined $972,000,000, and the amount of Federal Reserve notes in circulation had decreased about $376,000,000. This improvement in condition was not, however, uniform throughout the System, for banks located in agricultural sections found it necessary to make additional advances and renewals, while the liquidation had been most pronounced in the manufacturing and commercial sections of the country. Despite the reduction made in Federal Reserve Bank rates, reports to the Board indicated that banks throughout the country were making no corresponding reduction to their own borrowers. By July 1st, the rate on commercial and agricultural paper at all Federal Reserve Banks had been reduced to six per cent, except at Chicago and Minneapolis, where the rate was six and a half per cent on paper maturing within ninety days and seven per cent on maturities after ninety days. At that time the Kansas City Bank was the only one which continued the progressive rate, but under another modification, excess borrowings at the Federal Reserve Bank of Kansas City were subject to an additional charge of one per cent for the first one hundred per cent by which the amount borrowed by a member bank exceeded the basic line, and for any further excess an additional rate of two per cent was charged, making the maximum rate eight per cent. Later on in the month the progressive rate was discontinued entirely by the Federal Reserve Bank of Kansas City, and further reductions were made in the discount rates by some of the banks. The rate at the Federal Reserve Bank of Boston, New York, Philadelphia, and San Francisco was then five and a half per cent on commercial and agricultural paper; six and a half per cent at Minneapolis, and six per cent at all the other banks. There had, however, been no appreciable reduction in current rates for prime commercial paper. Reports made from the various cities in which the Federal Reserve Banks and their branches were located, showed that six per cent was the minimum rate, ten per cent the maximum, and average rates generally around seven per cent.

Congress met in extraordinary session shortly after President Harding's inauguration, and it was evident from the outset that agricultural problems would be given first consideration. A number of Senators and Representatives from agricultural States formed what is known as the 'Farm Bloc,' which proved to be a powerful factor both in that Congress and in the succeeding one. The Bloc was composed of Republicans and Democrats who coöperated usually without regard to ordinary political alignment. Senator Kenyon, of Iowa, was the leader of the Bloc when it was first formed, and, upon his resignation from the Senate to accept a Federal judgeship in Iowa, Senator Capper, of Kansas, succeeded him. At the behest of the Farm Bloc there was appointed, from the members of the Senate and House, a committee called the Joint Commission of Agricultural Inquiry. The personnel of this commission was as follows: Representative Sydney Anderson, of Minnesota, Chairman; Senators Lenroot, of Wisconsin; Capper, of Kansas; McNary, of Oregon; Robinson, of Arkansas; and Harrison, of Mississippi; Representatives Mills, of New York; Funk, of Illinois; Sumners, of Texas; and Ten Eyck, of New York. This commission was directed to investigate and report particularly upon the causes of the depressed condition of agriculture; to make a study of agricultural credits, transportation facilities and rates; and to recommend a plan for the amelioration of existing conditions.

Meanwhile, there was an active and systematic propaganda to discredit the Federal Reserve Board and its policies, and especially its Governor. Advantage was taken of the distress in agricultural sections of the country to enlist the sympathy of the farmers particularly in these attacks, and to have them believe that the Federal Reserve System was responsible for their troubles. On July 14, 1921, the former Comptroller of the Currency, Mr. John Skelton Williams, in a public address at Augusta, Georgia, made an attack upon the Federal Reserve Board, its personnel and policies, to which reference has already been made. In view of the charges made in this speech, the Board addressed a letter to Senator McLean, Chairman of the Senate Committee on Banking and Currency, requesting an investigation of its operations by that committee. Senator McLean introduced a resolution in the Senate to authorize the Banking and Currency Committee to investigate all complaints and charges which had been made against the Federal Reserve Board, but after the resolution had been reported favorably by the Committee on Audit and Control of Contingent Expenses of the Senate, to which it had been referred, objection was made by some Senators to an investigation by the Banking and Currency Committee. The matter was thereupon referred informally to the Joint Commission of Agricultural Inquiry, which had been created for an entirely different purpose.

About this time, July 8, 1921, I received a personal letter from Senator Smoot, of Utah, in which after referring to the current criticisms of the Board, he asked me to explain the discount policy of the Board, and to state its attitude toward agricultural credits. The reply, which was sent under date of July 11, 1921, was a condensed and concise review and recapitulation of the economic and banking conditions over the post-war readjustment period, and will be found in full in Appendix D, page 289.

The Joint Commission of Agricultural Inquiry began its hearings on August 2d, and Mr. Williams was the first witness to appear before it. He occupied two days in making his statements, and at the conclusion of his testimony, the Commission gave me a hearing. I was followed by Governor

Strong, of the Federal Reserve Bank of New York; Governor Miller, of the Federal Reserve Bank of Kansas City; and by a number of others who were not connected with the Federal Reserve System. The Commission adhered closely to a line of inquiry bearing upon agricultural conditions and credits and did not appear to be interested in the alleged inefficiency and extravagance with which the Board had been charged. A stenographic report was taken of these hearings and the report of the Commission was submitted to Congress in four parts at intervals from December, 1921, to March, 1923. Part 1 was entitled 'The Agricultural Crisis and Its Causes'; Part 2, 'Credit'; Part 3, 'Transportation'; and Part 4, 'Distribution and Marketing.' This report followed an exhaustive inquiry and is most comprehensive. It is replete with statistics, and covers every phase of the production, distribution, and marketing of agricultural products of every kind, including live stock. Together the four parts form a volume of 1350 pages, of which 159 pages are taken up with the discussion of credit. In the credit section of the report alone are there any references to the policies of the Federal Reserve Board.

While the Commission in its discussion of credit did not meet in all respects the expectations of the friends of the Federal Reserve System, the report as a whole was a distinct disappointment to its critics. The charges of alleged extravagance in buildings and salaries were ignored entirely, and the Commission confined itself to a discussion of the Federal Reserve Banks as purveyors of credit and the general discount policies of the Board and the banks. The most serious charge which had been brought against the Federal Reserve System was that it had deliberately discriminated against the farmer. In its discussion of credit conditions from 1914 to 1921, the Commission completely exonerated the Federal Reserve System from this charge. It reached the conclusion that the expansion of bank loans in rural districts during the period of inflation ending in June, 1920, was relatively greater than in the industrial sections, taken as a whole; that the action of the Federal Reserve Board and the Federal Reserve Banks during the so-called deflation period did not produce a greater curtailment of bank loans in the rural districts than in the financial and industrial sections, and that credit was not absorbed by the financial centers at the expense of the rural districts for the purpose of speculative activities. It was evident that agriculture and the depression of that great industry were foremost in the minds of the members of the Commission. In that part of the Commission's report which relates to 'Credit,' some statements were presented as facts which may well be disputed, but the actual facts were stated fairly, and much of the reasoning based on these facts was unquestionably sound. In parts of the discussion, however, opinions expressed by the Commission do not appear to be logical conclusions from the premises, but rather a concession to the bias of some of its members.

After remarking that the national and State banking systems were the principal agencies for furnishing short-time credit to the farmer, and that the State and national banks, together with the Federal Farm Loan System and the private farm mortgage companies, furnished the great bulk of long-time credit to farmers, the Commission noted the fact that short-time credits were usually extended for periods of six months owing to the fact that paper of longer maturity than six months for agricultural purposes was not at that time eligible for rediscount at the Federal Reserve Banks. The Commission also remarked that long-time credit could be secured only on the basis of farm mortgages, and even if it was possible to do so it would not be wise to make farm mortgages the basis of credit for production or marketing purposes. Of the recommendations made in the Commission's report, the only ones affecting the Federal Reserve Banks were these:

It is proposed that notes taken or discounted by a Federal Land Bank shall be eligible for rediscount with any Federal Reserve Bank, when such loans have reached a maturity of less than six months. In addition, any Federal Reserve Bank is authorized to buy and sell the debentures issued by the Farm Loan Board to the same extent and in the same way as they now buy and sell farm-loan bonds.

While Congress did not legislate to carry out the specific recommendations of the Commission, it did early in 1923 pass the Agricultural Credit Act which included an amendment to section 13 of the Federal Reserve Act, making agricultural paper of maturities up to nine months eligible for rediscount by Federal Reserve Banks, and authorized the establishment of Federal Intermediate Credit Banks and of National Agricultural Credit Corporations. By this legislation, notes discounted by Federal Intermediate Credit Banks which do not bear the endorsement of a non-member bank which is eligible for membership in the Federal Reserve System, and have a maturity of not longer than nine months, are made eligible for rediscount by Federal Reserve Banks.

It is evident that the Commission recognized the fact that the Federal Reserve Banks had no power, under the law as it stood in the years 1920, 1921, and 1922, to aid member banks in extending the particular form of credit which agricultural interests especially desired.

In summing up, the Commission said:

The position of Federal Reserve Banks and the Federal Reserve Board during the period of the war and throughout the business cycle of expansion, extravagance, speculation, deflation, and depression, which followed it, was extremely difficult. The banks were the fiscal agents of the Government. Through them and their auxiliary organizations the enormous issues of war bonds were floated. Their policy was not only interwoven with the policy of the Treasury Department, but subordinated to it. The decisions which had to be made were difficult and important. Doubtless in these circumstances mistakes of judgment were made which the clearer judgment of retrospect would change. The Commission believes that a policy of sharp advances in discount rates should have been inaugurated in the first six months of 1919, and cannot excuse the action of the Federal Reserve Board and the Federal Reserve Banks in this period in failing to take measures to restrict the expansion, inflation, speculation, and extravagance which characterized the period.

As a matter of fact, all legitimate steps were taken by the Federal Reserve Board to restrict expansion, inflation, speculation, and extravagance during the year 1919, except one — a sharp advance in the discount rates; and it is not at all certain that even that expedient would have been effective at a time when the public seemed to care little for expense. In all events, the necessities of the Treasury during this period should not be overlooked, and the Board felt that it was its duty to coöperate with the Treasury authorities. Failure to coöperate would have been tantamount to an undertaking by the Board to dictate the policies of the Treasury. In such a case I think the Board would have heard something of the Overman Act. Under this Act, which at that time was still in effect, the President could, by Executive Order, have transferred any of the functions of the Federal Reserve Board to the Secretary of the Treasury, or to any other officer of the Government.

The best evidence that the report of the Commission was not altogether satisfactory to extreme critics of the Federal Reserve System is that, in the attacks which continued to be made upon the Federal Reserve Board, there was never any reference to the Commission's report.

While the Joint Commission of Agricultural Inquiry was pursuing its investigation of agricultural credits, there were being made in the Senate, almost daily, speeches denouncing the Federal Reserve Board, and myself particularly.

The accompanying letter to Chairman Anderson, of the Joint Commission of Agricultural Inquiry, has reference to some of the insinuations made in speeches on the floor of the Senate:

September 19, 1921

DEAR MR. CHAIRMAN:

The attention of the Federal Reserve Board has been called to the speech delivered by Honorable J. Thomas Heflin, a Senator from Alabama, in the Senate of the United States on August 15th, which was published in the Congressional Record of August 22, 1921, in which the following paragraph appears at the top of page 5934:

> Mr. President, I am not advised as to whether or not any of the friends of the Federal Reserve Board were speculating in cotton at that time. The Senator from Georgia (Mr. Watson) reminded us the other day that they loaned to themselves in the System the sum of $18,000,000. I want to say just here, Mr. President, that if they invested any of that $18,000,000 in speculating on the bear side of the cotton market in the month of August last year, they made a lot of money.

I am directed by the Board to suggest that the Commission consider the propriety of inviting Senators Watson and Heflin to appear before it for the purpose of stating to the Commission what information, if any, they have on this subject, to whom the money was loaned, by whom the loans were made, and what reason they have for believing that members of the Board speculated either directly or indirectly in the cotton market.

W. P. G. HARDING
Governor

The Commission, however, was not concerned with personal attacks and did not act upon the suggestion made. Had the Senate Committee on Banking and Currency been authorized to investigate all complaints and charges against the Federal Reserve Board, critics would have been more careful in making such statements, for they would have been called upon to prove them. All such statements were designed to create an atmosphere of distrust and suspicion, and, although libelous, could not be resented by the Board because of the constitutional immunity which attaches to statements made in the halls of Congress.

About this time I had some correspondence with the Honorable Samuel R. McKelvie, Governor of Nebraska, who urged that the Federal Reserve Bank of Kansas City be directed to reduce its discount rate as a means of relief to the farming community. In his letter dated September 12, 1921, Governor McKelvie said:

As the result of an inquiry that I have just concluded among Nebraska bankers, I am convinced that financial and business conditions are improving throughout this State, but I am also convinced that there is need for credit relief for the farmers and cattlemen in this territory now, and it is regarding this situation that I address you. . . .

The simple fact is that the urgent demand for liquidation and the contraction of credit during the past twelve months has imposed unusual and extraordinary hardships upon the farmers and cattlemen. In order that these demands could be met, the farmer has taken heavy losses in the sale of grain and live stock. It is true that bank deposits and reserves have improved during this period, but this improvement has been accomplished at the expense of interests that should have been protected and conserved. . . .

I am not unmindful of the relief that is being offered now through certain private banking sources, as well as from the War Finance Corporation. These are good and the work that is being done by them should not in any sense be disparaged, but with the Federal Reserve Banks holding seventy per cent of the reserves, it seems apparent that here lies the medium through which additional credit may be afforded at a much more reasonable rate of interest than is now required.

Especial consideration should be shown to the cattle interests, both to breeders and feeders. If this is done, it will also greatly aid the grain-growers, for it will afford a profitable outlet for a product that must otherwise be sold at a loss.

Our last Legislature passed the Grain Warehouse Law, which provides for the taking of receipts for grain that is housed on the farm. I am wondering if these receipts may not be used as the basis for credit to farmers in this State.

I do not want to burden you with a further enumeration of these facts, though I may say that I have only touched the high spots. Nor would I have you believe for a moment that I would have the Federal Reserve Bank System encourage an extension of credit that would result in unwise inflation or speculation. Too much of that has been done already. But I would like to see the Federal Reserve System operate as an agency for financial relief at a time when it is most urgently needed. May I be advised of anything that you think may be done to help us out?

My reply, dated September 15th, contained the following:

The Federal Reserve Board has always stressed the importance of sustaining the agricultural and live-stock interests of the country, and its policies have always been shaped with a view of encouraging member banks to extend all reasonable accommodations to those engaged in these vital industries. . . .

Federal Reserve Banks are not permitted by law to make loans direct to individuals, firms, or corporations, and they can rediscount only paper which bears the endorsement of a member bank. Consequently, in order for a Federal Reserve Bank to render financial assistance to those engaged in agriculture or the raising of live stock, it is necessary that the loans first be negotiated with member banks. Neither the Federal Reserve Bank nor the Federal Reserve Board has any control over the loan policy of any member bank. We cannot compel a member bank to make a loan which it does not desire to make, nor can we restrain it from making a loan which it wishes to make.

About one third of the member banks in the Kansas City District have been very heavy borrowers during the past year, another one third have been only moderate borrowers, while the remainder have not borrowed at all. It is possible that the Federal Reserve Bank may have called the attention of some of the larger borrowers to the advisability of reducing their discount lines at the Federal Reserve Bank, but in no case has the Federal Reserve Bank undertaken to say to a member bank just what particular loans it should call or ask to be reduced.

I was formerly in the banking business myself and know something of banking psychology. Banks as a rule do not like to admit to customers that they are short of loanable funds nor do they like to stir up enmity in declining to make loans or in asking for reductions. I know that in many cases they have found the Federal Reserve Bank or the Federal Reserve Board a convenient buffer and have stated to borrowers or would-be borrowers that they would like to grant extensions asked for or to make loans desired, but that the Federal Reserve would not permit it. Such a procedure has a tendency to relieve the situation as far as the local bank is concerned, but it is not altogether fair to the Federal Reserve System. The Federal Reserve Board has repeatedly issued public statements calling the attention of the banks of the country to the importance of granting adequate credits to farmers and cattlemen. . . .

I understand that the laws of Nebraska authorize a maximum

interest rate of ten per cent per annum. The progressive rate which prevailed for some months at the Federal Reserve Bank of Kansas City was abrogated last June, and all rediscounts made by that bank are now at a flat rate of six per cent per annum, regardless of the amount of accommodation extended to the borrowing member bank. I have before me a report of bills discounted for member banks by the Omaha Branch of the Federal Reserve Bank of Kansas City on September 9, 1921. This report shows that 111 notes, aggregating $1,031,835.09, were discounted for 21 member banks, by the Omaha Branch Bank on that date, all at the rate of 6 per cent per annum. The report shows also the rate of interest charged the customers by the borrowing member banks. This report shows that in the case of 52 notes the borrowing banks charged their customers 10 per cent; on 21 notes they charged 9 per cent; on 2 notes 8½ per cent; on 14 notes 8 per cent; on 13 notes 7½ per cent; on 5 notes 7 per cent; on 2 notes 6½ per cent; and on 2 notes 6 per cent.

Under an ideal operation of the Federal Reserve System, it is not intended that a member bank should make a profit on its rediscount transactions with the Federal Reserve Bank. The object of the Federal Reserve System is to afford a ready discount market, but member banks generally, especially in the West and South, seem to have an idea that they should make a profit on such transactions. In some States, where the maximum legal rate of interest is six per cent and the Federal Reserve rate is also six per cent, no profit is possible, but in States where the laws permit of rates as high as ten and twelve per cent, there is, of course, an opportunity for a very substantial profit. . . .

The abrogation of the progressive rate has made it possible for banks in Nebraska to make a larger percentage of profit on their rediscount transactions with the Federal Reserve Bank, but the daily statements made to the Board do not indicate that the Nebraska banks, as a rule, have shared this advantage with their borrowers. Is there any reason to believe that in case the discount rate at the Federal Reserve Bank of Kansas City should be still further reduced the Nebraska banks would give their customers lower rates than they do at present?

In acknowledging, under date of September 22d, Governor McKelvie said:

The facts that you give regarding the rate of interest that is being charged by correspondent banks on loans that are rediscounted through the Federal Reserve Bank are intensely interesting. I am not prepared to say that these margins have given any unusual profit to the banks that have been patronizing the Federal Reserve System, but I do feel that there is something radically wrong with a system which requires such wide margins. Also, I am convinced that this and other hampering influences must be remedied before the System will be very useful to agricultural borrowers here.

I am further informed that the banks in this district are not generally patronizing the Federal Reserve System. It would seem that if the margins indicated in your letter are profitable to the correspondent banks, there would be a more general patronage of the Federal Reserve System. . . .

In conclusion, I desire to suggest the desirability of a close coöperation among all of the agencies that have a controlling influence over the handling of Federal Reserve funds in this district. This is not the condition that obtains now, and I am sincerely hopeful that something will be done to bring it about. May I anticipate your hearty interest in that direction?

In answer to this I wrote at length explaining how rediscounts and advances were made by Federal Reserve Banks, how discount rates were established, and showed how the reduction in the rates which had already been made had no apparent effect upon the rates of interest paid by the smaller borrowers to their local banks.

In order to promote a clear understanding of rediscount functions of Federal Reserve Banks, and of the principles which govern their rates, the reader's attention is directed to these fundamental facts:

(1) The law does not permit Federal Reserve Banks to compete generally for business with each other or with the national banks, State banks, and trust companies of the country. They are not allowed to receive deposits from the public, nor are they permitted to make loans or advances direct to individuals, firms, or corporations. In their rediscount operations they are limited to notes and bills defined as 'eligible' which bear the endorsement of a member bank. It follows, therefore, that Federal Reserve Banks cannot

extend any discount accommodations to the public except through the medium of a member bank, with which institutions the loans must first be negotiated. Federal Reserve Banks have no funds to lend the public through the instrumentality of member banks acting as brokers. A Federal Reserve Bank does not take the initiative in making loans to a member bank for the purpose of enabling the member bank to distribute the funds so advanced to its customers. The Federal Reserve Bank lends to the member bank against transactions already made for the purpose of enabling the member bank to restore its reserve to the legal requirement, after the reserve has been impaired or is about to be impaired because of increased loans or withdrawal of deposits.

(2) The Federal Reserve Bank has no direct control over the policy of its member banks with respect to loans and it cannot compel a member bank to make a loan which it does not desire to make nor prevent it from making one which it wishes to make. Neither can a Federal Reserve Bank control the rate of interest charged by member banks. In case of State banks the interest rate is regulated by the laws of the respective States, and in the case of national banks the Federal law permits those institutions to charge up to the maximum rates permitted in the States in which they are located.

(3) No Federal Reserve Bank can rediscount paper for member banks outside of its own Federal Reserve District. Its rediscount transactions are limited to dealings with its own member banks. The Federal Reserve Act does not require rates of discount to be uniform in all districts. Each Federal Reserve Bank is authorized by paragraph (d) of section 14 of the Federal Reserve Act 'to establish from time to time, subject to review and determination of the Federal Reserve Board, rates of discount to be charged by the Federal Reserve Bank for each class of paper, which shall be fixed with a view of accommodating commerce and business.'

One of the early drafts of the Federal Reserve Bill which was considered by Congress in 1913 provided that the Federal Reserve Board should each week fix the rates of discount to be charged by the respective Federal Reserve Banks and that it should notify each Federal Reserve Bank what its discount rates would be for the ensuing week. This provision was stricken out in a later draft of the bill and the Act as finally passed contains the language above quoted. It seems, therefore, to be the intent of Congress that the discount rates shall not be initiated by the Federal Reserve Board, but by the directors of the respective Federal Reserve Banks. This is consistent with the theory of the Act, which does not create a central bank, but a regional banking system, comprised of twelve independent units. This theory is based upon the presumption that the directors of a Federal Reserve Bank are more conversant with credit conditions and current rates for money in their respective districts than the Federal Reserve Board in Washington can be expected to be. While the Federal Reserve Board undoubtedly has power to direct any Federal Reserve Bank, which persists in maintaining a discount rate which is clearly not warranted by general conditions, to change that rate, the Board so far has had no occasion to initiate a rate for any Federal Reserve Bank.

In considering the proper level of discount rates, the directors of the Federal Reserve Banks have taken into consideration not only the reserve position of the bank, but also current local rates for money. It is the purpose of the Federal Reserve Banks to afford a ready means of rediscounting paper for member banks, but when artificially low rates have been established the result has been an unhealthy stimulation of loans by member banks.

It is, of course, most desirable that the Federal Reserve System operate as an agency for financial relief at a time when it is most urgently needed, but in order to keep the Federal Reserve Banks in position to extend such relief, it is necessary that a policy be adopted which will not encourage an undue expansion of loans made for the sake of the profit to be derived by rediscounting with the Federal Reserve Bank.

Coming back to the situation in Nebraska in the autumn of 1921, Governor McKelvie said that he was altogether convinced that the Federal Reserve System was not functioning as it should in that district, and that he was informed that the banks in Nebraska were not generally patronizing the Federal Reserve Bank. It is true that a large majority of State banks, for reasons satisfactory to themselves, had not deemed it advisable to apply for membership in the Federal Reserve System and there were also a number of member banks which had no occasion at that time to rediscount with the Federal Reserve Bank. Many of the non-member State banks, however, borrowed from their correspondents in Omaha, Kansas City, and other cities, and those banks in turn rediscounted with the Federal Reserve Banks.

On August 31, 1921, there were 203 member banks in Nebraska. At that time 74 of these banks were not borrowing from the Federal Reserve Bank. One hundred and twenty-nine Nebraska member banks were at that time rediscounting to the extent of $11,263,345. On June 3, 1920, 135 Nebraska banks were borrowing from the Federal Reserve Bank $30,068,992, and on October 30, 1920, 168 Nebraska members were borrowing $38,294,175. When it is remembered that the total rediscounts and bills payable of all national banks in the United States, as shown by the official report of the Comptroller of the Currency, on August 22, 1907, amounted to $59,177,000, it would seem that the advances, in October, 1920, of over $38,000,000 by the Kansas City bank to member banks in Nebraska alone would indicate very effective functioning on the part of that bank. Older bankers have not forgotten the panic of 1907, and remember that for several weeks before the panic developed credit conditions were most stringent.

CHAPTER XVIII

THE SENATE INQUIRY REGARDING EXPENDITURES BY FEDERAL
RESERVE BANKS — BEGINNING OF MOVEMENT FOR A FARMER
MEMBER OF BOARD — SENATOR GLASS DEFENDS FEDERAL
RESERVE SYSTEM — HOUSE COMMITTEE ON BANKING
AND CURRENCY CONSIDERS AMENDMENT TO
PLACE A FARMER ON FEDERAL RESERVE
BOARD — CONFLICTING VIEWS OF
SECRETARIES MELLON AND
WALLACE

SOME of the charges made by the former Comptroller of the
Currency alleged waste and extravagance in the erection of
the buildings of the Federal Reserve Banks and in the salaries paid their officers and employees. So much publicity
was given these charges, and they were repeated so frequently, that on October 4, 1921, the Senate adopted a resolution directing the Federal Reserve Board to furnish it with

the number of employees, together with their respective salaries,
employed by the Federal Reserve Bank in New York, as well as in
the other Federal Reserve Banks in the country, and the expenditures made by each branch bank in the erection of public buildings and the general expenses in the administration of each Federal
Reserve Bank, and how much of the net earnings have been paid
to the United States as a franchise tax.

In response to this resolution, the Board furnished the
Senate with a detailed report covering salaries paid and
other expenses, cost of building operations, and the amount
of franchise taxes paid. This report was printed as Senate
Document No. 75, and was also reprinted on pages 359–491
of the Board's Annual Report for the year 1921. In its reply
to the Senate's resolution, the Board called attention to the
fact that a full report covering the operations of each Federal
Reserve Bank had been made annually to the Speaker of the

House of Representatives in accordance with the provisions of the Federal Reserve Act.

Two paragraphs from the Board's letter to the President of the Senate are quoted below:

The Federal Reserve Act did not establish a central bank. On the contrary, it made possible the establishment of as many as twelve Federal Reserve Banks, each almost wholly independent of the others in operation as well as in local policies. From a legal standpoint these banks are private corporations organized under a special act of Congress, namely, the Federal Reserve Act. They are not in a strict sense of the word Government banks, but are only quasi-governmental institutions in that they are under the general supervision of the Federal Reserve Board and have on their boards of directors three men representing the Government, who are appointed by the Federal Reserve Board.

The directors (of each Federal Reserve Bank) are immediately responsible for the administration of the bank and are familiar with the requirements for its efficient operation, with the qualifications of the officers and employees, with local conditions, such as cost of living, competition for services by member and other banks of the community, and the fair value of the services rendered. . . . The Federal Reserve Board has not approved in a perfunctory way salaries proposed by Federal Reserve Bank directors. . . . But the Board has taken the position generally that, as the directors are primarily responsible for the operation of the banks, great weight must be given to their representations.

In order to bring out the difference in the average salaries paid to officers by the Federal Reserve Banks and by the larger member banks in the Federal Reserve Bank cities, the accompanying table, which was submitted by the Board as part of its reply, is presented here (page 234).

It will be seen from this table that in 1921 the average salary of officers in all Federal Reserve Banks was $7743, while the average salary paid by the larger member banks in Federal Reserve Bank cities was $13,092, or sixty-nine per cent in excess of that paid by the Federal Reserve Banks.

An investigation made by the Federal Reserve Bank of New York in 1919 showed that the average annual salary, including bonus, paid to employees by the bank was $1440, while the average annual salary, including bonus, paid to employees by ten of the large New York City banks ranged

AVERAGE ANNUAL SALARIES PAID TO OFFICERS BY EACH FEDERAL RESERVE BANK AND BY THREE OF THE LARGER MEMBER BANKS IN EACH FEDERAL RESERVE BANK CITY AS OF OCTOBER, 1921

(Bonus excluded)

FEDERAL RESERVE DISTRICT	FEDERAL RESERVE BANK	MEMBER BANKS	FEDERAL RESERVE DISTRICT	FEDERAL RESERVE BANK	MEMBER BANKS
Boston	$9,679	$14,745	St. Louis..........	$7,078	$11,675
New York.......	12,745	*17,331	Minneapolis	6,478	10,621
Philadelphia.....	10,125	15,733	Kansas City.......	6,147	10,313
Cleveland.......	7,792	10,061	Dallas	5,512	8,767
Richmond	6,696	6,473	San Francisco......	6,459	11,409
Atlanta.........	5,677	7,828			
Chicago	7,946	15,440	System	7,743	13,092

*Six national banks.

from $1620 to $2265. In fact, it was found that in six of these banks the average salary paid employees was in excess of $2100.

The buildings owned by the Federal Reserve Banks are not 'public buildings.' They constitute a part of the invested assets of the respective banks, the funds for their acquisition or construction were not provided by a congressional appropriation, the title is vested in the Federal Reserve Bank and not in the United States, and they are subject to State and local taxation. Amounts invested in buildings by Federal Reserve Banks are capital expenditures, and do not diminish the amount of their franchise taxes payable to the United States except to the extent that the Federal Reserve Banks are authorized to charge depreciation and amortization allowances on their bank premises to current net earnings. The cost of Federal Reserve Bank buildings will be discussed in a succeeding chapter.

In the autumn of 1921, there seemed to be some misapprehension in official circles as to the manner of appointment or election of directors of Federal Reserve Banks, and of the

'Class C,' or Government directors, particularly. It was evidently the intent of the framers of the Federal Reserve Act that the Federal Reserve Banks should be kept out of politics. While the law as finally enacted provides that members of the Federal Reserve Board shall be appointed by the President, by and with the consent of the Senate, it also provides that the Federal Reserve Board shall appoint the three 'Class C,' or Government directors, while the remaining six shall be elected by the stockholding member banks.

Members of the Board heard that applications were being filed with the President for 'Class C' directorships in Federal Reserve Banks, and before the end of the year it was openly asserted by applicants in two districts that their appointments had been promised by the President. Other selections, however, were made by the Board, which during my time never surrendered any of its prerogatives in this respect.

Late in October I received a letter from President Harding in which he said:

I am enclosing you herewith a note from —— expressing his personal interest in one of the members of the Reserve Bank of Chicago. I wish you would sit down and tell me about the situation relating to this bank. If Mr. —— is the only Democrat on the Board, and if he is a capable and acceptable member thereof, I quite agree with —— that he ought to be retained. At your leisure I would like a note outlining the situation to me.

My reply follows:

October 31, 1921

MR. PRESIDENT:

I acknowledge receipt of your letter of the 29th instant, with which you enclosed letter from ——. I have read his letter with interest and return it to you herewith.

I may say that Mr. —— is not a director of the Federal Reserve Bank of Chicago, but is only a subordinate officer . . . not appointed by the Federal Reserve Board.

The Federal Reserve Act provides that there shall be nine directors of each Federal Reserve Bank; three of Class A, who shall be representative of the stockholding member banks and may be bank officers and directors; three of Class B, who at the time of their election shall be actively engaged in their district in commercial, agricultural, or some other industrial pursuit, and who may own stock in banks, but must not be officers or directors; and three of Class C, who are designated by the Federal Reserve Board and who shall not be officers, directors, or stockholders in banks. Class A and B directors are chosen by the member banks and the board of directors of the Federal Reserve Bank appoints all officers and employees and fixes their salaries. The law does not give the Federal Reserve Board a voice in the appointment of officers and employees of Federal Reserve Banks, but requires that the compensation fixed for them by the directors must be subject to approval by the Federal Reserve Board.

(Then followed a list of the nine directors and the name of the two principal officers and the member of its Federal Advisory Council.)

I have no personal knowledge as to the politics of most of these gentlemen, but I have been told that they are all Republicans. . . .

I assure you that it will be a great pleasure to me to give you at any time any information that you may desire regarding the Federal Reserve System.

During the late summer and autumn of 1921 there were successive reductions in the discount rates of the Federal Reserve Banks based upon the improved reserve position and easier market rates; and on December 1st, the rates on all classes of paper and of all maturities were uniform. At the Federal Reserve Banks of Boston, New York, and Philadelphia the rate was four and a half per cent; at the Federal Reserve Banks of Cleveland, Atlanta, Chicago, Kansas City, and San Francisco, the rate was five per cent; and at the other Federal Reserve Banks it was five and a half per cent. These reductions, which were logical and were made in accordance with a definite policy, put an end to the clamor for lower rates, although critics still continued to denounce the

Board for having approved the higher rates which had prevailed when conditions were entirely different.

In January, 1922, Senator Glass addressed the Senate on the subject of the Federal Reserve System. His speech, which consumed parts of two days in its delivery, was a masterly exposition of the intent of the Federal Reserve Act, and was a straightforward discussion of the functions and policies of the Federal Reserve Board and of the operations of the Federal Reserve Banks. Fortified impregnably with facts, its reasoning was clear and cogent, and it was an effective and unanswerable defense of the Federal Reserve System. It was printed in due course in the 'Congressional Record,' and the Board was notified that reprints of that part of the 'Record' containing it were obtainable.

On January 28th, I sent a telegram to all Federal Reserve Banks advising them that copies were available and suggesting their distribution.

Early in July, 1922, the Senate adopted a resolution (S.R. 308) offered by Senator Heflin requiring the Federal Reserve Board to advise the Senate at whose instance this speech was distributed, how many copies were sent out by each Federal Reserve Bank, and to furnish a list of the names and addresses of those to whom copies were sent. The Federal Reserve Bank of Atlanta furnished a list of the residents of Alabama to whom copies were sent, but the other Federal Reserve Banks declined to make their mailing lists public.

The Board's reply to Senate Resolution 308 will be found in Appendix F, page 306.

It seems that some critics of the Federal Reserve System, who were making every effort to bring its administration into disrepute, took umbrage because representative citizens in the various States were afforded an opportunity of hearing the other side of the question as presented by a Senator of the United States on the floor of the Senate, who was, by reason of his experience as Chairman of the House Committee which framed the Federal Reserve Act, and his more recent experience in the administration of the Act while he was Secretary of the Treasury, certainly as well qualified to discuss the subject as any other man.

Shortly after the delivery of Senator Glass's speech, the Senate adopted, without prolonged debate, or reference to a committee, a resolution offered from the floor which provided that no Federal Reserve Bank should hereafter be permitted to expend more than $250,000 in the erection of a building without the specific consent in each case of Congress; but that this should not apply to buildings already in course of construction or for which contracts had been made. Subsequently, this resolution was incorporated in an amendment which passed the House and became a part of the law. The Federal Reserve Banks themselves were not affected by this action, with the exception of the Federal Reserve Bank of St. Louis, which, although it had acquired a site, had not at that time let its contracts; and plans which had been made for buildings for branches at some important points were delayed. Bills were introduced later, permitting the expenditure of the amounts required for the erection of these buildings and were passed without difficulty.

Early in the year 1922, a resolution was offered in the Senate by Senator Smith, of South Carolina, directing the President to fill the next vacancy which might occur on the Federal Reserve Board, by death, resignation, or the expiration of the term of a member, by the appointment of a man whose 'business and occupation' is farming. As the members of the Board were all in good health, and as none at that time showed any disposition to resign, it seemed that this resolution was directed against me, as my term was to expire on August 9th. I had already informed Secretary Mellon that I did not desire a reappointment, but I had been requested by him to make no public announcement of the fact, and he asked me not to close my mind entirely on the subject. A perusal of the foregoing pages is no doubt enough to satisfy any one that my position was no sinecure, and hardly more pleasant than that of a baseball umpire. I should have resigned several months before but for the attacks which were being made upon the Board. The governorship of the Federal Reserve Board does not carry with it any political prestige and from a material point of view offers no attractions. I had served in this capacity continuously since August, 1916, and had been a member of the Board from the beginning. I had seen the Federal Reserve System developed beyond the experimental stage to a point where it had become the strongest banking force in the world. There was nothing for me to gain by accepting a reappointment, nor did I feel that I was under any public obligation to do so. In deference, however, to the wishes of Secretary Mellon, I agreed to await developments.

Without any effort or solicitation on my part, resolutions were adopted during the spring and early summer by bankers' associations in all sections of the country requesting the President to reappoint me, and similar resolutions were adopted by chambers of commerce and other commercial bodies. Some members of the Cabinet and some of the officials of the American Farm Bureau Federation urged my reappointment upon the President, as did some members of the Farm Bloc in Congress, including the Honorable Sydney Anderson, Chairman of the Joint Commission of Agricultural Inquiry. To use the President's own language, the Secretary of the Treasury was for me 190 per cent, and the Secretary of War, 189 per cent.

The demand for the appointment of a farmer upon the Federal Reserve Board continued. Finally, a bill was introduced in Congress to increase the number of appointive members from five to six with the intent that the new member should be a farmer. The law as it had stood since its original enactment provided that 'in selecting the five appointive members of the Federal Reserve Board, not more than one of whom shall be selected from any one Federal

Reserve District, the President shall have due regard to a fair representation of the different commercial, industrial, and geographical divisions of the country.' The proposed amendment provided that 'in selecting the six appointive members of the Federal Reserve Board, not more than one of whom shall be selected from any one Federal Reserve District, the President shall have due regard to a fair representation of the financial, agricultural, industrial, and commercial interests, and geographical divisions of the country.'

The House Committee on Banking and Currency held a hearing on the bill on March 15 and 16, 1922. At this hearing statements were made by the Secretary of the Treasury, the Secretary of Agriculture, and the Governor of the Federal Reserve Board; Mr. Gray Silver, Legislative Agent of the American Farm Bureau Federation; Mr. A. D. Adams, Chairman of the Committee on Federal Legislation, American Bankers Association, and Mr. Thomas C. Atkeson, of the National Grange. Mr. Wallace, the Secretary of Agriculture, Mr. Silver, and Mr. Atkeson favored the amendment which was opposed by Secretary Mellon, Mr. Adams, and myself.

The official report of this hearing shows that Secretary Mellon saw no occasion for enlarging the Board. He believed that a board is more efficient when it is not too large, and that the larger the board is made, the more the responsibility of each member is lessened. He stated the Federal Reserve Board had been functioning very satisfactorily, and pointed out that the Board itself did not pass on the discounting of paper by Federal Reserve Banks. He suggested that if the idea of having an additional member on the Federal Reserve Board was to give more consideration to some particular branch of industry or to some particular region, that purpose could be accomplished better by membership on the boards of directors of the Federal Reserve Banks themselves which discounted the paper of the member banks. He saw no occasion for singling out any particular class for representation on the Federal Reserve Board and thought that, in the appointment of a member, his capacity should be considered. He need not necessarily be a banker, but he should have a general, comprehensive knowledge of trade, commerce, industrial and agricultural activities; but to require that he be engaged in any particular business did not seem to be logical. In reply to an inquiry as to whether any member of the Federal Reserve Board represented agriculture, he stated that Mr. Crissinger had one of the largest farms in Ohio. As to the policy of the Board toward agriculture, Secretary Mellon said that an analysis of the accommodations granted by Federal Reserve Banks to agricultural interests would show that these interests had been treated as liberally as any others, if not more so. To specific questions whether the members of the Board had paid due attention and given due consideration to the agricultural interests, and whether they represented the whole country irrespective of what the interests might be, he answered, 'Yes,' which was also his answer as to whether in his opinion this was true in May, 1920, and in September, 1920. When asked if there would be any objection, instead of increasing the number of appointive members of the Board, to adding the Secretary of Agriculture as an *ex officio* member, Secretary Mellon stated that there would be the same objection, as there would be an unnecessary enlargement of the Board, and the Board would be to that extent less efficient; that generally speaking a board consisting of seven members is better than a larger board. He did not advocate reducing the membership of the Board, but said plainly that he thought it should not be increased.

The Secretary of Agriculture, Mr. Wallace, who followed Mr. Mellon, stated that he did not regard the Federal Reserve Board as a purely administrative body, but rather as an institution which determines the general financial and credit policies of the country, and that the Federal Reserve Board would in time, through the exercise of its administration of the great credit machinery of the country, have a very direct

influence upon prices and upon business in general, and therefore it should be a cross-section of the country's industrial
life, including agriculture. He saw no force in the objection
to increasing the membership of the Board, which he thought
should be sufficiently large to bring into the councils of the
Board a direct personal knowledge of the business and industries in which the people in the various sections of the
country are engaged. He stated that he was in full sympathy
with the proposal to increase the membership of the Board
by adding a member recognized as being fully informed as to
agricultural interests and who would represent agricultural
interests.

I followed Secretary Wallace, and described the powers of
the Federal Reserve Banks as clearly defined in the law, and
I agreed with the Secretary of the Treasury that the duties
of the Federal Reserve Board are largely supervisory and in
a general way administrative, expressing the view that the
Board under the law could not exert such influence on prices
as Secretary Wallace had indicated. I called attention to the
advantage of having an odd number on any board, commission, or tribunal in order to avoid a tie vote. If the Board
were a central bank, I should favor a larger number of
directors, but I said:

The Board's functions are such that if you created a larger
board I think you would very materially decrease its efficiency.
There would be more talk and less action. The proposition to
have one member of the Federal Reserve Board from each Federal
Reserve District is, in my opinion, very unwise. Whether or not
the Board as at present constituted measures up to the requirements is a matter for you gentlemen to decide, but it is conceded
that the Board as at present constituted should have a national
viewpoint, should consider all interests, and give everybody a
square deal as far as possible. If you had one member from each
Federal Reserve District, then you would immediately localize
each member, and each man would say to himself, 'I do not represent the country at large; I represent my particular district.' We
should have meetings of the Board where each man might be

wanting something for his particular district, and there would be
the danger of a disposition to trade favors with each other.

In summing up, I said:

As to the increased membership, experience has shown that a
board of seven is of convenient size, and if it is desired — I see the
force of the argument — to have on the Board some man recognized as agriculturally minded, as you say, and broadminded
enough to know something about the general principles of finance,
if you could find a man of that sort, he would probably be a very
valuable man for the Federal Reserve Board.

There is no occasion to amend the law in order to get such a
man, because there is going to be a vacancy on the Federal Reserve
Board in August, my term expiring at that time, and if you leave
the law as it is, there is nothing to prevent the President from
appointing a farmer. Why do you want to amend the law? I am
not speaking from a selfish standpoint at all. You remember when
the agitation first came up in the Senate — the Banking and Currency Committee reported to the Senate a short bill adding the
word 'agricultural' — to require the President to consider agricultural as well as financial, industrial, and commercial interests
in making his appointments to the Federal Reserve Board; and
then Senator Smith, of South Carolina, offered an amendment in
a legislative session of the Senate providing that the President, in
filling the next vacancy to occur on the Board, whether by resignation, removal, or expiration of term of office, shall appoint a man
whose business and occupation is farming.

If I were concerned about my own position or ambition, I
should be here advocating the bill you are now considering, because its enactment would be the only possible chance for me to
get a reappointment. But the question of whether or not I continue as a member of the Federal Reserve Board is not a matter
of vital importance to me, and certainly of no consequence to the
country. I am talking from a purely disinterested standpoint,
based on eight years' experience on the Board, for what I think is
the good of the country and the Federal Reserve System. I think
you will all agree I am arguing against this bill, and am therefore
arguing against any possibility of my own reappointment. But
the issue lies a good deal deeper than that, you see.

Then why do you want to change the basic structure of the Act,
when all you have to do is to wait until August and get the man
you want?

CHAPTER XIX

NOTWITHSTANDING the evident reluctance of several members of the House Committee on Banking and Currency to enlarge the membership of the Federal Reserve Board, the bill which was discussed in the last chapter was favorably reported and was duly passed by the House; similar action having been taken in the Senate, the bill became a law on June 3, 1922, having received the approval of the President. While there is certainly no objection to the membership of a practical farmer on the Federal Reserve Board, provided he possesses other desirable qualifications, it would seem that, in amending the Act so as to require that one of the members be a farmer, a dangerous precedent has been established. Other classes as they acquire political power may also demand representation on the Federal Reserve Board. Senator Norris, of Nebraska, when the bill was being debated in the Senate, said that it had been given 'an importance vastly beyond what it deserves.' He also said:

The farmers of the country have been given to understand that they are going to get great relief by the passage of the bill and get representation on the Federal Reserve Board. They are going to be fooled again. There will be no relief any more than there is now so far as the Federal Reserve Board is concerned. After all, we cannot by a legislative act take away the discretion that is vested in the appointing power. Under the law as it stands now the President can appoint all farmers, practically, with the exception of two — yes; he could get all farmers as members of the Federal Reserve Board if he desired. . . .

It is said we shall have a farmer on the Federal Reserve Board, and after that everybody in agriculture will prosper. But, Mr. President, the appointing power could select a farmer who is more reactionary than any Wall Street banker that ever lived, if he wants to do that. There are plenty of them whom he could get. . . .

So, after all, in my judgment it is nothing but camouflage; and, while I may probably vote for some of the proposed substitutes, so far as I am concerned I shall do so more as a protest against the action of the Federal Reserve Board in the last two or three years than for any other reason. . . . Yet the bill itself cannot directly accomplish anything.

Senator Kenyon, the leader of the Farm Bloc, said:

If I had time to read the Republican platform of last year, I could cite a declaration in that platform that would sustain this legislation. In his speeches the President has committeed himself to the proposition, and has appointed a farmer, or a representative of agriculture, on the Interstate Commerce Commission, and will unquestionably appoint a representative of agriculture on the Federal Reserve Board. It is not going to accomplish a great deal, as the Senator from Nebraska and the Senator from Connecticut have said. It is not going to remedy all the ills that the farmer is suffering from. It will simply be helpful, and if this Federal Reserve System is to be a great superlord of government and a great supergovernment in this country building up this industry, destroying that one, then it is proper that all the various interests of the country be represented thereon.

As soon as the bill was signed by the President, the efforts of those who were opposed to my reappointment were redoubled, for it was felt that the passage of the bill had removed the principal obstacle to my reappointment. It was represented to the President by some of the practical politicians who were not concerned with banking and economic policies, that the office was one of the most desirable within his gift; and that it would be bad politics to confer it upon an appointee of the previous Administration. Others who had exerted their influence early in 1920 to induce farmers to hold their products for higher prices, and had since been unpleasantly reminded that the prices finally realized were much lower than those which could have been obtained had sales been made in a normal way, were strong in their opposition.

During the months of June and July and up to the expîra-
tion of my term on August 9th, speeches denouncing me were
made in the Senate two or three times a week; and the Senators who remained in their seats were regaled with speeches,
or rather with repetitions of the same speech, which, while
possessing less literary merit, were more bitter in invective
than the philippics of Demosthenes or the orations of Cicero
against Catiline. Even the newspaper correspondents in the
press gallery, who failed to see any news value in these orations
after they had been repeated a few times, were assailed for
their venality in not remaining in their places to report them.
In one of his speeches, made about ten days before my term
expired, Senator Heflin declared that I had been speculating
for a decline in the price of cotton and had for that reason
favored a policy of drastic deflation. This was a very serious
charge, and in substantiation no proof whatever was offered.
As this statement was made upon the floor of the Senate,
there was not open to me the usual course of demanding immediate retraction, and of instituting suit for libel if retraction was not made. I, therefore, addressed a letter to Senator
McLean, Chairman of the Senate Banking and Currency
Committee, in which I flatly denied the charge and made the
statement, which is now reiterated, that I had not during
my term of service on the Federal Reserve Board speculated
in stocks or bonds, cotton, or any other commodity, and
that I had bought or sold nothing whatever on any of the
exchanges; that the only bonds I had purchased had been
direct from the Government in the various Liberty Loan
campaigns, and that I had had only one transaction in
cotton, and that was to buy one bale at ten cents a pound
in the autumn of 1914 when a movement was under way to
induce purchases at that price for the purpose of aiding producers of cotton. Senator McLean very kindly had this
letter inserted in the 'Congressional Record.' Senator Heflin
declared that I was personally obnoxious to him, and I am
informed that the President was advised that senatorial

courtesy would be invoked to defeat my confirmation in case my nomination was sent in. The President did not send my name to the Senate; and some weeks after the expiration of my term, when upon his invitation I called at his office, he told me that he had never seriously considered doing so until these attacks on me became so frequent and intemperate.

During the first week in August most of the matters pending before the Board were disposed of, and on the afternoon of the 9th, I took official leave of the Secretary of the Treasury and my colleagues on the Board, and turned my office over to Mr. Platt, who had been redesignated by the President as Vice-Governor of the Board. For about nine months Mr. Platt was the acting governor of the Board, the organization of which was finally completed by the appointment of D. R. Crissinger, of Ohio, to be Governor of the Board; Henry M. Dawes, of Illinois, to be Comptroller of the Currency; and Milo D. Campbell, of Michigan, to be the farmer member of the Board. Mr. Campbell died suddenly a few days after taking office and was succeeded by E. H. Cunningham, of Iowa. In May, 1923, John R. Mitchell, of Minnesota, resigned as a member of the Board and was succeeded by George R. James, of Memphis, Tennessee. Comptroller Dawes resigned in December, 1924, and was succeeded by J. W. McIntosh, of Chicago.

In the foregoing pages an effort has been made to review in narrative form some of the principal problems encountered by the Board in the establishment and operation of the Federal Reserve Banks. No reference has been made to some of the routine work of the Board, such as the granting of trust powers to national banks, and giving permission to individuals to serve as directors in not exceeding three banks where the institutions concerned were found not to be in substantial competition; nor has it been attempted to enter into a full discussion of all the various amendments to the Federal Reserve Act. Much of the criticism of the Board and its policies was unscientific and intemperate; but there were some who, while expressing their disapproval of some things which were done or left undone, made friendly and constructive criticisms, which are well worth considering. The constructive critics in the main have been economists who have not always agreed among themselves as to what policies should have been adopted. Some of these, however, are in agreement that the Board had no consistent discount policy, and that it had no definite policy as to gold and open-market operations. Other critics believed that too much money was expended by the Federal Reserve Banks in the construction of their banking houses. In this connection it seems proper to state that the Board from the beginning was of the opinion that the Federal Reserve banking system was no mere experiment or temporary expedient, but that its usefulness would be so clearly demonstrated as to assure its permanence in the field of American banking. In this country experience has shown that public buildings and bank buildings which have been erected in growing communities are seldom large enough after the lapse of a comparatively few years to serve the purpose for which they were intended. In many cases either additions have been made involving inconvenience and greater expense, or buildings have been torn down and replaced by larger ones. Where an old building has been sold and a new site selected, the amount realized from the sale has frequently been the value of the land without any reimbursement for the cost of the building itself. As land values have a rising tendency in most American cities, the cost of a new site has usually been much greater than that of the original one. The directors of most of the Federal Reserve Banks, having these facts in mind and finding it impossible to acquire by purchase fireproof buildings suitable for their needs, determined to construct buildings large enough to answer requirements for a long period of years. In two Federal Reserve Bank cities where this principle was not followed, the buildings upon completion were found to be inadequate and were immediately enlarged, additional land being purchased in each instance.

The Federal Reserve Bank of New York has been most frequently cited as affording an example of extravagant expenditure in the construction of its bank building. The statement has been made on many occasions that the bank had entered into contracts amounting to $26,000,000 for the erection of its building alone, and that the amount expended for the land to be covered by the building, something less than $5,000,000, was excessive. The necessity for locating the Federal Reserve Bank of New York in the financial district should be apparent to any one who is familiar with that city and who is informed as to the operations of the Federal Reserve Bank. New York is the great financial center of this country and the daily cash transactions of the member banks with the Federal Reserve Bank are very large. Had the Federal Reserve Bank been located away from the financial district, not only would much inconvenience have been occasioned to member banks, but in their necessary dealings with the Federal Reserve Bank, which involve the transportation of currency and securities through the streets, there would have been incurred the additional danger of robbery and loss of human life. Within the past year the building of the Federal Reserve Bank of New York has been completed. Its cost was not $26,000,000, but about $14,000,000. The bank at one time had over three thousand employees and has now something more than twenty-five hundred, and as business expands it will probably have a larger number in the future. The laws of New York lay down certain requirements which must be observed in the provision of space in new buildings. Should the bank be obliged suddenly to abandon its building because of damage by fire, serious inconvenience, if not positive loss, would be experienced by the business of the entire country. Fireproof construction was, therefore, necessary, and in order to provide properly for the safe-keeping of the vast amounts of gold and securities entrusted to its care, it was necessary to use every means to make the vaults not only fireproof, but burglar-proof and mob-proof. It should be remembered that in the year 1919 Congress abolished the sub-treasuries and transferred to the Federal Reserve Banks as a part of their fiscal agency duties the functions which formerly had been exercised by the sub-treasuries. Since the Federal Reserve Bank of New York removed to its new building, it has held in its vaults always very large amounts of gold and currency, besides the large volume of Government bonds and other securities owned by it and held for account of its clients. The paid-in capital of the bank is about $30,000,000 and surplus about $59,000,000, making a total of $89,000,000. The investment of the bank in its building, including land, is something less than $20,000,000, or about twenty-two per cent of its capital and surplus. Has any commercial bank having a capital and surplus of say $5,000,000 ever been criticized for investing $1,000,000 in a banking house? The old Sub-Treasury Building in New York which occupies the historic site at the corner of Broad and Wall Streets is no longer in use as a sub-treasury; all business formerly transacted there is now carried on at the Federal Reserve Bank of New York, and the Government is able to use the building for any other purpose it may desire. The site, one of the most valuable in the world, is worth several millions of dollars. Those who think that the new building of the Federal Reserve Bank of New York represents too large an investment should bear this fact in mind and deduct from the amount invested the value of the old sub-treasury site.

Before the expiration of my term, the Board adopted the rule that each Federal Reserve Bank should charge off each year an amount equal to two per cent of the cost of its building in order that the amortization should be complete at the end of fifty years, and this rule has never been rescinded. Those who think that the bank buildings at the end of fifty years will still be too large are certainly not optimistic as to the future of America.

As to the gold policy of the Federal Reserve System, it may be said that the law as originally enacted provided that 'subscriptions to the capital stock of the Federal Reserve Banks shall be paid in gold or gold certificates.' Payments were made accordingly. Upon the announcement of the date set for the opening of the banks, the Board requested member banks so far as possible to pay in their required reserves in gold, and this request met with a gratifying response. Reference has already been made to the amendment which permits Federal Reserve Banks to issue notes in exchange for gold. As it became evident that this country would be drawn into the war, every effort was made to increase the gold holdings of the Federal Reserve Banks, for it was anticipated that a great expansion of credit would result and a large stock of gold was necessary as a foundation for these credits. It was not practicable during the war to put in practice any scientific policy covering the conduct of open-market operations by the banks. Embargoes on shipments of gold existed in all countries and open-market purchases were necessarily one-sided, being confined to the purchase of bills arising from imports or growing out of domestic shipments. Any purchase of foreign bills would have been a speculation in foreign exchange, and generally speaking would have been attended with heavy loss. These conditions in the main continued until a few months ago, and are still existent with respect to a number of foreign countries.

During the year 1919 and up to the beginning of the year 1922, the rediscounting operations of the Federal Reserve Banks for their member banks and for each other were so heavy that their open-market operations were systematized. A few months before I left the Board, however, a definite open-market policy was formulated, and it was arranged that there should be concerted action by the Federal Reserve Banks in the exercise of these powers. This policy has since been elaborated and standardized.

Despite the large issue of Federal Reserve notes outstanding, the gold reserves of the Federal Reserve Banks have been at all times sufficiently large to permit of the prompt redemption in gold of such notes as were presented; and of the money hoarded when the pressure upon the banks was greatest, by far the larger amount was in the form of currency. The purchasing power of the Federal Reserve note was always equal to its equivalent in gold. During the year 1922 the volumes of gold imports increased heavily and the policy was adopted of having the Federal Reserve Banks pay out gold and gold certificates instead of Federal Reserve notes, in order to minimize the effect upon their reserves of the large importations of gold.

Much can be said regarding the Board's discount policy and there has already been some discussion of it in these pages. No banking system has ever experienced so many vicissitudes within a few years as has the Federal Reserve System since its establishment. The World War was in progress when the banks began business and, as has already been shown, the rediscount transactions of the Federal Reserve Banks were negligible during the first year or two of their operation. The rate exerted but little influence. Even had conditions been normal, there were no established precedents in this country which could be followed in formulating a discount policy. When the United States entered the war, the Board felt that its duty was to coöperate with the Treasury. That it should or could have pursued a different policy is inconceivable. Right or wrong, the Treasury policies dominated the rate policy of the Board during the war. Many steps which were taken may have been unsound from an economic point of view, but it should be remembered that war itself is the most uneconomic of all processes, for it involves waste and destruction on a large scale. No attempt will be made here to explain the policy of the Treasury, but the reader is referred to an address which was delivered before the Academy of Political Science in New York on April 30, 1920, on 'Treasury Methods of Financing the War in Relation to Inflation,' by R. C. Leffingwell, Assistant Secretary of the Treasury under Secretaries McAdoo, Glass, and Houston. This address will be found in Appendix A, page 257.

The Joint Commission of Agricultural Inquiry expressed the opinion in its report that the Board, regardless of the apprehensions or wishes of the Treasury Department, should have seen that Federal Reserve Bank discount rates were advanced early in the year 1919. The Commission appears to have overlooked the fact that technically the country was still at war at that time. Had the Board undertaken to obstruct the Treasury, means were available of depriving the Board of power to interfere. Military operations, indeed, had ceased, but unpaid and unfunded obligations of the Government were very large early in the year 1919, and the financial necessities of the Treasury were as great as they had been a year before, and funding operations were perhaps even more difficult.

In its report the Commission referred also to the unwillingness of the Secretary of the Treasury to fix the interest on Victory notes at rates sufficiently high to induce the market to absorb them. The writer holds no brief for the Treasury, but would refer those who believe that the rate on the Victory notes was too low to Mr. Leffingwell's discussion of Treasury policies, to which reference has just been made.

Before the war, when the principal countries of the world were on a gold basis, one of the most important functions of a central bank was to regulate the movement of gold to and from the country which it served. If the movement was adverse, the official bank rate would be raised. With a heavy inflow of gold, the rate would be lowered. The gold movements were quickly reflected in current market rates which always followed them and sometimes anticipated them. Because of embargoes during the war, and the general suspension of gold payments abroad which continued after the Armistice, the rates of central banks no longer controlled gold movements, but they were still related to the market rates prevailing in their respective countries. Most of these countries looked forward to the time when they could with safety resume gold payments, but had their central banks disregarded market rates, and attempted to maintain rates below the market, such resumption would have been indefinitely postponed and made increasingly difficult.

Beginning with the year 1920, and continuing up to the time I left the Board, the discount rates which were approved from time to time for the various Federal Reserve Banks, while lower in some districts than the average going rate, were related to current market rates in the larger centers. In regarding market conditions and rates as the chief factors to be considered in the establishment of a Federal Reserve Bank rate, the Board and the banks adopted a principle which has long been recognized and put in practice by central banks in other countries. Some economists both in this country and abroad have during the last two or three years suggested that Federal Reserve Bank rates should be based upon the general price-level. In view of present conditions the Federal Reserve Board is perhaps in better position to consider the merits of such a suggestion than it was at any time during my connection with it, but so far it has given no intimation that it is willing to reverse a policy repeatedly declared, and try the experiment of making the general price-level the determining factor in the rate structure. It would seem that such a determination would put the Board in the attitude of assuming to be the arbiter of prices, and that then an advance or reduction in rates would reflect the Board's opinion that prices were too high or too low, as the case may be, and proclaim its intention to attempt to rectify them. The question then arises, Would the country be willing to commit so important a question as the fixing of a proper price-level to any board or commission? Any announcement by the Federal Reserve Board of a purpose to control prices by means of discount rates would, in my opinion, lead to the destruction of the Federal Reserve System. Nor is it certain that any advance or reduction in Federal Reserve Bank discount rates would synchronize with changes in the price-level. The substantial advances in rates which were made in January, 1920, were not followed by a decline in the general price-level until July, and the successive rate reductions which were made in the year 1921 and early in 1922 were not followed by a higher price-level until the autumn of 1922. Low discount rates have prevailed since July, 1923, but for a year there was no general advance in prices. Federal Reserve Bank rates usually have little effect upon the cost of credit to the small producer and distributor, and certainly the cost of credit is only one of the many factors which enter into the costs of production and the determination of prices. In recent years it has not been the fashion to say much about the old economic law of supply and demand; but nevertheless this law invariably asserts itself, whether the thing affected is an agricultural commodity, or a manufactured product, or credit. Because of the war emergency, and as their contribution to the inflation which the exigencies of war finance seemed to make necessary, the Federal Reserve Banks maintained artificially low rates through the years 1917 to 1919. Now that they are in position to maintain rates based upon actual or impending conditions in the money market, it would be the height of folly for them to disregard these conditions, and, in an effort to control prices, to resort to arbitrary and artificial rates entirely unrelated to market conditions. The law requires that Federal Reserve Bank rates be 'established with the view of accommodating commerce and business.' These rates when properly adjusted have a stabilizing effect and prevent violent fluctuations in the money market, and in this way may exercise a corrective influence; but it would seem that this influence can be exerted more safely and effectively by the maintenance of a proper relationship of Federal Reserve Bank rates to market rates and conditions which normally are responsive to the requirements and activities of commerce and business.

APPENDIX A

TREASURY METHODS OF FINANCING THE WAR IN RELATION TO INFLATION

ADDRESS BY R. C. LEFFINGWELL, ASSISTANT SECRETARY OF THE
TREASURY, BEFORE THE ACADEMY OF POLITICAL SCIENCE
NEW YORK, APRIL 30, 1920

I

FINANCING THE WAR

THE Treasury's war problem was to meet the financial requirements of the Governments of the United States and the Allies promptly and without stint, and to meet them so far as possible from the saved incomes of the people, avoiding avoidable inflation. These objectives must be pursued in such ways as would not interfere with, but on the contrary facilitate, the mobilization of the Nation for war purposes and the production and transportation of munitions and supplies. It was necessary that the Treasury should reach its determinations without the possibility of knowing the duration of the war or, consequently, the magnitude of the ultimate financial effort which the country would be called upon to make. The Allies had about reached the end of their tether because of their dependence upon imports for an important part of their munitions and supplies. They had nearly reached the limit of their ability to finance these through private channels in America and the neutral world. The Central Empires, more self-contained in fact and aided by the blockades maintained by the Allies, appeared to be less subject to the risk of economic breakdown. The United States, the last great nation to enter the war, was also the last great reservoir of available wealth which could be tapped in the Allied cause. If America failed to meet the financial and economic demands upon her, the war was lost.

For about a year after our declaration of war, our loans to the Allies were our principal effective contribution to winning the war which they were fighting. During the first six months the loans we made to Russia and the knowledge of our willingness to make further loans kept Russia in the war and held the eastern front for six months. It was the loan we made to Italy in the fall of 1917, when the great offensive broke on Italy, that gave the Italian people courage and enabled Italy to replace the lost munitions and supplies. In the spring of 1918 it was our silver that held India for the Allies. In the summer of 1918 American credits sustained the French when Paris itself was under gunfire.

As our own military effort grew, the demands of our own army and navy in large measure displaced those of the Allies in respect to American production and transportation, and consequently the burden which the Treasury had to bear came increasingly to represent the expenditures of our own Government and decreasingly those of the Governments of the Allies. The rapidity with which our financial and economic resources were mobilized made possible the termination of the war a year sooner than had been hoped by the most optimistic. Our military and economic effort was, I believe, planned to reach the peak in the spring or summer of 1919. Though hostilities ceased on November 11, 1918, the Treasury was called upon to meet expenditures to the average amount of about $2,000,000,000 a month in November and December, 1918, and January, 1919 — the full amount of the First Liberty Loan each month. The peak of the war debt was not reached until August 31, 1919 (when the floating debt amounted to over $4,000,000,000, and the total gross debt amounted in round figures to $26,596,000,000), and it was not until January, 1920, that the Treasury was able to reduce the floating debt to manageable amount and maturities.

In the period, lacking six days of three years, from the declaration of war to March 31, 1920, on the basis of Treasury daily statements, excluding transactions in the principal of the public debt, the Government's current expenditures amounted in round figures to $37,455,000,000, and its current receipts to $14,198,000,000, the difference being covered by a net increase in the public debt of $23,257,000,000. On March 31, 1920, the gross debt had been decreased by about $1,900,000,000 to $24,698,000,000 from taxes and salvage, including in the latter item the reduction of the net balance in the general fund made possible by the reduced ordinary and public debt disbursements. Though the current months of April and May will show an important increase in the public debt, in large measure due to the heavy burdens thrown upon the Treasury in connection with the return of the railroads to private control, the Treasury is hopeful that the ground lost in the first two months of this last quarter of the fiscal year will be regained in

June when another installment of income and profits taxes is payable, and that the end of the fiscal year on June 30, 1920, will show a reduction in the gross debt of somewhere near $1,750,000,000 from the peak in August, 1919, and that the operations of the whole fiscal year will show a decrease in the gross debt of some $600,000,000, which is more than accounted for, however, by the decreased balance in the general fund. This means that for the fiscal year beginning seven months after the cessation of hostilities, three days after the signing of a peace treaty which is still unratified by America, and two months before the peak of the war debt was reached, the United States should balance its budget within a couple of hundred million dollars — current receipts against current expenditures.

The total disbursements of $37,455,000,000 include expenditures for loans to the Allies and obligations taken from the Allies and other Governments upon the sale of goods on credit in the aggregate amount of, say, $10,000,000,000, and in addition several billion dollars' worth of more or less salvageable investments. To what extent and with what degree of expedition these investments may be liquidated depends upon questions of public policy as well as practical finance.

The most rigid economy in governmental expenditure should be enforced, adequate revenue from taxes should be maintained, and rigorous salvage methods adopted with a view to the rapid retirement of the floating debt and of a portion of the Victory loan before maturity. If due progress is thus made in reducing the floating debt, Victory notes should be accepted at par in payment of the five income and profits tax installments falling due in the calendar year 1922 and the first quarter of the calendar year 1923; or, if the notes are then selling at or above par, a portion of them should be called for redemption in June and December, 1922. This would raise the level of all other Government securities and make possible the refunding of the reduced balance of the Victory loan upon terms advantageous to the Government.

These measures are feasible and necessary. If, however, we reduce taxes, increase expenditures, and delay salvage operations, the Government's financial predicament will be grave, for the debt outstanding and maturing within three years amounts to $8,000,000,000.

The maturities and redemption dates of the Liberty bonds and Victory notes were arranged conveniently for the retirement of the public debt. The sinking fund will retire the entire funded war

debt (over and above the amount of obligations of foreign Govern
ments held by the United States) within less than twenty-five
years if, say, $1,250,000,000 a year is provided for the service of
the debt, including interest and sinking fund.

II

THE TREASURY'S METHODS

The methods pursued for accomplishing these results were intended to and did hold the inevitable war inflation in this country
down to a minimum. There are three ways of financing Government expenditures: taxes, loans, and paper money. The last and
worst of these methods was resorted to, to a greater or less extent,
by all the European belligerents, and, to a disastrous extent, by
some. It was avoided in the United States as a means of meeting
the Government's war expenditures. The Government did not
issue paper money; nor did it borrow directly from the banks of
issue except (a) temporary borrowings for a day or a few days at a
time which were promptly repaid by withdrawals from depositary
banks or out of tax receipts, and (b) certificates sold to Federal
Reserve Banks under the Pittman Act as a basis for the issue of
Federal Reserve Bank notes to replace silver withdrawn from circulation and sold to the British Government for India. There
have been a few instances of purchases of Treasury certificates of
public issues by one or more of the Federal Reserve Banks, but
these have been in such small amounts and of such brief duration
as to be negligible.

Taxation. The Treasury persistently and, on the whole, successfully insisted that one third of the current war expenditures
should be met from current taxes. The effort to go further would
probably have defeated itself and made the speeding-up of production for the winning of the war impossible. When tax rates
are low, the inequalities, injustices, and economic injuries from
errors in the incidence of taxation are slight enough, but as rates
go higher their consequences become graver. The income of the
business man in a period when the demand is for increased production ought to be turned back into his business. The income
of the *rentier* ought to be taken up to the point where the most
rigid economy in personal expenditures would be enforced. As a
practical matter the distinction cannot be made, so we impose
taxes as high as we dare upon both and seek to take the surplus
income of the *rentier* by loans.

The first War Revenue Act became law on October 3, 1917, about six months after the declaration of war. Six or seven months later, it became apparent to the Treasury that war expenditures were mounting very rapidly and, immediately after the third Liberty loan, the Treasury took steps to obtain additional revenue from taxation, demanding $8,000,000,000 in taxes against a rough estimate of $24,000,000,000 of expenditures. The proposal was resisted bitterly by leaders of both parties in Congress, who were anxious to adjourn for the summer and were looking forward to a general election in the fall. The issue was laid before the President, who, after careful consideration, sustained the Treasury, and on May 27, 1918, delivered a special message to Congress demanding an increase of taxes. After months of delay the House passed a bill estimated to produce $8,000,000,000 of taxes, but this bill was still before the Senate Finance Committee when the Armistice was signed. The Treasury, three days after the Armistice, reduced its estimates of expenditures for the fiscal year from $24,000,000,000 to $18,000,000,000 (a figure which proved to be correct within a few hundred millions of dollars), and advised the reduction of the taxes to be carried by the pending bill from $8,000,000,000 to $6,000,000,000 for the current year and $4,000,000,000 for subsequent years. These recommendations were ultimately adopted in the second War Revenue Act, which did not, however, become law until February 24, 1919.

The Treasury's tax policy measurably limited the inflation inevitably incident to the war. But we must not assume that to the full extent that Government expenditures are met from taxes inflation is avoided. There are good and bad taxes. Congress gave effect to the demands of the Treasury as to the amount of revenue required, but the House of Representatives and the Ways and Means Committee of that House are very jealous of the right and duty which they believe to be theirs to initiate revenue measures. The Treasury was consulted and given the most courteous consideration and the fullest opportunity to express its views, but the tax bills were written in Committee and the Treasury's views were overruled in many important instances.

The Treasury, though favoring, and indeed urging, the war profits tax as a tax upon profits roughly attributable to the war, strongly opposed the excess profits tax as a tax upon profits in excess of a given return upon invested capital. Experience has shown, what the Treasury always asserted, that the excess profits tax discourages initiative and enterprise, rewards overcapitalization and discourages conservatism in capitalization, confirms great corporations in their monopolies, encourages extravagance and wasteful management, and adds to the cost of living.

Similarly, the Treasury advised against excessive rates of surtax and urged heavier rates of normal tax. Excessive surtaxes do not produce revenue, but drive capital into the billions of exempt securities; and the manufacture of additional amounts of exempt securities is stimulated by the very existence of these high surtax rates. This encourages wasteful or deferrible expenditure by States and municipalities at a time when the world-wide shortage of capital makes it urgently necessary that our capital resources be conserved for productive business. Graduated surtaxes are necessary and desirable socially, but, particularly where there exist billions of dollars of securities carrying exemption from these taxes, excessive surtax rates defeat their own ends, and, in the last analysis, the burden is shifted to the community as a whole because of the consequent shortage of capital for useful and necessary purposes.

The departure from the Treasury's views concerning surtaxes and normal taxes has seriously impaired the market value of Liberty bonds, which are exempt from the normal taxes, but, within certain limitations, subject to surtaxes. It is within the power of Congress, by reducing surtaxes and increasing normal taxes, to lift Liberty bonds to practically any market level it chooses.

In the last analysis, taxes can only be paid out of income, and the best tax is a properly graduated income tax. When a tax is imposed upon something else, or measured in some other way, the taxpayer who has not current income available must shift the burden to some one else. If possible he will shift it to the ultimate consumer. Capital taxes, including retroactive war profits taxes, and excessive surtaxes, excess profits taxes, and sales taxes — all these must be shifted sooner or later — after much economic disorder in some cases — if possible to the consumer. Because the whole income of the poor man is spent on things he consumes, and the greater part of the income of the man of modest means, but a negligible part of the income of the rich man, taxes of this sort are unjust and unnecessarily burdensome.

There is an even greater evil in these indirect taxes, and that lies in the fact that Congress is perpetually urged to make expenditures out of the public purse for the benefit of some class or group in the community. A system of indirect taxation makes it possible to conceal from the great mass of the voters upon whom the burdens fall the fact that they are being mulcted in order to confer special benefits upon a part of the community. The notion that in some mysterious way the other fellow will pay, the profiteer or the plutocrat — or perhaps the general public without knowing it — leads to wasteful expenditure.

Thus, the beneficent effects of the Treasury's policy to pay as we go one third of the war expenditures from taxes were limited by the character of the taxes imposed. Inflation was avoided to an important extent because the spending power of the individual was curtailed and transferred to the Government without the issue by the Government of credit instruments. The full value, however, of these measures was not obtained because certain of the taxes imposed tended to dissipate or penalize capital and inflate prices.

Liberty loans. When the war began, the investment bankers of the country had, it is said, sold bonds of all kinds to some four hundred thousand persons. The Treasury grappled with the problem of loans boldly, relying upon the patriotism and capacity for self-sacrifice of the American people; it devised a sound plan of decentralized organization for mobilizing the financial resources of the country; and it promptly drew into its headquarters staff experts from the business and financial world, who gave to the fine old Treasury organization the necessary leadership for solving the problems of the war.

The Sixty-Fifth Congress convened on the 2d of April, 1917, war was declared on the 6th, and the First Liberty Loan Act was approved on the 24th. It was the third Act passed by the Sixty-Fifth Congress, being preceded only by two deficiency appropriation bills. Bankers differed in their opinions as to the amount of bonds which could be sold, some believing that the amount might run as high as $1,500,000,000, others that it must not exceed $500,000,000. The Treasury demanded $2,000,000,000 and the loan was oversubscribed fifty per cent. The Treasury disregarded all accepted methods of bond-selling, paid no commissions, employed the Federal Reserve Banks as fiscal agents, and called upon the leaders in the banking and business world in every community to form Liberty Loan Committees and lead the movement. In organization it pursued a policy of decentralization, vesting leadership in the Governor of the Federal Reserve Bank of each district and in committees appointed by him.

The first Liberty loan not only filled the Treasury for the moment, but it prepared the American people for the draft and made them realize the war. It taught millions of them what a bond is and how to save and pay for one.

From May, 1917, to May, 1919, the country was thrown by the Treasury every six months into throes of a Liberty loan campaign — five loan campaigns in two years. It is estimated that twenty million people or more subscribed for some or all of the loans, and that two million people took part as workers in one or all of the campaigns. During these two years, covering the whole period of our participation in the war and six months after the fighting stopped, no one in America was ever allowed to forget that there was a war, that he had a part in it, that that part included buying Liberty bonds, and that to do so he must save money. In the history of finance no device was ever evolved so effective for procuring saving as the Liberty loan campaigns. Every one was always buying a Liberty bond, or trying to pay for one, or getting ready to buy bonds of the next issue. The first, second, third, fourth, and Victory loan campaigns stand out in my mind as the most magnificent economic achievement of any people. For conception, direction, and detail the Treasury is entitled to credit and must assume responsibility, but for the actual achievement of one hundred million united people, inspired by the finest and purest patriotism, no man or group of men could be so foolish as to imagine themselves responsible. Those Liberty loans were the principal instrument in raising cash and getting the people to save for the war.

In fixing the terms of the loans the Treasury had always one major consideration in mind, and it perhaps accounts for some divergence of opinion between the Treasury and some of the bankers. It was not from a willful desire to make the sale of bonds hard, but from a determination to finance the war so that it should never be lost for financial reasons, that the Treasury sold long bonds, and sold bonds at low rates of interest. There must never come an end of the war in defeat because of lack of foresight, lack of courage to take the first steps in a careful, thoughtful way, looking to the possibility of a long war. In addition to the effect of high rates of interest and short maturities, in depreciating other securities and in causing apprehension as to the future, must be kept in mind the psychological effect at home and abroad.

As to maturity, the experience of the Governments of the Allies showed conclusively the grave embarrassment which must confront any Government in the course of a long war which failed to place long-time bonds. The theory that short bonds would keep themselves at par has not been sustained in practice. Very much the highest interest bases have been established by the short bonds and notes of this and other Governments. The explanation is simple. When bonds are sold, to the accompaniment of patriotic appeal, to an amount in excess of the normal investment demand, subscribers who have overbought sell first the bonds which they can sell with the least loss of principal. They do not bother much about the interest basis.

Given the necessity of selling bonds of long maturity, it was undesirable to burden the country with a high interest rate for a long period of time with the moral certainty that very high interest rates would drive the bonds to a premium long before maturity. But above all, the Treasury must give ground slowly, remembering that the limit of the task was not in sight and that the credit of the Government of the United States was the last financial resource of the Allies. We were engaged in war, not conducting a commercial operation. Indeed, there was no rate of interest which would float several billion dollars of Liberty bonds or notes as a commercial operation.

But the bankers differed as much with each other as with the Treasury, and I do not recall any instance when there was any considerable opinion in favor of a rate in respect to any Liberty issue more than one quarter of one per cent higher than the rate actually adopted by the Treasury. A comparison of the present opinions of some financiers and publicists with those expressed during the war, and of record in the Treasury, would furnish amusing reading.

When the Treasury fixed the terms of the Victory loan, I was told by a banker, who is second to none as an expert in the distribution of securities, that they were unnecessarily attractive. A leading newspaper criticized the issue bitterly on the same ground. The attractiveness of the issue was proclaimed by the financiers of the country with such unanimity that serious apprehension was aroused lest the people at large should get the impression that the Victory notes were so attractive that they might leave them safely to the bankers and business men and that no subscriptions involving self-denial on their part were necessary to assure the success of the loan. The head of the Publicity Bureau of the Liberty Loan Organization, after a tour of the country, told me that the Treasury had jeopardized the success of the loan and destroyed the patriotic appeal by offering notes upon such attractive terms.

Federal Reserve authorities became very apprehensive lest the banking institutions of the country should subscribe heavily for their own account, and the Treasury and the Governors of the Federal Reserve Banks were hard put to it to prevent their doing so. Recently the four and three quarters per cent Victory notes have been selling on an interest basis of about six and one quarter per cent.

The rates of interest determined upon by the Treasury were at the time fair rates for the Government to pay, having regard to the exemptions from taxation which the bonds and notes carry and their maturity. No one could foresee the probable course of the market for the bonds and notes in the immediate future with any degree of confidence. A year ago it was freely predicted by financial authorities that Victory notes would shortly go to a premium and that Liberty bonds would be selling at or near par within a year or two.

Every one knows why these sanguine expectations have not been realized. With the Armistice, and still more after the Victory loan, our people underwent a great reaction. Those who had bought Liberty bonds as a matter of patriotism, but not as investors, began to treat their bonds as so much spending money. Those who had obeyed the injunction to borrow and buy Liberty bonds ignored the complementary injunction to save and pay for them. A fifty dollar bond in the hands of a patriot turned spendthrift was to him a fifty dollar bill to be spent Saturday night, or, to her, a new hat, and if the fifty dollar bill turned out to be a forty-five dollar bill, small matter. This was the first and most immediate cause of the depreciation of Liberty bonds, affecting them particularly. I shall mention later other conditions affecting the general situation and them incidentally.

I doubt whether higher rates of interest on Liberty bonds, which would have meant more taxes for the taxpayer and more spending money for the bondholder, would have had any other effect than to increase the inflation which has been rampant since the Victory Loan.[1]

[1] 'Some people argue that a low rate of interest makes people save more because it is necessary for them to save more in order to acquire independence. Others maintain that a high rate of interest induces people to save because they can see the direct advantage of doing so. Both these arguments are probably true in some cases. But, as a rule, people who have the instinct of saving will save, within certain limits, whatever the rate of interest may be. When the rate of interest is low, they will certainly not reduce their saving because each hundred pounds that they put away brings them in compara-

Some critics say that the Treasury should have foreseen the after-the-war reaction and, in order to protect bondholders from the consequences of their own acts, issued the bonds and notes at rates of interest which would insure a market price for them at or near par even in the period of reaction. This is inflationist doctrine. The bonds and notes were never meant to be treated as spending money. The Civil War gave us our fill of interest-bearing currency. Depreciation in market price serves as a check upon those who wish to spend their bonds.

There was no plan of financing the war or of financing the period of readjustment which would protect the holders of the Government's securities or the Government's credit against subsequent folly and waste.

War savings. The Liberty loan campaigns were supplemented by the work of the War Savings Organization, which disseminated sound economic doctrine and produced some cash.

Treasury certificates. By selling Treasury certificates in anticipation of each Liberty loan and of income and profits tax installments, the Treasury provided current funds to meet outgo, made provision against the money strain which would have been involved if Liberty loan and tax installments had been paid on one or several days without anticipatory borrowing, and, more important in economic effect, tapped the credit resources of the banks and trust companies of the United States and mobilized them for the uses of the Government, thus limiting commercial inflation during the period when the Government was the principal buyer and needed to have the credit resources of the country placed at its disposal.

The Treasury issued as great and as frequent long loans as the market could absorb — in fact, greater and more frequent than the market could absorb. The point of saturation for long Government loans had been reached — and passed — with the fourth Liberty loan. Investors require diversification of their investments. In a little over two years we created $25,300,000,000 of debt (at the maximum). It was bad enough to ask the people to absorb that amount of the obligations of one Government. It would have been intolerable to insist upon their buying only bonds of one character — that is, long-time bonds. After Armistice the only way to get additional investment money into Government

tively little, and when the rate of interest is high, the attraction of the high rate will also deter them from diminishing the amount that they put aside.'
(Hartley Withers: *War-Time Financial Problems*, p. 7.)

securities was to offer some diversification of terms, and this was done by issuing Victory notes and thereafter by revolving Treasury certificates.

The result of forcing out more long loans would have been the perpetuation of the war debt. There is no greater influence toward economy of expenditure and maintenance of adequate revenue than the existence of short-dated debt. No Administration could have resisted the pressure for reduction of taxes and increase of expenditures if the war debt at its maximum of $25,300,000,000 had been funded, and it had subsequently appeared that taxes and salvage would more than meet current expenditure. The time to pare down war debt is immediately after the war.

During the war Treasury certificates were sold largely to taxpayers in anticipation of taxes. Since the Victory loan campaign, efforts to procure distribution of both tax and loan certificates among investors have been increased and marked success has attended them. The banking institutions of the country have been asked to buy the certificates and sell them to their customers, and their fine efforts to that end have been supplemented by mailing circulars describing each issue of certificates to a selected list of taxpayers and bondholders of the United States. The success of these efforts is evidenced by the fact that on April 16, 1920, of $2,693,808,500 loan and tax certificates outstanding only $462,114,000 were pledged with Federal Reserve Banks as security for loans and discounts. In view of the fact that the Reserve Banks were maintaining a preferential rate for paper so secured, it is safe to assume that the remaining $2,231,000,000 certificates were in the hands of investors, including banks which were not borrowers.

War loan deposits. Technically the Treasury's special depositary system is one of the most interesting, as it is one of the most valuable, devices for financing the war. Our problems were different from those of European countries. We had to deal with some thirty thousand independent banks and trust companies scattered all over the United States. The device of 'payment by credit' was worked out in connection with the first Liberty loan at a Sunday conference in May, 1917, between representatives of the Treasury, of the Federal Reserve Board, and of the New York Liberty Loan Committee. Unchanged in principle from that date to this, but simplified and perfected in the course of three years, it served to weld together and mobilize for war the banking resources of the United States, including in the Government's depositary

banking system ten thousand of the thirty thousand banking institutions of the country.

'Payment by credit' is a device for permitting the banking institutions which purchase Government securities to defer payment for them until the Government actually needs the money. It was adopted to prevent money stringency. It developed the further advantage that in the difference between the rate borne by the securities and the rate charged on the deposit, banks found some compensation for their time, trouble, and the loss of deposits resulting from the sale of securities to investors. If, instead of permitting the banks to make payment by credit, the Treasury had required them to make payment in cash and had held the cash, it is apparent that the operation simply could not have been carried out. A very modest increase in the balances in Treasury offices involves money strain. The attempt to make payment into Treasury offices in cash on one day of the proceeds of the smallest issue of Treasury certificates — not to mention a Liberty loan or tax payment — would create a panic. Bankers and the public have become so accustomed to the ease and smoothness with which Treasury operations are conducted that they take them for granted; yet two years ago the business and banking community was in an uproar because of the fear of money strain in connection with the first income and profits tax payment — a strain which never occurred because the Treasury's arrangements to deal with the situation were so complete.

'Payment by credit' was well calculated to limit inflation incidental to war borrowing. If, instead of permitting the banks to make payment by credit, the Treasury had required them to make payment in cash and had then redeposited the proceeds, to the extent that it did not require to make immediate use of them, it would have pursued a course more likely to create inflation. If the Government were to draw into the Reserve Banks and the Treasury offices cash in excess of its current requirements, the first effect would be to make money very tight, and increase money rates, with consequent interference with the Government's financial operations. The second effect would be heavy discounts by the Reserve Banks to meet the demands so artificially created. Discounts so made would be for periods from one to ninety days. Upon the redeposit of the proceeds of certificates depositary banks would be put in possession of loanable funds.

It was better to make one bite of the cherry and to avoid the money strain and inflation which would have been inevitable if the money had been first drawn out of the banks and then redeposited with them.

In order to sell Liberty bonds and Victory notes it was necessary to give subscribers the option of making immediate payment in full or of making payment in installments over a period of months. This injected an element of great uncertainty into the Treasury's calculations. It was quite impossible precisely to anticipate receipts under these circumstances. As a matter of fact, the privilege of making payment in full on the opening day was largely availed of, and the Government's balances were consequently swollen until certificates of indebtedness issued in anticipation of the loan matured or could be called for earlier redemption. This was done as promptly as possible, but the operations were on so huge a scale that it was a matter of two weeks after a payment was made before the Treasury could obtain really reliable information as to the amount of the payment.

The same principle (payment by credit) was employed in handling the great tax payment in June, 1918 (which was only about half covered by anticipatory borrowing), although modified necessarily in detail. Checks received, drawn on qualified depositary banks, were forwarded to them and the amount credited by them in the War Loan Deposit account. This was done instead of collecting the checks and redepositing the proceeds.

A similar problem, though not of such great dimensions, presents itself in connection with the current routine business of the Government under war and armistice conditions. The ideal thing would be to have the Government's receipts precisely equal its expenditures from day to day. That ideal, however, being impossible of attainment, the Treasury has consistently pursued the policy of borrowing sufficiently in advance to meet its requirements, without direct borrowing from the Federal Reserve Banks. The Treasury plans to sell certificates to an amount sufficient to cover the estimated requirements for some three weeks in advance. This is a small margin of safety in view of the impossibility of estimating closely. It is physically impossible to issue Treasury certificates more frequently than every two weeks, and it takes ordinarily two weeks from the date of the offering of an issue of Treasury certificates to the date of closing the issue for the ascertainment of its results. Sometimes it happens that the Treasury miscalculates its cash requirements and borrows in excess of the amount which turns out to be actually necessary at the time. That happened last September. Sometimes it underestimates its requirements. That happened only last month. Indeed, it is very much more difficult to gauge the current income and outgo now than it was during the period of active warfare. Expenditures increased at the rate of about $100,000,000 a month pretty regularly during the war. The physical limitations upon production and transportation prevented expenditures increasing by leaps and bounds — imposed a certain sobriety upon them. There has been no similar brake upon the decrease since Armistice. In consequence of settlements and sales of accumulated stores, receipts and expenditures have jumped about in such a way as to make them utterly impossible of calculation. The Treasury has no control over the expenditures or salvage operations of other departments.

A depositary bank, when it makes a 'payment by credit,' does not put itself in possession of loanable funds. What actually happens is that the bank becomes possessed of an asset, to wit, Treasury certificates, and is charged with a liability, to wit, an entry in the Government's War Loan Deposit account. It does not have any money to lend or to spend until it sells the certificates or borrows on them. Like most human devices, payment by credit may be subject to abuse, as, for instance, by the application of the proceeds of sale or borrowings on the certificates to other purposes than meeting the Government's calls, but the Governors of the Federal Reserve Banks, under the wise guidance of the Federal Reserve Board, have been alert to prevent such abuse.

The view that bank deposits are potential currency [1] is inapplicable to the deposits created in the Government's War Loan account. No checks are ever drawn upon or charged against the Government's War Loan Deposit account with depositary banks. Remittances are made by them to Reserve Banks on receipt of letters or telegram.

The number and amount of United States Government disbursing officers' checks outstanding or in process of collection at any given moment of time is not affected by the amount of the Government's deposits in depositary banks. The Treasury has no control over the drawing of these checks and the credit of the

[1] 'As many people may be puzzled by the assertion that the Government increases the currency by borrowing from banks, it is better to explain the process briefly here, though in another book I have already shown how loans made by banks produce manufactured money by adding to the banks' deposits, *which embody the right of their customers to draw the cheques which are the chief form of currency that we now use.*' (Hartley Withers: *Our Money and the State,* p. 61.)

Government of the United States has at all times been sufficient to float them regardless of its bank balances. These checks have involved an important expansion of currency. The Treasurer of the United States handled as many as three hundred thousand checks in one day during the war. He is now handling something like eighty thousand checks a day. This is not potential currency, but real currency. We have struggled to keep enough money in the bank to meet these checks as they come in, but the checks have been floated, not on the faith of our bank deposits, but on the general credit of the United States Government.

Collateral agencies. During the war many collateral agencies were created to conserve and mobilize the resources of the country and limit the inflation of prices and the expansion of currency and credit. Some were initiated by, others were quite independent of, though acting in coöperation with, the Treasury. The Capital Issues Committee discouraged issues for non-essential purposes. The Sub-Committee on Money of the New York Liberty Loan Committee fixed the price of call money and rationed credit to the stock market. The Division of Foreign Exchange of the Federal Reserve Board licensed imports and exports of gold, silver, and capital. The War Trade Board licensed imports and exports of commodities. The War Industries Board fixed prices and priorities for commodities. The Shipping Board, the Food and Fuel Administrations, and the Railroad Administration, were all parts of a comprehensive plan for mobilizing the resources of the country.

It was impossible to rely upon prices and rates to prevent inflation at a time when the first duty was the winning of the war. When the Government requires the services, the wealth, the productive capacity of all the people for the purposes of a great war, it must practically go through a process of condemnation and pay a price determined by properly designated functionaries. The law of supply and demand cannot be allowed to function in wartimes so as to permit some of the people to extort from all of the people, represented by their Government waging a righteous war, prices, whether for commodities or credit, based upon the fact that the supply is very limited and the demand for all practical purposes unlimited.

When the fighting was over, most of these controls were broken down one by one as rapidly as seemed possible, with a view to restoring natural conditions.

III

INFLATION

Before the war. Before we entered the war, we had what, for lack of a better short description, may be called, though inaccurately, gold inflation.

During the war. Currency expansion, as distinguished from credit expansion, has been very moderate in this country.[1] The Treasury has not manufactured currency at all. It has not manufactured credit directly with the banks of issue. It has limited the expansion of credit as far as practicable. The expansion of currency and credit which has taken place has been the result, not of Treasury methods of financing the war, but of the unlimited buying power of the Government of the United States when supported by the devotion of the people. Government expenditures and commitments were the cause of price inflation, rather than the methods which the Treasury employed to meet those expenditures. Expenditures and commitments always outran the provision made for them by the Treasury, whether in cash or credit. Government contracts covered future production for months or years ahead; but the Treasury never during the whole period of the war had provided money or bank credit sufficient to meet its requirements for more than a few weeks ahead. Prices rose in response to the effective demand of the United States Government sustained by the general credit which its resources and taxing power and the devotion of one hundred million people gave it. They were influenced by two conflicting forces, the desire of the Government to stimulate production and the desire of the Government to prevent profiteering. The expansion of currency and bank credit, which followed the Government's expenditures and commitments, sustained and distributed the price inflation. In much of the discussion of currency and credit inflation and their relation to price inflation, insufficient attention has been given to the practical difference between the operations of private persons and companies, on the one hand, and a government in war-time, on the other. A government in war-time may, as a private concern cannot, upset the balance between the supply and demand for commodities without first obtaining currency or bank credit.

[1] Letter of Governor Harding to the Chairman of the Banking and Currency Committee, United States Senate, dated August 8, 1919; *Federal Reserve Bulletin* for August, 1919.

The cost of living here has increased less than in any of the belligerent countries (including Japan [1] which assumed no appreciable part of the financial burden of the war) or in the neutral countries of Europe.[2] This was in no small measure due to Treasury methods of financing the war.

[1] Japan has a bank rate above eight per cent. Her inflation is a gold inflation. 'The cost of living has advanced threefold more than before the war. . . . The gold holdings of Japan have now reached the unprecedented total of 1,899,000,000 yen, of which 1,061,000,000 yen belongs to the Government and 838,000,000 yen to the Bank of Japan. Of this large sum only 545,000,000 yen is in Japan, 1,354,000,000 yen being invested or deposited in England and the United States.' (*Economist*, January 3, 1920, pp. 19–20.)

'The abnormal inflation of currency not only keeps up prices, but is lending impetus to speculative fever, which now knows no bounds. Investments in new enterprises between January and October this year amounted to no less than 2,859,000,000 yen, or more than for the whole of last year, when investments totaled 2,676,000,000 yen; and the expansion of capital is now such that the authorities can no longer regard the situation as wholesome. Banks have been officially instructed to restrict loans, and to preach economy and caution, but speculation continues rife. It is frequently reported that officials are interested in speculation, and that that is one reason why no control is exercised over note inflation. The same thing went on after the war with Russia, but it was followed by panic and numerous business failures, leading to prolonged business depression.

'The effect on industry and society is far-reaching and disaffecting. Many enterprises, such as weaving and shipping, continue to pay enormous dividends, though most of the mushroom enterprises can hardly pay their way. Industry is marked by increasing unrest, with frequent strikes for higher wages and shorter hours. Of late the greater part of this unrest has been in shipyards and mines. At one of the copper mines recently the troops had to be called out to put down violence when six thousand miners began to take matters into their own hands. This is the first time in the industrial history of Japan that troops have had to be called out to deal with strikes. The cotton mills, which are paying such big dividends, being manned mainly by women, have labor in their own hands, and so far they experience no labor unrest. In most cases mill work, so far as women go, is little less than a form of slavery, as the girls are not free to leave when they wish, and seldom get away until invalided out. On the other hand, the luxury and extravagance of the profiteers and the newly rich tend to demoralize society, and cause revulsion of the poor against the rich. The most prosperous concerns in cities are the restaurants, houses of questionable pleasure, and the dealers in jewelry and expensive ornaments. The wealthy are buying up whole lots of houses, and pulling them down to erect grand mansions with spacious gardens for themselves, to the great resentment of the poor, who cannot find dwelling accommodation. A great part of big cities like Tokyo is taken up with these gardens of the privileged and the wealthy, while space for common dwellings is at a premium, the poor being driven into the slums. This leads to social disaffection and encourages Socialism.' (*Economist*, February 7, 1920, p. 263.)

[2] British White Paper (Cmd. 434, 1919), *Statements of Production, Price Movements, and Currency Expansion*, in certain countries.

Since Armistice Day. Since Armistice Day the world has not only failed to make progress toward the restoration of healthy economic life, but in fact has receded farther from a sound position. We have failed to restore peace and peace conditions in Europe, and in America unsound economic ideas have in many instances prevailed, and the effort is being made, first here, then there, to improve the condition of some of the people at the expense of all of the people.

Inflation here since Armistice Day is attributable to three principal causes: (*a*) world inflation and the internationalization of prices; (*b*) heavy expenditures by our Government and Government Interference with business; (*c*) reaction and waste among our own people.

(*a*) For five years the world has been consuming more than it produced, living upon its capital, and the Governments of the world have been issuing evidences of indebtedness to represent the wealth destroyed. This has caused world inflation of prices.

The inflation which has taken place here since Armistice seems attributable in no small degree to the inflation of the Continental European currencies operating upon the optimism of the American people.

People have been led to believe that there is a mystery about foreign exchange, and that in some way America is at fault for not protecting the European exchanges from depreciation. In wartime the measures taken by the belligerent nations in respect to international trade and finance were more or less complete. Embargoes on the export or import of gold were accompanied by embargoes on the export and import of commodities, by domestic price-fixing, by fixing the price of money, by control over capital issues, by control over foreign exchange, and by Government loans in foreign countries. These controls probably should not have been removed if the gold embargoes were to be retained; for the gold held in Europe has been made a basis for further inflation there and the ever-expanding European currencies have been sold for dollars to be used to purchase things not needed as well as those needed. The depreciated price at which European currencies are taken in consequence of these methods means for them a rapidly increasing foreign debt which will make the ultimate resumption of a gold basis more difficult.

Our own prices are being inflated and our own banking and currency position expanded by the feverish speculation in European currencies, credits, and securities, including those of countries with which we are still technically in a state of war.

In the present position of the international balances and of the foreign exchange and because of gold embargoes, Federal Reserve Bank rates cannot function internationally, and will operate solely upon the domestic situation.

(*b*) Government expenditure is at the root of inflation all over the world. Wise methods of meeting it may mitigate the inflation, but they cannot prevent it.

The Government of the United States has been slow to realize upon its salvageable war assets and to cut down expenditures growing out of the war.

While Congress deliberated, the Government held control of the railroad systems of the country for a year and a quarter after fighting stopped, and furnished transportation at less than cost. Then Congress ordered the railroads returned to their owners with a new expenditure of $1,000,000,000 by the Government for their account and the deferment for years of $1,000,000,000 the railroads owe the Government.[1]

The interference of Government in railroad affairs, begun many years before we entered the war, has subjected business and industry to the gravest hardships for lack of adequate transportation and has involved a great additional strain upon our credit facilities. You can fix the price of capital, but you cannot make it work for that price. You can fix the price of labor, but you cannot make it work for that price. By holding down rates for the shipper, the railroads have been kept so poor that neither capital nor labor will work for them. The shipper has cheap rates, but he cannot get transportation. If the railroads had been allowed to charge reasonable rates, the Government would have lost nothing in their operation, and it would not have been obliged to invest any considerable amount of money in them, for, given reasonable rates, they could have obtained capital through private channels.

[1] The actual cash expenditures of the Railroad Administration for the six months ending June 30, 1918, were $120,000,000; for the fiscal year ending June 30, 1919, were $359,000,000; and from July 1st to March 31, 1920, were $776,000,000, a total of $1,255,000,000. The recent legislation and that now pending make specific appropriations to the amount of $800,000,000 and indefinite appropriations (including a gift to short-line railroads which were not taken over by the Government) which will involve expenditures to the estimated amount of $300,000,000. It is safe to say that the Government's expenditures and losses on account of the railroads and its investments in the railroads will shortly amount to $2,350,000,000.

The United States Shipping Board expended in the fiscal year 1917 $14,000,000; in the fiscal year 1918, $771,000,000; in the fiscal year 1919, $1,820,000,000; and in the fiscal year 1920 (to March 31, 1920), $433,000,000. The actual cash expenditures since Armistice Day amounted to approximately $1,600,000,000, while Congress deliberated as to our shipping policy. Notwithstanding the fact that it has been engaged in commercial shipping at a time when it is exceptionally profitable, the Shipping Board has made as yet no net return to the Treasury, its expenditures still exceeding its receipts.

Five billion dollars spent or invested in railroads and ships, the larger part of it after the fighting was over! Why are the railroads being run to-day at a loss at the Government's expense? To what end are we moving in our shipping policy?

Instead of telling the people frankly and boldly that prices are high because they are wasting, we fix prices and prosecute profiteers in order that the people may buy more and pay less.

Instead of telling the people that Liberty bonds have depreciated because they are treating their Liberty bonds as spending money, we clamor that the rate of interest upon the bonds is too low and urge a bonus to bondholders disguised as a refunding operation.

Instead of telling the young men who were drafted to fight the war, and who came back better and stronger and more fit to fight their own battles than they ever were before, to go to work and save their money and look out for themselves as any self-respecting man should, we listen complacently to their organized demands for a bonus, euphemistically called 'adjusted compensation.'

Penny-wise and pound-foolish, we leave the executive departments underpaid, and undermanned so far as regards supervisory employees. While Congress struggles to effect economies at the expense of efficient administration of the Government, it takes time to add $65,000,000 to Civil War pensions.

From November, 1918, to March, 1921, nearly two years and a half, the first two years and a half after fighting stopped and probably the most critical two years and a half in the world's history, the Government of the United States has been deadlocked against itself, a Government by obstruction. It is at least questionable whether the progress of reaction would have been so complete or so disastrous if our institutions had not given this country, during the most critical period of the world's history, a government divided against itself, and therefore incapable of effective leadership in national or international affairs.

(c) At this most critical moment in the history of Europe, when our own financial and economic stake in Europe's affairs is so great that disaster there could mean only disaster here, many of our own people have turned gamblers and wasters. For plain living and high thinking we have substituted wasting and bickering. We enjoy high living while we grumble at the high cost cf living — of silk stockings and shirts for the poor, of automobiles for men of small means, of palaces for the profiteer and the plutocrat.

Unhealthily stimulated, commercial business appears to prosper and commercial expansion proceeds unchecked. From March, 1919, to March, 1920, though holdings of, and loans upon, Government war securities of all reporting member banks of the Federal Reserve System (about eight hundred member banks in leading cities believed to control about forty per cent of the commercial bank deposits of the country) decreased from $4,000,000,000 to something over $2,000,000,000, their other loans and investments increased from $10,000,000,000 to over $14,000,000,000. For every dollar of credit released by the Government, two dollars were extorted by business. From May 2, 1919, to March 19, 1920, though the Reserve Banks reduced their loans and discounts upon Government war securities from $1,800,000,000 to $1,400,000,000, they increased their other loans and discounts from $350,000,000 to $1,400,000,000.[1]

High rates of interest and discount, limitations of currency and credit, these and all other traditional methods should be used courageously; but they will not suffice under the abnormal world conditions now prevailing.

[1] On the other hand, though Federal Reserve Banks' loans and discounts secured by Government war obligations rose from about $250,000,000 at the end of 1917 to a high of over $1,800,000,000 in May, 1919, their other loans and investments never during the war rose above about $850,000,000 (in November, 1918) and were down as low as about $350,000,000 in May, 1919. All reporting member banks' holdings of, and loans upon, United States war securities increased from a low of about $1,250,000,000 in December, 1917, to a high of about $4,000,000,000 in May, 1919. Their other loans and investments increased from about $9,500,000,000 in December, 1917, to a high of about $10,750,000,000 in August, 1918, and contracted to less than $10,000,000,000 in March, 1919. A smaller number of banks (about 630 controlling about thirty-five per cent of the commercial bank deposits of the country) were reporting in December, 1917.

IV

REMEDIES

We must get together, stop bickering, and face the critical situation which confronts the world as we should a foreign war. We must recognize our responsibility to and our stake in Europe, and in one way or another lend her our moral support and leadership and economic assistance, but without Government loans. We must cut Government expenditure to the quick, abjure bonuses, and realize promptly upon all salable war assets, including ships, applying the proceeds to the war debt. We must have a national budget with teeth in it, which means, among other things, that no appropriation shall be made by Congress without a critical examination and report on ways and means by the Treasury, representing the financial end of the executive branch of the Government, and the Ways and Means Committee of the House and the Finance Committee of the Senate, representing the financial end of the legislative branch. We must promptly revise our tax laws to make them more equitable and less burdensome without reducing the revenue. We must restore the railroads to a self-supporting basis by establishing rates which will insure a return for capital and labor commensurate with the return to be had elsewhere at a time when there is a world-wide shortage of both. And, above all, we must work and save. We must produce more, but, more important still, we must consume less.

APPENDIX B

MEMORANDUM

Issued by the Federal Reserve Board Relating to the Operations of the Call-Money Market in New York During the Years 1919 and 1920

THE principal supplies of money for collateral call loans are loanable funds of banks and bankers located both in and outside of New York City, including foreign banks and agencies of foreign banks; and similarly the loanable funds of firms, individuals, and corporations seeking temporary investment. The proportion of the whole fund loaned by these several interests varies seasonally and in accordance with the attractiveness of other opportunities for investment, either locally or in other markets. . . .

In the matter of the supply or attraction of funds to the call-money market, there is generally a definite and well-understood obligation on the part of banks to accommodate first their own commercial clients, so that it is only the excess of loanable funds which they may have from time to time that is available for the collateral call-money market or for the purchase of commercial paper in the open market. This excess of loanable funds available for employment in the securities market varies, therefore, according to the commercial requirements of the country. It has long been recognized that for assurance of a sufficient amount of money to finance the volume of business in securities, reliance cannot be placed on a rate of interest limited to the rates which obtain or are permitted in commercial transactions whose prior claim on banking accommodation is universally conceded. . . .

Prior to the institution of the Federal Reserve System, bankers, especially in reserve centers, were accustomed to look upon call loans as their principal secondary reserve on the theory that, inasmuch as those loans were payable upon demand, funds so invested could always be promptly obtained on short notice to meet withdrawals of deposits or for other use. In these circumstances there was ordinarily available for collateral call loans a supply of funds sufficient for ordinary market requirements and at low rates, although at times the rates rose to high levels as the supply of funds diminished or the demands increased.

This attitude of the banks toward call loans as their chief sec-ondary reserves has been greatly modified by two causes. The first was the closing of the stock exchanges at the outbreak of the European war in the summer of 1914, when it became practically impossible to realize on call loans secured by investment securities, which became, therefore, 'frozen loans.' This resulted in a more or less permanent prejudice against dependence upon call loans as secondary reserves. The second and more important factor was the creation of the Federal Reserve System. Under the terms of the Federal Reserve Act provision is made for the rediscount of commercial paper, but the rediscount of loans for the purpose of carrying investment securities, other than United States Government obligations, is excluded. Consequently, in order to maintain maximum liquidity, with suitable provision for secondary reserves that can be immediately availed of, banks, including foreign agency banks, now invest a greater proportion of their resources in assets that can be realized upon at the Federal Reserve Bank. Another changed factor in the present situation grows out of the fact that the war and post-war conditions have rendered unavailable supplies of money which formerly came from foreign banks. Since the summer of 1914, while total banking resources have largely increased, the volume of bank money available to the securities market at low or normal rates has not increased proportionately, but, on the contrary, has probably decreased. All of these circumstances explain in some measure the increased rates which have often been required during the past year for money loaned in the securities market.

Changed conditions are also present in the factors governing the demand for money. Prior to the Armistice, agencies of Government were employed to restrict the issue of new securities for purposes other than those which were deemed essential for carrying on the war. At the same time, as the Treasury undertook to sell large amounts of certificates of indebtedness and Liberty bonds bearing low rates of interest, the question arose as to whether the competition of the general investment markets might not prejudice the success of the Government issues. In these circumstances, with full understanding on the part of the Treasury Department, the officers and members of the New York Stock Exchange undertook to limit transactions which would involve the increased use of money for other purposes in consideration of which the principal banks of New York City endeavored to provide a stable amount of money for the requirements of the security market.

After the Armistice, these restrictions were removed and ordinary market forces reasserted themselves. The issuance of new securities was resumed in unprecedented volume and consumed a vast amount of capital and credit when bank credit was already expanded by the necessity of carrying large amounts of Government securities which the investment market was not prepared to absorb. Thus arose a further cause for the increased cost at times of accommodation on collateral call loans. . . .

The volume of money outstanding on call is more or less constant, fluctuating only over relatively long periods, and the amount which is loaned from day to day is but a small proportion of this constant volume. The constant volume of outstanding call loans bears a rate of interest which is determined daily and is known as the 'renewal rate.' The daily borrowings, either in replacement of loans called for payment or representing new money borrowed, are made at rates which may or may not be the same as the renewal rate and which frequently vary during the same day. . . .

At a time of such heavy credit requirements as the present the greater volume of borrowings, not only in the aggregate, but in the day-to-day demands, naturally often results in high rates for the money loaned. Indeed, so reluctant have the bankers been during the past few months to supply the large demand for credit based on securities that the occasional loaning of relatively small amounts of money at very high rates often represents a desire, not to secure the high rate quoted, but to prevent the rate from going very much higher with the consequent demoralization which might result.

The operation of the law of supply and demand is equally effective in determining the rate for commercial loans and all other borrowings. In fact, rates for commercial loans and rates for collateral call loans have a common root in the law of supply and demand, and the conditions which affect one, in the main affect the other, although not in like degree, as is demonstrated by the far wider fluctuation of call rates and the higher points to which they go. The rates for call money do not determine, and have not exerted an important influence on, the rates for commercial borrowings. It is the universal custom of the banks to satisfy first the commercial needs of their customers. They feel an obligation to customers, but none to those who borrow in the open market on securities. Besides, as the resources of the banks mainly come from the commercial customers, their own self-interest compels a preference in favor of their commercial borrowers, since failure to grant them reasonable accommodation would induce them to withdraw their deposits and so reduce the ability of the banks to do business. . . .

An attempt to control the rates for call loans by the establishment of an arbitrary limit at a low level, without the ability to modify the causes above enumerated which operate to increase rates, would be distinctly hazardous, for the reason that up to the point where the arbitrary rate would limit the supply of new money, speculation and expansion might proceed unchecked and the natural elements of correction or regulation would not obtain. In other words, high rates act as a deterrent to overspeculation and undue expansion of credit. On the other hand, should the supply of money available to a fixed maximum rate become exhausted, liquidation might suddenly be forced because the demands for additional accommodation for the consummation of commitments already made could not be met. The effect of such liquidation would be to embarrass not only investors and dealers in securities, but frequently might affect dealers and merchants in commodities as well. As an example of the latter, the case might be cited of a commitment to purchase a round amount of cotton on a certain day. Many of the houses on the cotton exchange are also members of the stock exchange and frequently borrow very largely on the stock exchange against investment securities to provide funds for settling their transactions in cotton. If, therefore, when an important cotton settlement is imminent, borrowings on securities could not be availed of, the cotton transaction could not be consummated and a drastic liquidation through sale either of securities or of the cotton might be required to avoid default. Similar consequences might obtain in the cases of transactions by members of other commodity exchanges who are also members of the stock exchange and have recourse to the call-money market.

APPENDIX C

ADDRESS OF W. P. G. HARDING

GOVERNOR OF THE FEDERAL RESERVE BOARD, BEFORE THE ANNUAL
CONVENTION OF THE AMERICAN FARM BUREAU FEDERATION AT
INDIANAPOLIS, DECEMBER 7, 1920

THE impression exists in the minds of many that the Federal Reserve System has adopted a policy of radical deflation and that the farming interests have been the chief sufferers from this policy. No such policy has ever been undertaken, and as a matter of fact there has been during the past year an increase, and not a reduction, in the net volume of bank credit and currency. There has been no policy looking toward a broad curtailment or deflation of credit, but efforts have been made to correct abuses and to bring about moderation and better judgment in the use of credits which a year ago were being diverted into all kinds of speculative and non-productive channels. Efforts have been made also to conserve the resources and credit power of the member banks and of the Federal Reserve Banks, in order that they might better respond to the seasonal needs occasioned by the harvesting of the crops. . . .

On September 19, 1919, the total earning assets of all Federal Reserve Banks were in round amounts $2,350,000,000, while on January 27, 1920, the total was nearly $3,300,000,000, an increase of almost $1,000,000,000, or nearly fifty per cent within a period of four months. There is no banking system strong enough to sustain itself very long at so rapid a rate of expansion of credit, and while no drastic deflation was attempted, measures were taken to regulate the credit expansion. Discount rates were advanced, and this action was followed by a moderate amount of liquidation, the earning assets of the Federal Reserve Banks being reduced in the course of sixty days by about $100,000,000. By the middle of May, however, the total loans and investments of the Federal Reserve Banks approached again their previous high level, and the Board called the attention of the banks and the public to the importance of marketing the crops of 1919 before those of 1920 were harvested, and of reducing borrowings at the Federal Reserve Banks until the seasonal requirements of the autumn should develop. . . .

On July 23d, just before the crop-moving demands began to be felt, the total loans and investments of the Federal Reserve Banks had declined from the high point about $150,000,000, and stood around $3,150,000,000. Since that date they have advanced steadily, with occasional slight recessions, until December 3d, when the total amount reached $3,333,792,000, as compared with $2,933,082,000 on December 5, 1919. Federal Reserve notes in circulation on December 3, 1920, amounted to $3,312,039,000, as against $2,881,359,000, on December 5, 1919. You will see, therefore, that as far as the Federal Reserve Banks are concerned, no contraction of credit or currency has been had during the past twelve months, but, on the other hand, there has been an increase in Federal Reserve Bank credit of $400,000,000 and in currency of $430,000,000.

You are, however, most interested in knowing to what extent credit has been available for agricultural purposes. It will be impossible to give precise information on this point until the reports recently called for by the Comptroller of the Currency from national banks have been tabulated and the digest made public. The Comptroller has asked each national bank for a statement both of direct and indirect loans to farmers. The Federal Reserve Banks in agricultural districts have been rediscounting heavily for several months past with Federal Reserve Banks in the industrial districts. Three banks, the Federal Reserve Banks of Boston, Philadelphia, and Cleveland, have advanced at times as much as $250,000,000 to seven other Federal Reserve Banks, whose districts are largely agricultural. The total amount of bills discounted by Federal Reserve Banks in distinctly agricultural districts is about $1,500,000,000. Early in the season Federal Reserve Banks in these districts were asked to estimate the proportion of their total loans directly in support of the agricultural and live-stock interests. The estimates for September 3, 1920, were as follows: Federal Reserve Bank of Richmond, 27.3 per cent; Atlanta, 23.7 per cent; Chicago, 48.3 per cent; St. Louis, 22 per cent; Minneapolis, 65.6 per cent; Kansas City, 59.8 per cent; Dallas, 50 per cent; and San Francisco, 58.7 per cent. In some of these banks the proportion of agricultural paper held is much greater now than on September 3d. It is certain that there has been no curtailment of agricultural credits by the Federal Reserve Banks and while, as I have stated, exact figures of member bank transactions are not yet available, it seems reasonable to assume that there has been a very large volume of credit extended by member and non-member banks in support of the agricultural interests. . . .

I am a firm believer in the policy of gradual and orderly methods of marketing our great agricultural staples. All will agree that agriculture is a basic and fundamental industry, for upon its fruits depend the lives of those engaged in all other industries. The farmer is a great consumer of manufactured products, and anything that affects his buying power is soon reflected in the business of the merchant and manufacturer. Conversely, a depression in manufacturing and other lines of business is reflected in the reduced demand for farm products. I cannot conceive of any one questioning the fact that farming as a business must be remunerative or production will languish. It is highly desirable that the efforts of the farmer be supported and stimulated in every proper way, and that he be aided in preserving the full measure of his harvests, and that he be given an opportunity of marketing his products on terms sufficiently profitable to warrant his staying in the business of farming. It is well to remember, however, that, in other lines of business, profits are not always continuous. This is also true with respect to farm industry. The farmer, however, as a rule, has only one turnover a year, while those engaged in other enterprises have the advantage of more frequent turnovers. Great staple crops, the production of which extends over a period of several months, must meet the requirements of consumption until the next season's crops are produced. In order to prevent possibility of shortage, it is desirable that there be a moderate surplus held over from one crop pending the marketing of the next. It is important, however, that the surplus held over be not too large or unwieldy, for the marketing of a crop and a half, when the ordinary requirements call for only one crop, means a loss unless an unforeseen abnormal demand should develop. The gradual and orderly marketing of great staple crops is a matter of importance both to producer and consumer. The dumping upon the market within a short period of time of a large part of a crop, the consumption of which extends throughout the year, means not only loss to producers, often to those who can least afford it, but involves also a great strain upon our transportation facilities and upon the banks in providing the funds necessary for large purchases in advance of actual requirements for consumption. The dumping of farm products promotes speculation and often results in higher prices to the ultimate consumer.

I take this occasion to say that the members of the Federal Reserve Board have a keen sympathy for the farmers in their present predicament and are desirous of doing everything they can legitimately and properly to help them. It is impossible, however, for any banking system to provide funds for withholding all staple crops entirely from the market for any length of time. The volume of our great staple crops is so large and their value so great that any efforts to valorize them by means of bank credits would inevitably result in disaster to the community in general and to the farmer especially. Orderly marketing means marketing; it means steady sales and steady purchases. Gradual sales make possible the gradual liquidation of debts, and as the maturity of so many obligations synchronizes with the marketing of staple crops, it is probably no exaggeration to say the liquidation of a million dollars of farmers' indebtedness means the liquidation of four or five million dollars of general debts. Your convention will no doubt consider means of preventing in future a repetition of present conditions. I assume that you will consider coöperative marketing, greater diversification of crops, and the maturing of farmers' obligations over periods extending from October to March. I suggest also that you do not overlook the importance of minor crops as a means of giving the farmer an additional turnover. I assume also that you will consider the processes of marketing and ascertain why in many cases commodities which are sold by the farmer at less than the cost of production are sold to the ultimate consumer at high prices. . . .

I am aware also that there is much apprehension on the part of farmers as to their current indebtedness. The present crops were produced at abnormally high costs, and many farmers, no doubt, have stuff on hand for which there is now no ready market, or which cannot be sold for enough to liquidate their debts. Such a situation calls for the closest coöperation between the farmer and the merchant and banker with whom he deals. I have no authority to speak for the banking business in general, but I do know that as a rule the banker realizes that the welfare of his own institution depends upon the prosperity of the community in which his bank is located. The average banker is averse to foreclosures or other drastic methods of liquidating indebtedness, except as a last resort, and my opinion is that if the farmer will go to his banker or merchant creditor and make a frank statement of his condition, giving additional security if available and if required, and agree to make gradual sales of his produce as the market develops, applying the proceeds on his indebtedness, he will be able to make arrangements for present pressing needs and for requirements for another season. Many farmers have had this experience in years when there has been a crop failure. This is a year of physical plenty and the farmers' troubles arise from price derangements. The decline in prices of all agricultural staples has been very marked, and some may not be salable in the present circumstances at any price. Such commodities, of course, must be carried over for account of some one, and they had better be carried for the account of the producer. Other staples can be sold at a price, and gradual sales of these staples will, in my opinion, stabilize the entire situation. The resumption of activity on the part of woolen mills and cotton mills will revive the demand for wool and cotton, and continued employment of labor will stimulate the demand for foodstuffs and all other farm products. . . .

While it is true that the greater volume of our staple crops and the larger part of our manufactured goods are consumed at home, the maintenance of our export trade is of the greatest importance to farmers and manufacturers, for ability to dispose of surplus products abroad is a potent factor in the determination of the price at which goods are sold at home. The great need of the world to-day is peace and revival of the industries of peace, the reëstablishment of trade relations between the nations, and in my judgment the surest means of relieving present conditions permanently lies in the development of our foreign trade upon a basis of assured permanency.

APPENDIX D

LETTER

OF THE GOVERNOR OF THE FEDERAL RESERVE BOARD TO
SENATOR REED SMOOT, JULY 11, 1921

MY DEAR SENATOR:

Some of the charges which have been made against the Federal Reserve Board and against its members personally, which have appeared in certain papers and in some public speeches, do not appear to me to be susceptible to argumentative reply. They are made without giving any facts to support them and show either total ignorance of the subject on the part of the proponents or else wanton disregard of actual facts.

Owing to the exigencies of Treasury financing, the war-time Federal Reserve rate of four per cent was not advanced until November, 1919, although after the first of July, 1919, there was a rapid advance in the market rate for money and the best grades of commercial paper sold in the open market at from seven per cent to eight per cent. The customers of the member banks were willing to pay full rates for accommodation, and urged upon the banks as a reason for easy credits that they were willing to pay high rates, and the banks in turn could rediscount with the Federal Reserve Banks at a very substantial profit. On or about September 15, 1919, the total amount of invested assets of the Federal Reserve Banks, including bills rediscounted for member banks, acceptances bought in the open market, and Government obligations held, amounted to about $2,350,000,000. An expansion of bank credits was going on all the time at a rate which has never been equaled in the history of the country and far in excess of any war-time expansion. Federal Reserve Bank rates were advanced to four and three quarters per cent early in December, 1919, but the advance was negligible and had no effect. The latter part of January, 1920, rates were advanced to six per cent. On January 23, 1920, the total rediscounts and earning assets of the Federal Reserve Banks amounted to about $3,030,000,000, an increase since September 19, 1919, of $680,000,000. The rate of expansion for that period was nearly thirty per cent. At the same time the reserves of the Federal Reserve Banks had declined to about $2,090,000,000, of which only about $2,030,000,000 were gold reserves. The pyramiding of credits was proceeding at an alarming degree, and it was evident that, if expansion should continue to proceed at such a rapid rate, it would be merely a question of time until the credit structure of the country would explode.

It should be noted that even after the rates were increased the expansion of loans and currency continued in a more moderate degree. On January 16, 1920, the total loans and earning assets of the Federal Reserve Banks amounted to about $3,000,000,000. These increased gradually and steadily until November 5th, when they amounted to $3,400,000,000. On January 16, 1920, the volume of Federal Reserve notes outstanding was about $2,800,000,000, and this note issue also increased steadily until it reached the peak on December 24, 1920, of $3,400,000,000. You will remember that the great price reactions which took place all occurred before November 5th or December 24th. Wholesale prices reached their peak about the middle of May, 1920, being at that time about 272 as against 100 for the year 1913. After the middle of May, wholesale prices declined steadily, although the loans of the Federal Reserve Banks and Federal Reserve note issues increased until November 5th and December 24th, respectively.

Since the close of the year 1920, there has been a marked reduction in the loans and note issues of the Federal Reserve Banks combined, although this reduction has been by no means uniform at all the banks. As a matter of fact, the liquidation in the New York District has been about equal to that in all other districts combined. The rediscounts and advances of the Federal Reserve Bank of New York, at the close of business on June 30, 1921, were lower than they had been since July 10, 1918. I would call your attention to the fact that on July 9, 1920, the Federal Reserve Bank of New York had total bills discounted and bought amounting to $1,001,864,000, while on July 6, 1921, total bills held at the Federal Reserve Bank of New York were $461,585,000, a reduction of $540,279,000. If comparison should be made a week earlier in each case, it would be seen that a reduction took place of $578,695,000. Bills held at the Federal Reserve Bank of New York increased from June 29, 1921, to July 6, 1921, from $423,169,000 to $461,585,000, a net increase for the week of $38,416,000. The detail is as follows:

	July 9, 1920	*July* 6, 1921
Secured by United States bonds and certificates.............	$544,229,000	$212,999,000
Commercial paper, etc.........	303,454,000	236,970,000
Bills bought in open market.....	154,181,000	11,616,000
Total	$1,001,864,000	$461,585,000

Some of those who have complained of the curtailment of credit live in the Richmond and Atlanta Districts, and it may be interesting, therefore, to ascertain just what the Federal Reserve Banks in those districts are doing. On July 6, 1921, the Federal Reserve Bank of Richmond had total bills on hand amounting to $105,974,000 against $110,052,000 on July 9, 1920, but there was a reduction between these dates of $15,830,000 in the amount of notes secured by Government obligations, which probably represents sales of bonds and certificates, while loans on commercial and agricultural paper increased from $58,344,000 on July 9, 1920, to $74,280,000 on July 6, 1921.

The Federal Reserve Bank of Atlanta shows between July 9, 1920, and July 6, 1921, an apparent reduction in total loans of about $17,000,000, but commercial and agricultural paper increased from $61,611,000 on July 9, 1920, to $65,754,000 on July 6, 1921. When the difference in the value of cotton is considered, it is evident that the real amount of accommodation given is considerably greater now than was the case a year ago. It should be noted, however, that the decrease in the total loans of the Federal Reserve Bank of Atlanta is not so great as it appears, for the bank on July 6, 1921, reports United States bonds and notes owned amounting to $10,142,000, against $117,000 on July 9, 1920. This increase represents bonds and notes purchased under resale agreement from certain member banks which had previously been using the bonds as collateral for loans with the Federal Reserve Bank of Atlanta, so the actual reduction in the amount of the bank's total loans is only about $7,000,000 instead of $17,000,000.

As your State is in the San Francisco District, some figures relating to the Federal Reserve Bank of San Francisco may be of interest to you. The total loans of the Federal Reserve Bank of San Francisco on July 6, 1921, amounted to $161,203,000, as against $199,003,000 on July 9, 1920. This reduction, however, is made up as follows: a decrease of $4,446,000 in the amount of paper secured by Government obligations and a decrease of $44,687,000 in the amount of bills and acceptances bought in the open market. Commercial and agricultural paper under rediscount for member banks amounted on July 6, 1921, to $114,623,000, against $103,290,000 on July 9, 1920, an increase in commercial, agricultural, and live-stock loans of $11,333,000.

Let us now consider the figures for the System as a whole. On July 9, 1920, the total bills on hand at all Federal Reserve Banks amounted to $2,934,184,000. On July 6, 1921, this total amounted to $1,832,499,000, a decrease of $1,101,685,000. The detail of this decrease is as follows: on paper secured by Government obligations, $621,973,000 (which can be accounted for in part by Government redemptions of bonds and Treasury certificates and private purchases for investment account); in bills bought in the open market, $341,455,000. (While the volume of the acceptance business has declined during the past twelve months, this decrease is accounted for principally by the greater demand for first-class acceptances on the part of member and non-member banks and trust companies.) The total of agricultural, commercial, and livestock paper on hand, rediscounted for member banks, on July 6, 1921, was $1,126,986,000, as against a total of $1,265,243,000 on July 9, 1920, a decrease of only $138,257,000, which is more than accounted for by the decrease in the holdings of paper of this kind by the Federal Reserve Banks of Boston, New York, and Chicago.

The Federal Reserve Board has made no suggestion whatever that any Federal Reserve Bank should undertake to force farmers to sell their cotton before the new crop comes in, and telegraphic inquiry made of the Federal Reserve Banks in the cotton-producing districts shows that no such restrictions have been made by the Federal Reserve Banks.

Recent correspondence between the Federal Reserve Bank of Atlanta and one of its member banks shows that the Governor of the Federal Reserve Bank calls the attention of his correspondent bank, which writes that it has notified its customers who are borrowing on cotton to sell it and pay their notes by July 1st, to the fact that this is a matter which the Federal Reserve Bank has nothing to do with and that it has made no such demands.

The Comptroller's Abstract No. 130, made up from reports rendered as of April 28, 1921, shows that the total rediscounts with the Federal Reserve Bank of Richmond by national banks in South Carolina on that date were $12,506,000, while total loans and discounts of the South Carolina national banks on the same date, exclusive of the amounts rediscounted, amounted to $75,208,000. Adding these two items together, we find that the South Carolina national banks had total loans and discounts on April 28, 1921, of $87,714,000, and of this amount they had rediscounted with the Federal Reserve Bank $12,506,000. They had also borrowed $6,759,000 from the Federal Reserve Bank on their own collateral notes. The total accommodation granted to national banks in South Carolina as of April 28, 1921, was therefore $19,265,000, or twenty-two per cent of their total loans. At the same time the total reserves carried by all national banks in South Carolina with the Federal Reserve Bank of Richmond amounted to $3,829,000. Deducting the loans to State member banks, $2,285,000, the loans of the Federal Reserve Bank of Richmond to national banks in South Carolina on June 30, 1921, amounted to $18,820,000, and the total loans to all member banks in South Carolina on June 30, 1921, by the Federal Reserve Bank of Richmond amounted to $21,105,000, against $17,316,000 on June 30, 1920, and yet the Federal Reserve Bank of Richmond is charged with restricting loans in South Carolina. I may add that the Federal Reserve Banks of Richmond and Atlanta were both heavy borrowers during the latter half of 1920 from other Federal Reserve Banks, and the Federal Reserve Bank of Richmond has recently shown loans as high as $25,000,000 from the Federal Reserve Bank of New York. It is worthy of note also that the Federal Reserve Bank of Richmond has never had the progressive rate and has never had a higher rate than six per cent. The legal rate of interest in South Carolina is eight per cent. So you can see that there is a margin of profit to member banks in that State of two full points, or thirty-three and a third per cent, in their rediscount transactions with the Federal Reserve Bank.

In conclusion, I wish to say that the attitude of the Federal Reserve Board toward agriculture has been greatly misunderstood and grossly misrepresented. The Board has always advocated as liberal a policy as possible, consistent with the terms of the Federal Reserve Act and with reasonable banking prudence toward agriculture, which it recognizes as the basic industry of the country and the foundation upon which all other industries necessarily rest. The trouble is that the loans made by the member and non-member banks throughout the country are not well distributed and in a number of cases have not been judiciously made. Something over a third of all member banks are not borrowing from the Federal Reserve Banks at all, and of the two thirds which are borrowing, more than one half are borrowing very large amounts. Many of these banks have extended themselves so far that they do not feel warranted in making any new loans, regardless of the disposition of the Federal Reserve Banks to rediscount the paper. They do not want their names on any more paper than they already have. They do not like the idea of increasing their contingent liability. In view of the fact that the twelve Federal Reserve Banks are independent bodies corporate and are controlled and directed each by its own board of directors, subject only to the general supervision of the Federal Reserve Board, whose authority with respect to discount is confined principally to defining eligible paper in accordance with the terms of section 13 of the Federal Reserve Act, it seems to me that the statement which many, both in Congress and on the outside, urge be issued by the Federal Reserve Board, stating that the Federal Reserve Banks will adopt certain policies in connection with the rediscounting of agricultural paper, would have to be made by the Federal Reserve Banks themselves. The Federal Reserve Board has no power to interfere with the discretion given or the responsibility imposed by law upon the directors of a Federal Reserve Bank with respect to passing upon the merits of eligible paper offered for discount.

Congress did not establish a central bank in this country. It established twelve banks under the general supervision of the Federal Reserve Board, which does not exercise banking functions. These functions are exercised exclusively by the Federal Reserve Banks. The Board has taken up repeatedly with the various Federal Reserve Banks complaints of a general nature regarding the restriction of agricultural credits and the banks have always made a good showing of what they have done for agriculture. Very few specific cases have been brought to the attention of the Board where eligible agricultural paper has been refused for rediscount, and in those cases it seems that the management of the Federal Reserve Banks have justified themselves in the refusal.

In some agricultural States there was two years ago, unfortunately, great speculation in farm lands, and member and non-member banks in those localities loaded themselves with a large volume of real estate mortgages, which paper is not eligible for discount under the terms of the Federal Reserve Act, and many of them have sustained losses in deposits. In the present circumstances, they are endeavoring to work out from under the tremendous load which they ought never to have taken on, and do not feel able or else are indisposed to extend accommodations for agricultural purposes which ordinarily they would be glad to do. In almost every State, however, there are a number of ultra-conservative banks which have strong reserves which are not borrowing, and which ought to do their part in assisting agriculture at the present time.

In the present condition of the country it seems to me that the strong position of the Federal Reserve Banks should be a source of comfort rather than the cause of so much reckless criticism. The Federal Reserve Banks cannot be expected to encourage their member banks to make loans to the public on the basis of values which obtained eighteen months ago. The inability of any banking system to maintain values in the face of a world-wide decline is evidenced by the plight of the banks in Cuba, which were heavily loaded up with loans on sugar at high prices. Surely, the return of better conditions in this country would not be expedited by having American banks in the same condition that Cuban banks are to-day.

By way of summary, let me state that, while the Federal Reserve Act imposes a general limitation upon the maturity of paper eligible for discount of three months, it is provided in section 13 'that notes, drafts, and bills drawn or issued for agricultural purposes or based on live stock and having a maturity not exceeding six months, exclusive of days of grace, may be discounted in an amount to be limited to a percentage of the assets of the Federal Reserve Bank, to be ascertained and fixed by the Federal Reserve Board.' Had the Board been unfriendly to agriculture, as many of its critics claim it has been, it could easily have limited the amount of six months' agricultural paper which could be discounted by a Federal Reserve Bank to a very small percentage of its total assets. But in order to offer the fullest possible accommodations to agriculture, the Board more than five years ago fixed this percentage at ninety-nine per cent and has never changed it. It has already been pointed out that the decrease of more than $1,100,000,000 which has taken place in the loans and earning assets of the Federal Reserve Banks is represented mainly by a reduction in loans secured by Government obligations and by bills and acceptances bought in the open market. The actual reduction in commercial, agricultural, and live-stock paper, rediscounted for member banks, from July 9, 1920, to July 6, 1921, was $138,257,000. This reduction is more than accounted for by the decrease of paper rediscounted by Federal Reserve Banks in Boston, New York, and Chicago. The bank liquidation which has taken place has been mainly in financial and industrial centers, and the figures of the Federal Reserve Banks do not indicate that there has during the past twelve months been any decrease in Federal Reserve accommodations to banks in the agricultural and live-stock districts, but, on the contrary, there has been a considerable increase, as you will see from the official statements enclosed herewith.

APPENDIX E

EXCERPTS FROM THE REPORT ON CREDIT

By the Congressional Joint Commission of Agricultural Inquiry, January, 1922, and the Minority Opinion of Ogden L. Mills

The Commission has also carefully considered the policy of the Federal Reserve Banks and the Federal Reserve Board during the period of the recent crisis, with special reference to the effect of the policy adopted upon agriculture.

The regulation of the volume of credit and currency within the Federal Reserve System is accomplished in part by the automatic operation of the System and in part by the discount policy of the various Federal Reserve Banks.

The discount rates of Federal Reserve Banks in accordance with the policy of banks of issue, in almost all of the countries, having a central banking system, should normally be slightly above the rates carried by the class of paper to which they apply, in order that the lending power of the Federal Reserve Banks may be preserved for times of financial stringency and crisis and in order that this lending power shall not be depleted by member banks borrowing from them for purposes of profit only. The rates of the Federal Reserve Banks were for the most part above going rates on prime commercial paper from the beginning of the operations of the Federal Reserve Banks to the date of our entrance into the World War. With our entrance into the World War, the rate policy of the Federal Reserve Banks was subordinated to the requirements of the Treasury and the Treasury policy of borrowing the funds necessary for the conduct of the war at rates of interest below the market rate, and discount rates thereafter were below the market rates on the character of paper to which they applied.

The cost of the war could not be paid out of collection of current taxes; it was necessary to provide for immediate payments by means of the expansion or manufacture of credit. This manufacture of credit necessitated the use of the lending power of the Federal Reserve Banks through loans to member banks at a rate of interest below the rate carried by the bond and certificate of indebtedness issues of the Government. This policy induced large borrowings on the part of member banks from Federal Reserve

Banks and larger expansion of loans and discounts of the member banks. . . .

In the early part of 1919, following a short period of price deflation and business contraction, the question of increasing the discount rates of the Federal Reserve Banks in the direction of the sounder policy of maintaining these rates above the going rates for commercial paper and above rates on Government bonds and certificates of indebtedness, arose. At this time the Government was considering the flotation of the Victory loan, which it was then thought would involve $6,000,000,000. The Treasury Department was unwilling to undertake the flotation of the Victory loan at a rate of interest comparable with commercial rates on account of the possible effect which that action would have upon existing issues of private securities and its possible effect in requiring the refunding of the issues of Government bonds already floated.

The discount policy of the Federal Reserve Banks was again subordinated to the Treasury policy in securing its credit requirements, although at this time the tendency toward expansion, speculation, and extravagance was beginning to be apparent.

This was clearly the time for a policy of advancing the discount rates of the Federal Reserve Banks with a view of curtailing the expansion, speculation, and extravagance which was then beginning.

It is the opinion of the Commission that a policy of restriction of loans and discounts by advances in the discount rates of the Federal Reserve Banks could and should have been adopted in the early part of 1919, notwithstanding the difficulties which the Treasury Department anticipated in floating the Victory loan if such a policy were adopted.[1]

It is also the opinion of the Commission that had this policy been adopted in the early part of 1919 much of the expansion, speculation, and extravagance which characterized the post-war period could have been avoided.

The Commission also believes that had such a policy been adopted in 1919 the difficulties, hardships, and losses which occurred in 1920–21 as a result of the process of deflation and liquidation would have been diminished.

No action in the direction of restriction of expansion, inflation, and speculation by increases in discount rates was taken by the Federal Reserve Banks or the Federal Reserve Board until December, 1919, when slight advances were made in discount rates,

[1] The Commission appears to have overlooked the possible effect of the Overman Act, had the Board undertaken to upset the policies of the Treasury.

followed in January by more radical advances and by further increases during the remainder of 1920.

In the meantime there began and continued a period of expansion, extravagance, and speculation, the like of which has never before been seen in this country or perhaps in the world.

This era of expansion, speculation, and extravagance resulted in the making of a large volume of debts which was reflected in large increases in the borrowings of the member banks from Federal Reserve Banks. When finally the Federal Reserve Banks and the Federal Reserve Board adopted the policy of restriction of expansion of loans and discounts and of speculation and extravagance, loans and discounts, currency and prices had reached such a point that deflation was a process accompanied by perpendicular and very material declines of prices accompanied by great losses and hardship upon banks, communities, and individuals alike.

The reserves of individual Reserve Banks and of the System as a whole began to dwindle rapidly. In some of the Reserve Banks the reserves fell as low as nine per cent, and at one time it is said that the reserves of one of the banks were entirely exhausted. The tremendous drain upon the credit resources of the country brought about the overextension of many of the banks of the country, and with some of these banks loans and discounts had advanced to a point where the banks were utterly unable to loan additional funds to their customers without rendering themselves in great danger of insolvency.

From 1915 to 1920 the ratio of loans and discounts of national banks to capital and surplus had increased from 3.8 to 1 to 4.5 to 1, and in many instances capital and surplus would not permit of further expansion of loans and discounts of banks without endangering the interests of depositors and stockholders alike. The policy of the Federal Reserve Banks, therefore, during this period underwent a change. Discount rates were raised, particularly upon certificates of indebtedness and Government bonds, resulting in the liquidation of this class of paper by the member banks and the freeing of the funds invested in them for other purposes.

With the exhaustion of the credits of European Governments in this country, the purchasing power of Europe in our markets began to fail. This resulted in a sharp decline in exports, particularly of farm products. The exhaustion of credit and capital, coupled with the decline in exports, gave the first impetus to the decline in prices. With the beginning of this decline the forces of reaction and depression began to operate. Goods were thrown on the market, orders were cancelled, the buyer's strike developed, unemployment ensued, and complete industrial depression followed.

As the purchasing power of the domestic population diminished and unemployment began, more and more goods began to congest the channels of commerce and more and more credit was required to carry these goods until they could be marketed. It was necessary, by a high level of discount rates, to keep these credit requirements in such a relation to the prices of goods that bank failures would not result and a financial crash increase the inevitable industrial depression resulting from declining prices.

As the pressure of liquidation developed, there began to be demands on the part of the public for amelioration of the policy of the Federal Reserve Banks with respect to discount rates, based upon the assumption that lower discount rates and freer money would arrest the tide of liquidation and reduce the hardships of those who are compelled to sell in a declining market. The Commission believes that a policy of lower discount rates and greater liberality in extending credits could have been adopted in the latter part of 1920 and the early months of 1921, and that such a policy would have retarded the process of liquidation and thus spread the losses incident to the inevitable decline of prices to a lower level over a longer period, and that the adoption of such a policy at that time would have been advisable.[1]

About one third of the banks at this period were greatly overextended, and it was the position of the Federal Reserve Board that a policy of cheap money at this time, coupled with an invitation to them to further extend themselves and the ratio of loans and discounts to capital, might have resulted in bank failure involving the industrial and commercial institutions and that the Federal Reserve Board and the Federal Reserve Banks were confronted with a choice between continuing the high discount rates and the consequent pressure and hardship upon the commercial and agricultural industries of the country, on the one hand, and a policy of lower discount rates involving a possible financial crisis in the midst of an industrial crisis. The Federal Reserve Banks, with the approval of the Federal Reserve Board, took the first choice, and discount rates were continued upon practically the same level as before.

It seems probable that a change in the policy of the Federal

[1] Federal Reserve Bank rates were generally below current discount rates in 1920 and 1921, and were reduced in April, 1921. The dangerous expansion of bank loans is admitted in the preceding paragraphs.

Reserve System with reference to discount rates would have accomplished a reversal in part of the psychological and economic factors which at this time were moving in the direction of lower prices, and at the same time would have tended to induce on the part of banks a more liberal attitude toward furnishing additional credit.

It is without doubt true that the pressure of discount rates and of liquidation in the agricultural sections of the country resulted in great hardship, loss, and sacrifice among the agricultural population of the country. The hardships, sacrifices, and losses of the period, however, were not confined to agricultural sections.

The pressure was greater upon the agricultural sections because of the peculiar conditions surrounding the marketing of agricultural crops, and as a result of the fact that the crops of 1920 had been produced at costs greater than those applicable to any other crops in the history of the country. These hardships were also greater because the prices of agricultural commodities declined to a greater degree and with greater rapidity than the prices of other commodities. The investigation of the Commission shows that liquidation of bank loans and discounts in the agricultural sections of the country was less than in the industrial sections, and in fact that but little actual liquidation of loans and discounts had taken place in the agricultural sections of the country as a whole up to May, 1921. . . .

It was also contended before the Commission that high rates for call money on the stock exchange during this period brought a withdrawal of funds, sorely needed by industry and agriculture during this period, of New York for purposes of stock speculation. The rates for call money in New York during the period from January, 1920, to June, 1921, were continuously below ten per cent, with the exception of the period from January to March, 1920.

Beginning with November, 1919, and continuously throughout 1920 and the first half of 1921, the loans of New York banks made on the stock exchange for out-of-town correspondents, as well as the balances of country banks with New York banks, continuously declined, and an examination of the clearings of the Federal Reserve Bank of New York through the gold settlement fund shows a continuous flow of money on ordinary transactions from the Federal Reserve Bank of New York to other Federal Reserve Banks during this period. The very great demands for money by industry and agriculture resulted in withdrawal of funds from

New York, causing higher interest rates instead of the demands of the stock exchange resulting in a withdrawal of funds from the banks serving industry and agriculture.

At this time the total expenditures of the Government for ordinary and war purposes from the beginning of the war had reached a total of $27,806,546,698.23, of which $6,933,524,926.13 had been raised by taxation. In view of the enormous drain on the resources of the country, in credit, savings, and current production for war purposes, a further bond issue could not be floated without added inflation or manufacture of credit, which could only be accomplished through the medium of the Federal Reserve System.

Again, inasmuch as a willingness on the part of the Federal Reserve Banks to furnish the money necessary to carry the bonds to the member banks at a rate of interest lower than the rate carried by the bonds was thought by the officials of the Treasury Department to be essential to the success of the issue, a policy of raising the discount rates in advance of the flotation of the Victory loan might have greatly diminished the success of that loan, if, indeed, it had not compelled its failure.[1]

A policy of higher discount rates could have been adopted by the Federal Reserve Banks, notwithstanding the flotation of the Victory loan, if the Treasury Department had been willing to float this loan at a rate of interest high enough to permit an increase in the rediscount rate. Great difficulties were foreseen by the Treasury Department in this undertaking. If the Victory loan had been floated by the Treasury Department on a basis of an interest rate comparable with current rates on other taxable investments, or on certificates of indebtedness, which at that time was about four and a quarter per cent or on commercial borrowings, which at that time was about five and a half per cent, the pressure already felt at that time by the Treasury Department to refund the prior issues of Government bonds on the basis of a high interest rate on the Victory loan issue would have greatly increased and possibly been irresistible. In addition, the flotation of the Victory loan at this time on the basis of a high interest rate would have had a tendency to ultimately increase interest rates all along the line, and to depreciate the value of the bonds previously issued at the lower rates of interest. Again, it might have resulted in precipitating a

[1] See address of the Honorable R. C. Leffingwell, Assistant Secretary of the Treasury, before the Academy of Political Science at New York, April 30, 1920, *ante*, page 257.

liquidation of large amounts of securities other than Government bonds, and the depreciation of vast quantities of general securities held by savings banks, trust companies, insurance companies, etc. Thus, the advantages of the high discount rates, which might have been used to prevent speculation and inflation during this period, yielded to the apprehensions of the Treasury Department.

The Commission is of the opinion that the difficulties anticipated by the Treasury Department should not have controlled in this period and that the discount policy of the Federal Reserve Board and the Federal Reserve Banks should not have yielded to the apprehension of the Treasury Department.

The Commission believes that had discount rates been raised by the Federal Reserve Banks promptly and progressively beginning with the spring of 1919, much of the inflation, expansion, speculation, and extravagance which characterized the following twelve months or more might have been greatly retarded, if not wholly prevented.

Loans and discounts of member banks and of Federal Reserve Banks continued to expand in spite of the policy of direct remonstrance and repeated warnings of the Federal Reserve Board and the Federal Reserve Banks. Yet no action in the direction of restriction of expansion, inflation, and speculation by increases in discount rates was taken by the Federal Reserve Banks or the Federal Reserve Board until December, 1919, when slight advances were made. These advances were followed in January by more radical increases and by further advances during the remainder of 1920.

In the meantime expansion, inflation, extravagance, and speculation continued and prices soared to previously unheard-of levels. Sharp advances in discount rates at the beginning of this period would not only have served as a warning to banks and their customers, but would also have served to check the forces, both economic and psychological, that were combining to produce an era of expansion, inflation, speculation, extravagance, and high prices unparalleled in the history of this country, or perhaps in any other.

It does not, of course, follow that deflation must be equivalent to inflation, but it is altogether probable, if it is not wholly certain, that had a sound policy been adopted by the Federal Reserve Board and the Federal Reserve Banks at the beginning of this period the processes of liquidation would have been less precipitous and the decline less abrupt and the attendant hardships and losses upon banks, communities, and individuals correspondingly diminished.

[Representative Ogden L. Mills, a member of the Commission, filed a minority opinion as follows:]

I concur in the report with one exception. I cannot agree with the statement that late in the year 1920 'a change in the policy of the Federal Reserve System with reference to discount rates would have accomplished a reversal in part of the psychological and economic factors which at this time were moving in the direction of lower prices.' Such a suggestion is out of harmony with the balance of the report and inconsistent with the facts brought out by our investigation.

Higher rediscount rates charged by Federal Reserve Banks did not produce the break in prices, and it is inconceivable that their reduction could have counteracted the economic forces that were leading to inevitable deflation:

(1) Federal rediscount rates were below market rates throughout the year 1920.

(2) There are some 28,210 banks in the United States, only 9840 of which are members of the Federal Reserve System. Any number of these banks are to a great extent free from competition, and charge rates largely the product of local custom and local circumstances. For instance, what efficacy can the decrease in the rediscount rate of a Federal Reserve Bank from seven to six per cent have on a Western or Southwestern bank charging eight, ten, or twelve per cent? Furthermore, it must be obvious that rediscount rates can only be effective in the restriction of loans and discount against a bank which was borrowing from its Reserve Bank. And by no means were even all member banks borrowing. For example, in September, 1920, in the New York District there were 454 non-borrowing banks, as against 323 borrowing ones.

(3) In so far as agricultural counties were concerned, far from receiving less credit from the Federal Reserve Banks during the period referred to, the figures show that from May 4, 1920, to April 28, 1921, rediscounts by banks in the agricultural counties with the Federal Reserve Banks actually increased 56.6 per cent.

Incidentally, it may be noted that during the same period borrowings from Federal Reserve Banks in non-agricultural counties decreased 28.5 per cent. If the statement which I question be true, it would seem to follow that a lower rediscount rate would have tended primarily to maintain industrial prices to the further disadvantage of the farmer.

(4) Finally, while it cannot be conclusively proved that credit stringency was not an initial contributing factor to price deflation, there is no evidence to show that it was. By this I do not mean to state that once prices started to drop, it was not the cause of much hardship and, in many cases, of increased losses. Quite the contrary. It was. But I do not believe that increased interest rates and contracting credit were the primary causes of the sharp price deflation which characterized the second half of the year 1920.

(*a*) The price peak of the all commodities index was reached in May, 1920, while loans of all reporting banks and discounts of Federal Reserve Banks did not reach their maximum until October, and currency issues until January, 1921.

In so far as the following agricultural commodities are concerned, prices reached their peak as early as 1919, and declined rapidly thereafter some months before Federal Bank discount rates were materially raised or any credit stringency felt: hogs, bacon, cattle, mutton dressed, and butter. There was in practically every one of these cases a direct relationship between the peak of the export trade and the price peak. Thus, the peak of hog exports was reached in June and the price peak in July; and the same is true of bacon. The cattle export peak was reached in August, 1919, and the price peak in November. The cotton export peak was reached in April, 1920, and the price peak the same month. The export peak of the total farm index was reached in March, 1920, and the price peak in April of that year.

If a careful study be made of chapter 5 of Part I of this report, numerous instances will be found in which a relationship can be' shown between the peak of production and consumption and the peak of prices. But no such relationship can be established between increased discount rates and the drop in the price of any single commodity.

(*b*) Agricultural prices broke more sharply than any other, and yet from May, 1920, to May, 1921, the liquidation of loans in agricultural counties was relatively much less than in industrial counties.

(*c*) Interest charges as an element of expense in the cost of production and marketing must not be exaggerated. They are usually a small percentage of the total outlay, which is largely accounted for by the cost of labor, material, transportation, and distribution.

(*d*) The price-deflation movement was world-wide. The crisis began in Japan late in 1919. The price-level of all commodities began to decline in the United Kingdom in April, 1920; in France and Italy, in May; in the United States, Germany, India, and Canada, in June; in Sweden, in July; in the Netherlands, in August; and in Australia, in September.

I may add, in conclusion, that I think it desirable to present this minority opinion, because of the view apparently held by a considerable number of people that the increase in the discount rates of the Federal Reserve Banks was one of the primary causes of the sharp break in prices which occurred during the second half of 1920 and which so disastrously affected the agricultural communities. Such a view inevitably leads to the conclusion that the Federal Reserve Board and Banks constitute an agency by means of which prices may be raised or lowered. This opinion is so contrary to economic facts and to the purposes of the Federal Reserve System that any expression of opinion which seems to support it, even indirectly, should not be permitted to pass unchallenged.

APPENDIX F

REPLY OF FEDERAL RESERVE BOARD TO SENATE RESOLUTION 308

FEDERAL RESERVE BOARD
WASHINGTON, July 8, 1922

SIR:

The Federal Reserve Board transmits herewith letters from the Federal Reserve Banks of Philadelphia, Richmond, and St. Louis, in reply to Senate Resolution 308. Replies from the other banks will be forwarded as soon as received.

In transmitting this correspondence, the Board trusts that it may, without impropriety, avail itself of the opportunity to invite the attention of the Senate to certain matters which have a direct bearing upon the subject of the inquiry.

The corporate powers of the Federal Reserve Banks are defined in section 4 of the Federal Reserve Act, which provides, *inter alia*, that 'Every Federal Reserve Bank shall be conducted under the supervision and control of a board of directors' and that such directors 'shall perform the duties usually appertaining to the office of directors of banking associations and all such duties as are prescribed by law.'

The banking business is one which rests peculiarly upon the foundation of confidence. While true in the case of any bank, this is particularly true with respect to a Federal Reserve Bank which is the sole custodian of the legal reserves of its member banks and the instrumentality through which is issued the country's fiduciary currency. Anything which tends to undermine public confidence in a bank, and in a Reserve Bank particularly, impairs its ability to perform its functions, and unless counteracted may defeat entirely the purposes of its organization. Therefore, those charged with the administration of a bank have the right, and are impressed with the duty, of using all legitimate means, when necessary, to protect its good name and to prevent any impairment of public confidence.

Criticisms of policy cannot be objected to and have always been welcomed by the Federal Reserve Board, which has never imputed to itself infallibility of judgment. The Board has been charged with the administration of a new and untried law and has from the beginning been confronted with a series of difficult and unprecedented situations. When criticism is based upon the solid foundation of fact, and understanding of the Federal Reserve Act and of banking principles, it is useful; it is helpful to those charged with the duties of administration. To the Federal Reserve Board it has appeared, however, that for the past two years much that has been said under the guise of criticism of policy has not been intended to help, but to discredit, the management of the Federal Reserve System through attacks upon the integrity and purpose of members of the Federal Reserve Board and of officers and directors of Federal Reserve Banks.

These attacks have been so repeatedly made and have had such publicity as to justify the suspicion that they are part of a concerted movement against the Federal Reserve System. The patience and forbearance with which members of the Federal Reserve Board and officers and directors of Federal Reserve Banks have borne these repeated attacks, many of them personally abusive, have been cited as an admission of the truth of charges made and have tended to raise in the minds of some, who endorse the principles of the Federal Reserve Act, but who had no means of informing themselves as to facts, a question as to whether there may not have been some foundation for the charge that members of the Federal Reserve Board and officers and directors of Federal Reserve Banks have been incapable and corrupt.

Beginning last summer, insinuations and charges which had been made on the outside were repeated and amplified on the floor of the Senate of the United States, not merely once or twice, but at frequent intervals up to the present time. This circumstance has caused a great amount of correspondence with persons asking for information, and Board members, as well as officers and directors of Federal Reserve Banks, have had occasion frequently to consider whether there were any means which might appropriately be employed to inform the public as to the operation of the Federal Reserve Banks and the character of their management.

Respecting the constitutional prerogatives of the members of the Senate, care has been taken to make no criticism of any member thereof in any reply to letters of inquiry. This circumstance also has been construed as an admission of the truth of charges so frequently made on the floor of the Senate, some of which would have been resented as libelous but for the constitutional immunity above referred to.

Many quotations could be made from statements which have been printed in the 'Congressional Record' during the past twelve months, which are misleading and untrue, but their insertion would unduly extend this communication. The Board has seen nothing to indicate that those who made these statements have ever corrected them.

Last January the junior Senator from Virginia, who was Chairman of the Banking and Currency Committee of the House of Representatives which reported the bill creating the Federal Reserve System, and who was afterwards Secretary of the Treasury and *ex-officio* Chairman of the Federal Reserve Board, made a speech on the floor of the Senate, in which he discussed at length the operation of the Federal Reserve Banks and the attitude of the Federal Reserve Board during the recent period of economic reaction and financial stress. The speech was delivered during parts of two days. A brief report of it appeared in the daily papers and requests followed for complete copies of the speech. Officers of Federal Reserve Banks, who for several months had felt themselves obliged to maintain silence while their motives and integrity were being assailed, deemed it not improper to avail themselves of the opportunity then presented to give to their correspondents and to others in their respective communities who had evinced an interest or who were supposed to be interested in the economic questions dealt with, information which would enable them to draw their own conclusions.

The speech was a public document. Having been delivered on the floor of the Senate and having been published in the 'Congressional Record,' the Federal Reserve Board felt that there could be no impropriety in the distribution of copies by the Federal Reserve Banks. The speech dealt so comprehensively with charges and statements which had been made in the same place and printed in the same publication that the Board believed it should be given wide publicity. Having been informed that copies might be obtained from the Public Printer if ordered promptly, it was decided that the Governor should send to each Federal Reserve Bank the following telegram:

January 18, 1922

Think Senator Glass's great speech defending Federal Reserve System should be widely and promptly circulated. Government Printing Office will print special copies of it Friday 20th and additional orders should be given to-morrow. Printing Office estimates cost of copies at from five to seven cents each.[1] Please wire promptly how many copies your bank wishes.

HARDING

---

[1] This estimate of cost was too high. In view of the great demand for the speech and the large number of copies printed, the cost per copy to each Federal Reserve Bank was approximately one and three quarters cents.

The Federal Reserve Board assumes responsibility for commending this speech to the Federal Reserve Banks for circulation. Neither the Board nor the Federal Reserve Banks regarded the speech as being an attack upon any Senator and they were not interested in it from that point of view. This speech was and is regarded by the Board as a fair presentation of facts. It was commended to the banks for circulation because it was an answer made in the Senate Chamber to charges which had been made on the floor of the Senate. It is a clear exposition of the policies, functions and operations of the Federal Reserve System during a critical period and is an important contribution to current economic discussion.

Respectfully
(Signed)   W. P. G. HARDING
Governor

THE PRESIDENT OF THE SENATE

INDEX

92, 93; applications for shipment of, passed upon by Board, 93–95, 98; one case of application for shipment of, described, 95–97; amplification of order restricting export of, 98; the purpose of the restriction placed upon the exportation of, 99, 100; removal of embargo on, 149; reserves and deposits on December 26, 1919, and on December 20, 1920, 194; reserves in 1920–21, 199; policy of Federal Reserve System in regard to, 251, 252.

Gold exchange fund, 18, 19.

Gold fund, established by Board, 46–48.

Great Britain, declares cotton contraband, 40–43; sterling exchange maintained by, 101.

Gronna, Senator, discusses Victory Note Bill, 143.

Hamlin, Charles S., appointed member of Board, 4, 5; Assistant Secretary of the Treasury, 4; Governor of Board, 5; appointed member of Board for full term of ten years, 61; accompanies Lord Cunliffe on visit to cities, 89; appointed to the Capital Issues Committee, 120.

Harding, Governor W. P. G., interview with Colonel House, 1, 2; appointed member of Federal Reserve Board, 2–5; his view as to number of districts, 35, 36; member of committee on redistricting, 36; interview with Sir Cecil Spring-Rice, 42, 43; his advice as regards declaration of embargo on cotton, 43; designated to succeed Hamlin as Governor of the Board, 61; speaks before Committee of Senate on bill to provide credits for industries, 108, 114–16; of the War Finance Corporation, 120; resigns from War Finance Corporation, 120; address before Conference of May 18, 1920, 172–75; blamed for cotton situation, 188; addresses annual meeting of American Farm Bureau Federation, 189, 284–88; congratulated by Comptroller Williams on his birthday anniversary, 211; communication with President Wilson, 213, 214; reply to letter of Senator Smoot, 219, 289–95; witness before Joint Commission, of Agricultural Investigation, 219; denounced in Senate, 223; letter to Chairman

Anderson of the Joint Commission, suggesting investigation of charges, 224; correspondence with Governor McKelvie of Nebraska, 224–28; letter to President Harding on member of Reserve Bank of Chicago, 235; resolutions urging his reappointment, 239; disapproves of bill to increase membership of Board, 240, 242; attacked in the Senate, 245, 246; retires from Board, 247.

Harding, Warren G., President, becomes President, 215; first month of his administration, 215, 216; letter to Governor Harding on member of Reserve Bank of Chicago, 235.

Harrison, Senator, member of the Joint Commission of Agricultural Inquiry, 218.

Heflin, Senator, speech of Comptroller Williams delivered by, 209; his resolution concerning mailing of Senator Glass's address defending the Federal Reserve System, 237; accuses Governor Harding in the Senate, 246.

Henry, Robert L., his suggestion for relief of cotton market, 21.

High Cost of Living, 149, 180.

Holland, American exchange in, during the War, 102.

House, Colonel E. M., interview with Governor Harding, 1, 2.

Houston, David F., becomes Secretary of the Treasury, 160; on War Finance Corporation, 191; succeeded as Treasurer by Andrew W. Mellon, 215.

India, gold shipments to, 93.

Inflation, effort to avoid, 75, 78, 166; in the War, 118, 119; Treasury methods of financing the War, in relation to, 252, 253, 257–79.

Interbank rediscounting, 45.

Interest, advance in rate of, 106, 107, 169; proposed to fix maximum rate of, 192; Senator Owen appeals for lower rates of, 196.

Investments, on December 26, 1919, and on December 30, 1920, compared, 194.

James, George R., appointed member of the Board, 247.

Japan, panic in, owing to falling off of demand in silks in United States, 163.